Elisabeth Schwarzkopf

Elisabeth Schwarzkopf

a career on record

Discography with commentary
by Alan Sanders

Elisabeth Schwarzkopf in a discussion
of her records with J.B. Steane

Amadeus Press
Reinhard G. Pauly, General Editor
Portland, Oregon

First published in North America in 1995 by
Amadeus Press (an imprint of Timber Press, Inc.)
The Haseltine Building
133 S.W. Second Avenue, Suite 450
Portland, Oregon 97204, U.S.A.

ISBN 0-931340-99-3

Printed in Great Britain

Contents

(plates between pages 88 and 89)

To Walter Legge

Preface

In January 1995 Geoffrey Parsons died, my accompanist for fifteen years, all over the world, and a dear friend of the finest sort. He was at the piano when we recorded 'Der Erlkönig' (Schubert) in Berlin – which, as you may now gather, I regard as my finest recording of a Lied. The circumstances were so different from all other recording procedures, since neither of us had any idea at all that Walter Legge would startle us with a sudden announcement through the loud-speaker: 'And now, my children, you are going to do the Erlkönig!' We did – in a very short time and with very few takes.

I think I should stress that throughout my singing days I have been spoilt by the pianists who played for me, as by the conductors under whose guidance I had the honour to perform. More than once I have been terrified that I would not live up to their standards.

Most of all, I endeavoured to meet the standards of Walter Legge – whose credentials surely do not need to be spelled out for the readers of a book on recording!

A long time after I could put my ears to good use in producing better performances myself – and I mean ears, not voice – I now want young singers to benefit from my experience. With all the talent and care in the world, one could and should try to do better.

July 1995

Elisabeth Legge Schwarzkopf

Elisabeth Schwarzkopf

Walter Legge[*]

I did not even notice her when Sir Thomas Beecham and I were recording *Die Zauberflöte* in Berlin in 1937. She was in the chorus – Favre's *Solistenvereinigung*, the German equivalent of the Robert Shaw Chorale. I must have been blind!

In the later war years her name – Elisabeth Schwarzkopf, as an exceptional young soprano – seeped through to me in letters from young friends serving in the Mediterranean and North Africa who had heard her on German Services broadcasts. She went on my list of artists to be heard and perhaps engaged for EMI when the war was over. By January 1946, when I first reached postwar Vienna, the State Opera had collected the cream of Austrian and European singers into their company. The Theater an der Wien, where *Leonore, Fidelio* and *Die lustige Witwe* had had their premières, was then and for years to come the State Opera's temporary home, and it was there that I first heard her, as Rosina in *Il barbiere di Siviglia* – a brilliant, fresh voice shot with laughter, not large but admirably projected, with enchanting high *pianissimi*. She was a lively, winning actress and evidently very musical. I listened to her in two or three other roles, and once at a party at a friend's house (despite near-starvation, the Viennese still maintained their traditions of *Hausmusik*), before inviting her to discuss an exclusive recording contract. Some singers internationally famous from prewar years, others yet to win renown, pursued me with uncapped fountain pens ready to sign anything. Schwarzkopf was made of sterner stuff and insisted on 'a proper audition – two or three hours. I don't want you to buy a cat in a sack and regret it, and I don't want you to offer me less than you think I am worth.' I ought to have recognised in this frank tenacity, which invited detailed criticism and even possible rejection, the firm will and guts necessary to make an exceptional career in what Toscanini described as 'the primeval jungle we call the world of music'. Sir Terence Rattigan has recently written, 'What makes magic is genius, and what makes genius is the infinite capacity for taking pains.'

[*] This article first appeared in *Opera News* in 1975 and is reprinted here with the kind permission of the Editor.

Her stubbornness rattled me, and the audition was severe. After she had shown what she could do in her own choice of a variety of arias from both opera and oratorio, I started to work with her on a very difficult little Hugo Wolf song, 'Wer rief dich denn?', bar by bar, word by word, inflection by inflection, a song demanding changing emotions often on one syllable, one note: it was the beginning of the way we were to work together for the next thirty-two years. I soon realised that in this unflinching perfectionism I had found my match. After an hour-and-a-half, Herbert von Karajan, who was sitting with me, said, 'I'm going. Don't crucify the girl. I told you weeks ago she is potentially the best singer in Central Europe.' Half-an-hour later she demonstrated her diverse musical skills by accompanying, either at sight or from memory, other singers who had been waiting for auditions. That evening she signed her first recording contract, and so began the longest and happiest musical association of my life.

Schwarzkopf was evidently too intelligent to waste her natural endowments – which also included patrician bearing and rare beauty – as a high soprano. As you can hear from her 1946 recording of Handel's 'Sweet Bird' from *Il penseroso*, high D's gave her no difficulties. Blondchen and its top E had led Karl Böhm to engage her for Vienna, and Zerbinetta had been her first triumph in a major role. She demonstrated hair-raising agility as Constanze in *Die Entführung*, but the voice was by nature a lyric soprano. At my urging she was soon singing Agathe in *Der Freischütz* and the Countess in *Le nozze di Figaro*; the younger Rosina was a girl of the past.

She had been rescued from a series of so-called singing teachers by Maria Ivogün and Michael Raucheisen, who tenderly laid the foundations of her technique and sense of style. She was born with a fine, analytical ear and that rare gift – the *sine qua non* for international fame as a singer – an immediately recognisable and unforgettable personal timbre. At that time she had not hoped to be more than a principal soprano in Vienna or Berlin, perhaps to be engaged for Salzburg and Bayreuth. She was soon to be surprised.

Her first records for EMI were made in the autumn of 1946 – Bach, Handel, Mozart, and a few Arne songs. Some of these have never been issued, but a plan is afoot to publish the best of her recordings, starting with the period 1946-1953.* We selected the contents recently and were ourselves astonished at the consistent quality, artistically and technically, achieved even before the days of tape and splicing. In 1947, Karajan recorded the Brahms *Requiem* with Schwarzkopf and Hans Hotter. Recovering from a recent operation, she came to the sessions

---

* These were eventually issued, along with some slightly later material, in autumn 1981 as LP: RLS 763 and cassette: TC-RLS 763.

white and wan. Noticing that Karajan and I were desperate because the chorus sopranos could not keep in tune, she volunteered to stand in their midst to keep them up to pitch. Back to the chorus! That was only her first anonymous rescue operation in important recordings. There would be no Furtwängler-Flagstad *Tristan*, for my taste still the supreme *Tristan* recording, unless Schwarzkopf had promised to sing the top B-flats, B's and C's for her friend, as she had done in earlier Flagstad duets with Svanholm. She also spoke Marzelline's dialogue in Christa Ludwig's *Fidelio* recording and sang some words for a colleague in Karajan's *Falstaff*, which have not yet been detected.

Schwarzkopf's breakthrough to her international career came quickly and on a broad front. It began at the 1947 Lucerne Festival, the Brahms *Requiem* with Furtwängler. A few weeks later came her London début at Covent Garden as a member of the visiting Vienna State Opera – Donna Elvira in *Don Giovanni*, then Marzelline, which became one of her best roles.

On the strength of her London success and the spreading fame of her records, Covent Garden engaged her as guest member of its resident company. It was not a generous contract – sixty pounds a week, if I remember rightly – and everything was to be sung in English, which she had learned at school and as a teenage League of Nations student in the English provinces. Between 1948 and 1951 she sang Pamina, Sophie, Mimì, Violetta, Susanna, Marzelline, Eva, and – much against my will, but at the management's insistence – Manon and Butterfly, neither of them her cup of tea. All these roles except Eva were soon to be dropped from her repertory, but she accepted the Covent Garden offer because it enabled us to work together. This caused a break with Vienna – the music director, Josef Krips, and general manager, Egon Hilbert, told her that if she left their theatre even for three months a year she would lose her voice and be useless to them. But she and her voice survived it, in exile from the Vienna opera stage until Karajan took over the State Opera and welcomed her back.

Now her international career raced apace: Countess Almaviva at the 1948 Salzburg Festival with Karajan; her La Scala début with the same company five months later; and from then until 1963 two or three roles every season at La Scala, probably the longest and most distinguished career of any German singer in that Italian theatre.

At that time the *stagione* system worked perfectly, and there in 1952 she first assumed the Marschallin, a part we had been preparing for years. This music and text are honey for a fine Lieder singer's subtle art. After a month's intensive rehearsal, often ten or twelve hours a day, Karajan conducted a series of performances still unforgotten in La Scala's history.

There she sang her only staged Mélisandes, under Victor de Sabata; her only Elsas; the *Tannhäuser* Elisabeth; the première of Carl Orff's *Trionfi d'Afrodite*; even Marguerite in *Faust*, in which she, like Goethe, sank without trace. To her usual Mozart-Da Ponte parts she added Fiordiligi for Mozart's bicentenary at the newly inaugurated Piccola Scala. Giorgio Streher was to have directed it, but at the sight of Eugene Berman's murky décor he stormed out of the theatre belching clouds of quadrilingual obscenities, leaving poor Guido Cantelli to conduct (and produce!) an opera for the first and last time in his life with a cast nearly all new to the subtlest and most difficult Mozart opera. It turned out to be an exquisite, unaffected performance.

Schwarzkopf had already fulfilled her Bayreuth ambitions when she took part in the postwar reopening with Beethoven's Ninth Symphony under Furtwängler. She sang Eva there with Karajan then Knappertsbusch; Woglinde (as an example to her generation by reverting to the old Bayreuth tradition wherein leading singers lent their lustre to small parts) and a recital in the beautiful old Margraves' Theatre, designed by Galli Bibiena, to aid the Foundation of the Friends of Bayreuth. Between performances she learned the words and music of Stravinsky's *Rake's Progress*, whose première lay close ahead. That year the Venice Festival opened with the Verdi *Requiem*, conducted by De Sabata, with Schwarzkopf, Di Stefano, Stignani and Siepi. A few days later Stravinsky, his head buried in the score, conducted the first performance of his new opera.

She bided her time to make her U.S. début, but in 1953, after we had rehearsed for nearly a week with the pianist Arpad Sándor, she gave her first New York recital, in the Town Hall – and returned the same evening to Switzerland. On the flight home she studied Leonore in *Fidelio*, which she had promised Karajan to sing in a series of concert performances. The effect of young, impulsive voices in the two leading parts had moving overtones, but Leonore demands more vocal weight than she ever carried.

We had been warned that it was impossible to make a successful concert career in America without having first established oneself at the Metropolitan. That fallacy had to be disproved. Concert engagements came in plenty after the Town Hall recital, and the perceptive Kurt Herbert Adler immediately engaged her for his San Francisco Opera, where she sang for ten years before the Met condescended to engage her. In the meantime, we had proved that without a Met background it is possible to give Lieder recitals entirely in German and pack large halls even with all-Hugo Wolf programmes, events beyond the comprehension of New York impresarios but much to the taste of the intelligent

American musical public. Her subsequent American concert career, having finished its last lap, is already history.

In the 1930s Titta Ruffo had told me that though he had sung something like a hundred operas, if he could start his career again he would restrict himself to five or six parts, study and polish them in every vocal and dramatic detail and sleep happily without fear of competition. He was a wise man.

For the stage, Schwarzkopf whittled down her repertory to three Mozart parts – Fiordiligi, Donna Elvira, Countess Almaviva; two Richard Strauss parts, the Marschallin and the Countess in *Capriccio*; and because she delights in playing comedy, Alice in *Falstaff*. All are intensely human characters, with wide emotional ranges, expressing themselves in distinguished texts and free from conventional operatic fustian. She hankered after Desdemona and Strauss's Ariadne, but no theatre could give her both the three weeks' rehearsal and the conductors we wanted at the times she was free.

There are interesting disparities between Schwarzkopf's recorded opera repertory and the works she sang in public. She recorded but never publicly sang *Hänsel und Gretel* (our 1953 recording is still unequalled); *Ariadne auf Naxos*; *Der Barbier van Bagdad*, an exquisite score and diverting text but box-office poison; *Les contes d'Hoffmann*, which I had planned to record with Callas, Schwarzkopf and De los Angeles, a project that lost much of its sparkle after I resigned from EMI; Carl Orff's *Die Kluge*; *Arabella*, of which only highlights were recorded, but which Lotte Lehmann, Viorica Ursuleac and Clemens Krauss repeatedly urged her to put into her public repertory; *Troilus and Cressida*, which our friend William Walton wrote for her, but which she regretfully declined because the text was Ivor Novello-ish and in English. And the operettas.

I had set my heart on recording the best Johann Strauss and Lehár operettas since the 1930s, when Bruno Walter conducted *Die Fledermaus* at Covent Garden with Lehmann, Elisabeth Schumann, Maria Olczewska, and Gerhard Hüsch. To launch the recording project and attract the widest possible public, I intended to start with *Die lustige Witwe*. I had the cast, but Karajan declined to conduct, and a year passed before it struck me that Otto Ackermann was the man I had been searching for, a conductor of near-genius with marvellously flexible rhythm, a light hand, vast experience and sound theatrical instinct. Everything we had all learned from lives dedicated to the greatest music was gaily devoted to restoring the elegance, tenderness and infectious high spirits needed to make real the unreal world these masterpieces inhabit. Their launching as Angel's Champagne Operettas was carried out with the usual unparalleled flair of the promoters of the series, Dario and Dorle Soria. The nearest Schwarzkopf came to public performance of operetta was a few concerts at American summer festivals and at London's Royal Festival Hall.

Since Schwarzkopf has so often spoken of herself as 'Her Master's Voice', casting me as Svengali, let me give some indication of how we worked together. My predecessor in the recording world was Fred Gaisberg. He believed that his job was to get the best artists into the studio and get onto wax the best sound pictures of what those artists habitually did in public, intermittently using his persuasive diplomatic skill as nurse-maid and tranquilliser to temperaments. Having watched him at work, I decided that recording must be a collaboration between artists and what are now called 'producers'. I wanted better results than are normally possible in public performance: I was determined to put onto disc the best that artists could do under the best possible conditions. From the start of the Hugo Wolf Society, when I began to exercise my craft (with Alexander Kipnis, Herbert Janssen and others), the new approach was a success. After the war I found in Schwarzkopf, Karajan and Lipatti (to mention but three) ideal and incurable perfectionists — self-critical, hungry for informed criticism, untiring and acutely aware that their recorded performances were the true proof of their qualities and the cornerstones and keystone of their careers.

When Schwarzkopf came to London in 1947, she had never owned a gramophone. My first and favourite toy had been an ancient cylinder model; I had learned to read from record labels and catalogues, saved my pocket money to buy records and over the years built up a mammoth collection. Her father's profession, teaching the classics, meant that he and she changed schools every two or three years through the German provinces. She was nineteen before she heard decent singing. She had started with piano at seven, viola and organ at ten and taken part in school opera performances, including Kurt Weill's *Der Jasager*.

First I set out to widen by recorded examples her imaginative concept of the possibilities of vocal sound. Rosa Ponselle's vintage port and thick cream timbre and noble line; the Slavic brilliance of Nina Koshetz; a few phrases from Farrar's Carmen, whose insinuations were later reflected in Schwarzkopf's 'Im chambre separée'; one word only from Melba, 'Bada' in 'Donde lieta'; some Rethberg and large doses of Meta Seine-meyer to show how essentially Teutonic voices can produce brilliant Italianate sound. Then Lehmann's all-embracing generosity, Schumann's charm and lightness, McCormack's incredible octave leap in 'Care Selve', Frida Leider's dramatic tension — all these were nectar and ambrosia for Schwarzkopf's musical appetite. Instrumentalists, too; Fritz Kreisler for the dark beauty of his tone, his nobility and elegance, his vitality in upbeats, his rubato and cavalier nonchalance; Schnabel for concentrated thinking over long musical periods, firmly rhythmical, seemingly oblivious to bar lines. From the analysis of what we found most admirable in these diverse models we made our own synthesis, most adaptable to what we believed would best develop her voice for the repertory we were to concentrate on.

We made it our aim to recreate to the best of our abilities the intensity and emotions that music and words had in their authors' minds in the moment of creation. Therefore utmost obedience to every composer's markings – he knew best. This has involved and still does involve hours of merciless rehearsal, domestically known as 'Walter crucifying the pianist'. She has had rare luxury in pianists as partners – Furtwängler and Karajan, Sawallisch, Ackermann and Rosbaud, Edwin Fischer, Gieseking and Ciccolini and the incomparable London-based pair, Gerald Moore and Geoffrey Parsons. And in the summer of 1975 Sviatoslav Richter, for three recitals after twenty days' rehearsal.

From the outset I sat in with a secretary in opera rehearsals and performances, quickly dictating detailed notes on musical and acting nuances, sometimes having these passed to her in the wings. At performances I sat whenever possible in a stage box to watch both what she was doing and how the audience reacted – the exact moment when women fumbled in their handbags for handkerchiefs and men tugged them from their breast pockets. This is not calculation; it is in my view obedience to composers' intentions, to involve the audience in the action. We tried for years and once or twice succeeded in achieving Pamina's 'Ach, ich fühl's' so heartbreakingly that there was no applause. The length of the silence after Strauss's 'Morgen' is more eloquent than clapping.

We have tried to communicate and stir emotions like painters, by beauty and truth of line and colours in the voice. From what we have heard, most of her best younger colleagues have different aims. In two consecutive evenings at the Paris Opéra we listened to galaxies of stars singing beautifully, obeying every dynamic, marking and conveying nothing but the glory of their voices and their technical skill – no trace of emotion or the meaning and overtones of the words for which composers had so tenaciously wrestled with their librettists. For this the producers and conductors are most to blame.

More farewell concerts in Europe – finally, in 1976, three in London, the city where she has sung more than any other; some new recordings and then ...? She will play tennis, ski, and walk in her beloved Austrian mountains. Then, perhaps, we shall teach. But where shall we find pupils like her? What we would *really* like is to run an opera house with the musical and artistic standards Elisabeth and I have maintained in all the records we have made together.

Part I

Listening with Schwarzkopf

John Steane

Listening with Schwarzkopf

Nobody with any knowledge of Elisabeth Schwarzkopf, even at second-hand, would expect a listening-session in her company to be merely a matter of smiles and nods, an anecdote or two and a round of pleasantries at the end. She is famously self-critical, so much so that Gerald Moore, who worked with her for many years in concerts and recordings, wrote that he sometimes thought the only way of getting a record passed for publication was 'to prevent her at all cost from hearing her own play-backs' (*Am I too Loud?*, London, 1962). The quest for exact intonation, the devoted study of the score, words and music, the comprehensive insistence on standards: all of this is common knowledge. Yet, encountering it myself, and now at first-hand, I was still unprepared for the intensity and utter sincerity of it: it could in fact be alarming.

Often, when famous people say deprecatory things about themselves, there is an implicit subtext: 'That was very modest of me, wasn't it, but I can afford to be modest because of my well-known and unique attainments.' The disarming admission to having come short of absolute perfection will often connote something of that sort. With Schwarzkopf there is none of it, but only a plain and unsparing statement of what she hears as fact. My own first instinct was to outsmile the criticisms and jolly things along. That, needless to say, did not work, and at times we both had to face it, that this listening – the whole scheme as it had been planned – carried with it a fearful risk. It could have threatened confidence in a life's work.

Gradually, but only gradually, delight arose too. Sometimes it would take us – but her especially (since my delight is far more easily aroused) – by surprise. A song we had very nearly overlooked, an aria almost dismissed without a hearing, might suddenly bring a pleasure as genuine and acute as any of the criticisms. At other times we might go for a long stretch without comment, and this was most likely to signify approval, with which would often come a great happiness.

* This chapter is dedicated with gratitude and affection to Lily Reenvig.

❁

The notion of listening systematically to her records, sifting and making a personal evaluation, had probably been with Schwarzkopf for some years before the first experimental attempts. It originated in her teaching. After her retirement, which followed immediately upon the death of her husband in 1979, her strongly surviving musical and creative interests centred on her pupils. Perhaps a brief word may be said here about her work as a teacher, for it has commonly been misrepresented. Television viewers watching a masterclass seek entertainment, and the form they prefer it to take is the sight of a talented youngster singing a song or aria and then getting a pat on the back with perhaps a hint or two from the celebrity-instructor. But that is not teaching. Schwarzkopf will stop a pupil when she notices something she thinks needs correction; that is how pupils learn. It's no use leaving it till the end, when both pupil and teacher have forgotten *exactly* what happened. When it's done there and then, the pupil has the sense of it fresh in the system, can recapture what happened and adapt to a suggestion of how it might be done differently. Viewers may find this stopping-and-starting a restless business, and they tend to feel sorry for the student. But pupils (or at any rate the genuine ones) go to these classes to learn from them. All the Schwarzkopf pupils with whom I have had contact have expressed gratitude. They do not come to a lesson in order to give a concert and take a few comments: they want teaching, which means being stopped when something is amiss and trying it again. Teaching certainly involves discipline, but that does not exclude humour and laughter. The relationship between teacher and pupil is close and human, and a generous care for her pupils has been a principal concern of Schwarzkopf's life. The 'stop-and-start' procedure is itself both a product and a cause of this closeness. The teacher reacts (to what is beautiful as well as what is faulty), and the pupil responds. The immediacy of reaction and response is like spontaneous conversation, which is the lifeblood of friendship. As for the audience or the television viewers, they would feel a great deal *more* sorry for the pupil if they could see in four or five years' time the ruin of a promising career because lessons were not taught and learnt at the right time.

Naturally a singer's first instinct is to teach by example. That may not always be wise, and, in any case, is not always possible. A man, a retired baritone most of all, may still have the singing-voice intact; for a variety of reasons, a soprano is rarely in this position.[1] Schwarzkopf may still use her voice to make an occasional point (and I have heard her sing a high G of unflawed purity in the head-voice), but the recordings, she felt, should in many instances be a vitally useful aid in making the point for her; and that is where the listening-project began.

She quickly found that it was no use playing a record to herself and making comments (whether written or into the tape-recorder). Some other person – or, as it turned out, two other people – would be needed. Finding the records, putting them on (LP or CD), stopping, starting again, adjusting the volume for 'presence': this of itself was a full-time job. She also needed someone to talk to, preferably a listener with knowledge of the repertoire, and one who would not look completely blank if names such as Ivogün, Gieseking or Ackermann were mentioned. It might help too if this person would ask questions, risk an observation (however foolish) and even possibly advance a counter-argument. The role was a mixture of devil's advocate, *agent provocateur* and village idiot, and it fell to me. The work reported in this chapter was done during the course of three visits, each lasting rather under a week, the first in October 1991, the last early in 1994. I shall try to tell it, as they say, 'like it was'. The first visit is recalled from written notes, the second from taped recordings of Schwarzkopf's own words, the third (also from tapes) tying up loose ends and bringing out what seem to be the salient points.

❋

Our first record was Wolf's 'Elfenlied'. The relentless firing of objections to the singing in these two recordings[2] might conceivably have been half-humorous, and I hoped that it was, for here we had one of the songs commonly thought of as 'hers' in recordings well-known and well-loved for over thirty years or so; meanwhile, there at my side was their singer taking them to task over matters of tempo, intonation and diction. We heard other recordings she had made of the same song, better in some respects, less good in others, and then went on to the Goethe-Lieder. These included the Mignon songs culminating in 'Kennst du das Land?'

[1] Schwarzkopf points out that the range of the speaking-voice in men normally corresponds to the singing-range of a baritone, and that this generally remains so throughout life. The soprano's singing-voice rises well above the normal speaking-range (even of the extended range used in reciting poetry), which in age tends to deepen, and eventually the disparity becomes so great that the singing-voice is effectively lost.

[2] The records referred to in this chapter are identified, page by page, in notes on pages 39-41.

where the criticism became so severe as to call the wisdom of this whole project into doubt from the start. Intermittently during that first morning the listening brought happiness, and, interestingly, the recordings which gave most delight (Mozart's 'Un moto di gioia' and Wolf's 'Philine') were of happy songs. There was much that she could enjoy elsewhere in the Wolf recordings. But the faults, as she perceived them, nagged away; and when it came to 'Kennst du das Land?', the song with which she is most closely associated, it was dismaying to find her own pleasure so bruised and undermined.

The objections raised in this first session took several forms, but the initial and most insistent concern at that time was with an aspect of German pronunciation. In English, as in Italian, words such as those I have just written ('in English', 'in Italian') normally elide; in German, the vowel introducing the second word is separated from the preceding consonant. An example occurs early in Goethe's poem, 'Nur wer die Sehnsucht kennt':

> Allein und abgetrennt
> Von aller Freude

The 'a' of 'abgetrennt' is separated from the 'd' of 'und' by a light glottal stroke, as is that of 'aller' from the 'n' of 'von'. Schwarzkopf was at that time making a special point of this, particularly with foreign students, to whom it did not come easily.[3] So it was one of the first items for inspection as she listened to her own recordings, starting with the 'Elfenlied'. In this she does indeed separate in the second line ('Ein ganz kleines Elfenlied') but not in the third ('Wohl um die Elfe'), and she wished it had been more precise, more sharply defined. Other examples were the elision of 'was ich' in the second line of 'Nur wer die Sehnsucht kennt' in Wolf's setting, 'vielleicht in mir' from Mozart's 'Als Luise die Briefe ... verbrannte' and 'Abends ist' in 'Abendempfindung', also by Mozart. To the suggestions that, first, this was a side-track, secondly a matter that did not trouble the non-German-speaking listener, and, thirdly, that it was arguably a feature of German pronunciation inimical

---

[3] The problem (Schwarzkopf would add) concerns German singers also. They will have been taught, as are all properly trained singers, to bind the vowels and equalise the sounds in a way which ensures the legato style, an utterly essential feature of the singer's art. Correct pronunciation places the singer in a predicament, and German singers will frequently go back to 'binding' rather than 'separating', even with the knowledge that correct pronunciation requires it. It is difficult to make foreign students come to grips with this when Germans themselves are inconsistent. Ideally, it is a matter of achieving a very clean 'take' (this is the *Ansatz*, and is quite distinct from the forbidden *coup de glotte*).

to the legato line in singing, Schwarzkopf's answer was very simple: 'What is right is right, and this is wrong.'

Other matters arose concerning pronunciation and the general handling of words in song. After this insistence on vowel-separation, it was surprising to find that another criticism was of 'over-exactness'. The rolling of the 'r' in the word 'der' ('in der Weite') was noted in 'Nur wer die Sehnsucht kennt' and ('wenn die rasche, lose Knabe') in 'Philine'. This had been correct in the not-so-remote past, but in modern times sounded pedantic and old-fashioned, rather like the speech of actors recorded early in the century.[4] Moreover, 'Philine', she thought, needed a more colloquial style than it had in this 1956 recording: she remembered how vital it had seemed to get the words clear, only to find now that such clarity was not really necessary.

The balance between song and speech was another pre-occupation and a more fundamental one. While 'Philine' (Goethe's poem about the flighty girl for whom every day has its quota of boredom and every night its pleasure) is essentially a lyric, nevertheless its words are directed towards an audience. So it is in all songs, that the elements of public and private utterance have to be weighed. It was a consideration that became prominent in the very different context of Walter Gieseking's *Kinderlieder*, which Schwarzkopf recorded to the composer's accompaniment in 1955. She noted how particularly close in this instance song is to speech ('French music to a German text'). Here, pure singing has to sound like conversation, the notes still needing to be well and truly *sung*. In the success of these recordings she took some heartfelt satisfaction: the difficult balance had been achieved.

It goes without saying that another prime concern was with intonation. Several writers have told of the pencil-markings in Schwarzkopf's scores used for recording sessions: arrows pointing up or down to correct a note she heard as flat or sharp. For myself, I have to admit to finding it something of a thrill to be handling these legendary copies, often the ones used for the recording we were hearing at that very time. There were several arrows in the copy of 'Elfenlied', more in 'Die Spröde' where she detected a sharpness on the word 'fort' ('Dann sie sang und lachte fort'). Momentary flatness troubled her in 'Kennst du das Land?', with the very first word heard as flat in one performance, the 'Land' in another, and 'glühn' ('die Gold-Orangen glühn') in a third.

Right from the start (and this was still in the first session) it became clear that we were dealing with essential features of technique. The fine ear for intonation was exercised as part of the singer's equipment; but

[4] Her own tendency to produce a sharp 'r' sound may (she suggests) derive from her origins in East Germany, near the Polish border, where a particularly clear German was spoken.

simultaneous with this pinpointing of individual notes ran an equal care for the *line*, the melodic phrase, and the legato which should bind it firmly and smoothly.

Even the score of 'Elfenlied' (a song of light, darting movement) had 'legato' pencilled-in at certain points. The song which proved to be the most severe test in this respect was Mozart's 'Abendempfindung'. Here the pencil had marked 'Legatissimo!' in letters large enough to serve as a reminder for all life long. Listening to the Carnegie Hall performance as well as the studio recording made with Gieseking, she gained satisfaction up to a point. 'Legato, legato,' she would say, as though actually finding it and approving – and then almost immediately adding 'But it isn't *really*!' The tiniest of indentations in the smooth line would be sufficient to smudge the ideal. A third version, with the difficult phrase 'Und will Himmel auf euch wehn' particularly successful, proved more completely acceptable. Yet the recording which most delighted her in this matter of legato was not of Mozart but Bach. The Cantata 199, *Mein Herze schwimmt im Blut*, played on our second day, gave her for once a straightforward, unalloyed pleasure, and at the end of the B section in the opening aria she turned with a triumphant 'Now *that's* legato!'

Schwarzkopf would take it as axiomatic that legato extends to the singing of runs. Like her husband, Walter Legge, and her teacher, Maria Ivogün, she is an implacable foe of the intrusive 'h'. Aspirates and other 'separation' devices in florid music are anathema. Strangely enough, there were two aspirates in that very first song we played, Wolf's 'Elfenlied', and I remarked on them. They were introduced, she said, for laughter – and that is 'the one circumstance in which it's permissible'. The total avoidance of aspirates is so basic to the whole notion of legato that in its grosser manifestations the offence and its condemnation were concurrent. I was to find, however, that it also involved more than the crude 'addi-hio' 'le-hebe wohl' of operatic convention. It might in fact be an almost unnoticeable impediment in the completely smooth joining of notes on the same syllable. A full (or fuller) exposition of legato came with my second visit, while listening to the 'Laudamus te' of Bach's *Mass in B minor*. Comments on that are given in a later section of this chapter, but they concern us at this point because they also link the subject of legato with another essential problem for singers and for all who aspire to an understanding of their art.

This 'Laudamus te' is of course a mezzo-soprano or even a contralto aria. Schwarzkopf does not recall why she was asked to sing it in the Karajan recording; but sing it she did, and in a manner that now dismays her. The legato is, in her view, severely flawed or non-existent. But the cause, as she analyses it, was the demand made upon an area of the lyric soprano's voice which nature had not equipped it to meet. And therein lay an important lesson.

An awareness of what is right for the voice, and right for it at a given time in its development, also played a large part in these listening-sessions. This is hardly surprising, as Schwarzkopf's voice went through many phases. Remember that she had two famous teachers, and that the first, the contralto, Lula Mysz Gmeiner, trained her as a contralto, while the second, the high coloratura-soprano, Maria Ivogün, retrained her as a *leggiero* or coloratura. It was only gradually in the late 1940s and early '50s that she adjusted to the pure lyric soprano repertoire. Eventually, with the deepening of tone and loss of high notes that come with age, she made further adjustments, and so is very well aware of the choices singers have to make in drawing the voice-colours from their singer's palette, merging the vocal registers, and recognising the music appropriate to the various stages of development.

We listened, for instance, to some of the earliest recordings. These have come to light mostly from wartime radio archives, published on the Acanta label, and made (as Schwarzkopf recalls) not as records at all but as broadcasts which happened to be recorded. There would be a quick run-through with the pianist, and then straight into the studio. These are products of Schwarzkopf's time with Ivogün, and the pianist was Ivogün's husband, Michael Raucheisen, to whom she is ever-grateful for doing so much to teach her the song repertoire and deepen her understanding.[5] Happily, in these listening-sessions she was able to enjoy them all, quite frankly and simply, adding critical observations throughout but not seeming to be troubled by them. One of these, 'Schlagende Herzen', was the first song of Richard Strauss studied with her great teacher, and, listening to it, she remarked wryly that Ivogün 'didn't bother much about intonation'. In 'Morgen' she was fascinated by the word 'Glücklichen', where the 'Glück' sounds in the young voice, the 'chen' in the older. Verdi's song of the chimney-sweep, 'Lo spazza-camino' (sung in German), with its smile and birdlike high notes, she thought 'the most Ivogün of all': and it was Raucheisen whom she credited as being most responsible for the Viennese lilt in the 'G'schichten aus dem Wienerwald'.

These were the right songs for her voice and art at that stage. It was at the time of the change-over from light roles that the voice-character became more complicated: in the early 1950s the development of voice and the roles that went with it was still so recent that in her recording

---

[5] Many of the songs in these recorded broadcasts were studied intensively with Ivogün, and had in that sense been prepared very thoroughly indeed. On Ivogün, Raucheisen and their importance in Schwarzkopf's life and career see Alan Sanders' commentary on the wartime recordings, pp. 54-5, 58-9.

of 'Deh, vieni, non tardar', Susanna's aria from *Le nozze di Figaro*, it is not surprising to find an incidental lapse into the voice of the Countess, which by that time had become her role in the opera (she hears it in the last line of the recitative, 'i furti miei'). In the complete *Hänsel und Gretel*, where the girl-voice is so well established, she detected very occasionally the intrusion of an older, fuller and darker sound: in the Evening Prayer, for example, she found what she calls 'the Marschallin voice' momentarily present, as it never was in the 1947 recording she made with Irmgard Seefried – 'amazing what those few years did to the voice'. The 'Marschallin sound' also intrudes to weaken the consistency of Wolf 's 'Die Spröde', at the words 'und der dritte bot sein Herz'.

Another and more obvious factor that affects the aptness of a voice within its chosen repertoire is, of course, that of sheer power: the volume or 'size' of a voice. She was clear in her own mind, for instance, that her recording of the aria 'Non mi dir' with its recitative shows that it would never have been right for her to move in *Don Giovanni*, as many have done, from the role of Donna Elvira to that of Donna Anna. 'No reserve of power,' was her comment: 'I still find the beautiful things, the sound and so forth, but what it *should* be ...' That, she implied, is a different matter. Listening to her record of Elisabeth's Greeting, 'Dich, teure Halle', in *Tannhäuser*, she said: 'It *sounds* like the genuine thing ...' but again the implication was one of doubt. For Strauss's Ariadne she felt it was just about right. 'We know it isn't a Brünnhilde voice' and 'it isn't the double-bedded voice of Lotte Lehmann', but that has its advantages here, for 'it's the character of a *vulnerable* creature', and, from this point of view, 'No, it doesn't strike me as too small.'

It was at about the time of the *Ariadne auf Naxos* recording, in the mid-1950s, that Schwarzkopf 's voice and art were probably at their point of best equilibrium as far as operatic work was concerned. Immediately one then thinks of *Der Rosenkavalier*, recorded in 1956, and this she feels was in some ways premature, both vocally (wanting more fullness in the middle voice) and dramatically (wishing that it had come after she had 'worked it in' on stage). We returned to this famous recording on my third visit, when she spoke of the dangers inherent in forcing the naturally weaker areas of the voice, and also of how valuable 'live' experience proved in helping the voice to carry over the orchestra: 'I wish we had rehearsed more, and then I would have been more aware of when the orchestra comes over my voice – I should have studied that, and I didn't know.' She also faulted it for lack of a proper aristocratic Viennese pronunciation: the word 'heutig', for example, should end with less of the soft 'ch' sound and more of the hard 'g'. Perhaps it should be added that (matters of pronunciation apart) these criticisms gained little support from me, and that once the first pages of Act I were over it was only very rarely that I shared the misgivings about 'size' of voice (after all, no such doubts had arisen during repeated hearings at Covent Garden). In the last third of the first Act the criticisms began to diminish, and we listened more or less in silence. At the end, I said 'I won't hear a word against it' – which made her smile and content herself with adding 'But the real thing was at Salzburg.'

It is good to recall that the first visit came towards its end with confirmation of the *Vier letzte Lieder* in the 1965 recording under Szell. The earlier versions, with Ackermann and Karajan, had advantages in what is usually taken as the first of the songs, 'Frühling'; yet even in this, she argued, the singer is 'the same woman ... it's the same person's view of spring, and you don't really want a springlike voice'. In 'September' the voice in those earlier recordings is 'too young for the text', and a much greater depth of feeling is tapped in the final version, the one with Szell.

If the advantages of a mature voice were recognised in that recording, the premature assumptions of early middle-age were given short shrift as she listened to the recital of Schubert Lieder recorded in 1952 with Edwin Fischer. 'Die junge Nonne' was stopped abruptly: 'external ... theatrical ... should be much more private.' In 'Wehmut' there was again to her mind (not to mine) a lack of 'living' behind it: 'you have to have experience in the voice, which must also be felt as a "thinking" voice'. This and the 'Gretchen am Spinnrade' (again to my dismay) were heard as the performances of 'an opera singer singing Lieder ... it's wishful thinking'. She brightened somewhat at the Carnegie Hall performance of 'Gretchen' ('Yes, lady! aha!'), and then the much later version with Geoffrey Parsons brought something very like satisfaction: 'the pauses are right, the acceleration, the blackout at climax after you've piled one on another. At least it's my *idea* of what it ought to be.' And then, finally and with feeling, 'Thank God it's there!'

That was the end of our week. For her, the sessions must have been a strange mixture. Some tired her (the Schubert did); some quite alarmed me (particularly the Wolf session with its recognition of what to her were serious faults in that central part of her repertoire). Sometimes there was sheer delight. Those occasions would usually take her by surprise, and I shall not forget the radiance of her enjoyment – the smile, the laughter – that lit up at these moments. 'Un moto di gioia' (happy title) was the first that provoked it: 'my best Mozart singing ever – despite the fast tempo, the gaiety and rhythm, they're all there and I can't think I have done anything better.' Then there was the Bach cantata, where she loved the 'inner feeling for rhythm' and various technical felicities, such as the short trills that are present as incidental graces in a performance blessed with spiritual grace from first to last.

Loewe's 'Kleiner Haushalt' brought satisfaction both in the recording and in the memory ('We would use it as an encore in Japan, where they loved it even though they couldn't understand the words'). Sometimes a real pride would come upon her and no words were spoken. 'You don't hear me object to that,' she said at the end of Strauss's 'Waldseligkeit'.

She did not object (and that in itself was praise); but neither did she analyse. No doubt she could have gone into detail, both technical and interpretative; but at the time it sufficed that the music had gone to the heart and that the performance had been worthy of it. Schwarzkopf is sometimes described, often in association with Fischer-Dieskau, as an intellectual singer. It is a description which she herself utterly repudiates. A highly *intelligent* singer, beyond question; but 'intellectual' is a term that suggests analytical thinking about concepts, a concern with literary, historical or philosophical connotations, a ratiocinative, theoretical view of the concrete particular which it transmutes into the general and abstract. That is not Schwarzkopf's way, either in her professional work or in her reactions to the music she hears. The reader will have noticed that her comments throughout have been very much those of a *singer*, not (to use the common but misleading term) an 'interpreter'. Acutely attentive as she is to matters of technical detail, and thoroughly articulate in defining her perceptions as they arise, she is nevertheless very clear that there is a point where words end. It goes with her artistic practice in opera and song, where, after meticulous preparation, spontaneous feeling takes over.

As we came, in one of these listening-sessions, to the last scene in *Ariadne auf Naxos*, she was remarking on various features such as the vibrato ('we used quite a lot of vibrato in those days, but it's quite apt here'). Then came the long crescendo and Ariadne's 'Wie schaffst du die Verwandlung?', which she liked greatly and on which she was about to comment. Then, clearly moved by the music and, frankly, by her own singing from those many years ago, she gestured as though to push words aside. 'Don't try to describe,' she said. And then: 'It was one of those things I did by instinct.' When the record was over, she returned to this passage. 'I always wanted that my own bit of fantasy should be there,' and then, wise words, which were also a commentary on the very project we had in hand: 'a book or written explanation would only obstruct.' She then quoted Goethe (a bit of an intellectual after all). It was from the passage in which Faust insists upon the importance of feeling: only if there is a true inner feeling will the artist win the hearts of others.[6] This Schwarzkopf fervently believes. Essentially, it is the Romantic creed, not only of Goethe but of Wordsworth ('It is the hour of

[6] Goethe: *Faust* Bk. I. Nacht. 'Wenn ihr's nicht fühlt …'.

feeling') and Keats ('We murder to dissect'). It does not deny the value of disciplined study and preparation (quite the contrary): but ultimately it acknowledges that art thrives upon the spontaneity of the moment.

✴

From the second visit, Schwarzkopf's comments are given verbatim. They were made while listening or when the record had just finished, and the 'style' has not been polished as for a written expression. Dots indicate that the record is continuing to play. A square bracket encloses words from the text or some other guidance to a point or reference or tone of voice. Items are arranged in approximate chronological order of composition.

Monteverdi: 'Io son pur vezzosetta pastorella'; 'Ardo e scoprir'; 'Baci cari' (with Irmgard Seefried)

ES: We did it by instinct ... We didn't hear anything before. It may not be right for musicologists but it was right for us and the listeners ... It has the vitality, voices like instruments, the musical weave, staccato/legato ... Yet we were not *told* to do it, we just did it, by listening one to the other. In musical things we had the same imagination. Not in the expression – she was much better than I was expressing things. But musical – we had the same training and the same approach to these things. And the voices match, they have no wobble, and they have their own short vibrato. Seefried had the much thicker, bigger speaking-area than mine, but she could keep it lightly and calmly as if she was speaking ... Of course we didn't choose which voice we sang. Walter decided that and we just did it ... ['Ardo'] Incredibly together, even the dividing of 'mio' for instance ... uncanny ... wasn't easy for me down there, singing the under-voice. ['Bari caci'] Don't you think that's better than having everything sung without vibrato? Without vibrato, it's so hideous[7] ... To me, when you hear two mature voices who can sing light, and can colour it ... You see, it isn't children's voices ... Miss Kirkby and whoever ... I wouldn't listen to two bars of it. It may be our generation that says that, but we had the best of it ... Normally vibrating, normally produced, women's voices just singing as a beautiful string instrument would do ... And I don't like it

[7] In her own singing, Schwarzkopf did find a place for the vibrato-less tone, which she finds right for (for example) the sick girl in Wolf's 'Das verlassene Mägdlein'. Yet even here, she insists, it has to be delicately, sparingly applied, and not, as she puts it, 'wallowed in'.

when the string instrument doesn't vibrate ... It's a mode; but the other sounds are so much more ingratiating, without being syrupy.

Bach: *Mass in B minor*: 'Laudamus te'

ES: Slow isn't it? ... Ooh! it's *very* slow! ... Is that Karajan? Oh my God isn't it slow! ... no, no ... Very German Latin ... Flat, God almighty! It's terribly flat ... It's the 'ah' vowel in the middle ... That's not legato at all, a jerky legato, I call it step-walking ... It sits nicely on the voice, but it's so jerky ... [laughs] No, that is a great disappointment. The sound is very sweet, it's a 'laudamus' sound, but it's no way legato ... It's not 'h's but it's like a jerk on the bow of a violin. [later] It shows it *should* be sung by a mezzo, because it needs all that reserve, and I can hear that I'm cautiously husbanding the voice. It should be long bow, long bow, and not jerking the bow to interrupt it all the time. And there in that record it's done, not by martellato or 'h's but what in English we call 'hairpin legato'. And it's on no account to be imitated. And if that aria is to be sung by a soprano it should be by a Seefried, who had a stronger, lower voice ... but better still by a Christa Ludwig.

Handel: *Hercules*: 'Father of Hercules, great Jove'

ES: The colouring: that's what I'm trying to teach them all the time. When there comes a repeat of the words (and sometimes there are many repeats) one must give it a meaning. It wouldn't be repeated if it wasn't felt differently. And that's a fine example of how to colour ... of how to sing classical music with expression. It's expressive by style, not pulling the music to pieces, not altering the tempo. No 'veristic' touch to it, though in expression it strikes you as terribly true to life.

Mozart: *Die Entführung aus dem Serail*: 'Welche Kummer ... Traurigkeit'
[There were two recordings here: the first a broadcast from Vienna in 1944 conducted by Moralt, the second a studio recording (1946) with the Vienna Philharmonic Orchestra conducted by Krips. Schwarzkopf's first comments relate to the exceptional use of appoggiature in the recitative. In the aria she is concerned with the way in which, as a young singer, she took certain vowels on high notes with an open sound rather than in head-voice.]

ES: [1944] The appoggiaturas, two of them, are there on account of the music being very full of feeling. [on the 'ig' syllable of 'Traurigkeit'] I wouldn't have done that later: I'd have used head-voice, but I was afraid of people saying 'she doesn't sing the right vowels'. And again. It comes out sharper in sound than it should be, or would have been if I'd taken the head-voice ... It's too uncovered ... and that also makes it the wrong vocal colours ... It's musical, goes like an instrument, very honest singing. But wrong colour, wrong colour! ... I'm sure I *had* the head-voice then. Uncovered ... it's good to hear maybe, but only as long as the voice is young ... Woe if my students did it like that!

[1946] Now that would be a demonstration record of how not to do it. It sounds right to a layman, but I should have been singing slim and light in the lower range of the voice and calmer and rounder in the upper. Not that you can *hear* anything wrong – but technically it *is* wrong, and you will lose the ability to sing that role in no time ... Everybody liked it: I had nobody to tell me ... Not to know that it was the end of my light voice, to be too thick in the middle. How often Ivogün told me: 'Slim, slim, slim.' I wouldn't have been doing it like that if Ivogün had been by my side. The others could help me musically, but not technically.

Mozart: *Don Giovanni*: (a) 'Ah, chi mi dice mai'
                        (b) 'In quali eccessi ... Mi tradì'
[In both of these excerpts, the studio recording under Giulini was heard and then compared with the 1954 performance under Furt-wängler. In 'Ah, chi mi dice mai', the 1950 Salzburg performance was added.]

ES: (a) Very good tempo ... chest voice, you have to have it there.[8] [afterwards] It's well sung without consciously exhibiting singing; it's exhibiting the dramatic figure. But in the recit it's not matching. It becomes a waspish character ... I'm not saying the recit should be *sung* more, but it should be more in the voice of the entrance.

[Salzburg 1954] A bit too slow. It hasn't the drive of Giulini ... *Without* chest here: I didn't have it then ... No, it's too slow ... Ah! there was the chest for once ... very clean. [recit] Fine! I wish I could have heard that before doing the Giulini ... That's much better. There's many more colours ... The other one is much more a harridan, a shrew. More class

---

8 Schwarzkopf is very clear that this use of the chest voice is exceptional. Here, on the low Fs, it is needed to make Elvira's scorn more vivid (and, to take another and still more exceptional example, in the 'Libera me' of Verdi's *Requiem* it extends to the G and has within it the menace of hell-fire). But essentially it must be heard as an integral part of the voice: 'The moment it becomes noticeable, changing from a thin little middle-voice into a thick chest-sound, you know that the end of the voice is coming. There comes a great big hole, and many a mezzo-soprano who has been using it to satisfy the public (who have a great taste for blood) has soon found herself in trouble. For a soprano it is *terribly* dangerous.'

here, not lowering herself to the standard of a servant, shouting at everybody – with Giulini there's the better pace, but there's much less fidelity in the recitatives. Less theatrical reality. Walter wanted my voice as a foil to Sutherland who sang Donna Anna in the Giulini recording. So my voice gets hard, as it never did on stage. She was made into an unsympathetic woman – who's rightly abandoned!

(b) [Salzburg 1954] [a quiet passage in recit] That's the Furtwängler touch, which none of the others had ... [aria] Very good ... splendid. [in first run] Legato ... [second] Breathed once but good enough ... [return of 'Mi tradì'] Now there should be crying in the voice because of what has gone before ['tormento'] That was my view of the dramatic development, and now anger takes over. [afterwards, going back over the recitative] There's one very big portamento and then one very bad appoggiatura ... I eliminated a lot of them [appoggiature] because they weaken the character ... The musicologists are quite wrong there – they haven't been on stage!

[Salzburg 1950] [recitative] The fermata and portamento are terrible. Not in taste ... [quiet passage] Better than the other one! It's a marvellous touch ... [a further pianissimo] No, no, that's Puccini! That's terribly slow now, I must say [Mi tradì] It lacks the attack. I didn't have it then ... [long run starts] That won't last ... Two notes earlier to breathe, and that was simply because I didn't start with the head-voice. [after high B flat at end] Furtwängler wanted that! Awful! But he preferred it. We never did it before, with Krips in Vienna, or with any other conductor later.

[Giulini] [recitative] Much faster ... [Mi tradì run] That did start in head-voice: good. [at end] Stylistically, vocally, in expression, it's better ... The others are a bit wild against this, apart from the recit where I find Furtwängler better still with the slowing down, which Giulini didn't want (Walter proposed it to him but he didn't want it). An Italian always thinks forward instead of giving *time* for emotion. Otherwise I find the beginning better because it's faster, more dramatic. I'm glad I sang that coloratura in one breath, because I often did on stage. It's depending on whether I would slip into the head-voice at the beginning, because the head-voice takes so much less air. Good.

Mozart: *Così fan tutte*: 'Ei parte ... Per pietà'
    [The recordings used here were the two studio versions, under
    Karajan and Böhm respectively, then live performances under
    Böhm and Cantelli.]

ES: [Karajan] Fine, but it's very slow. You can tell I hadn't done it on stage at that time ... Much too many portamenti. Dragging! It's all wrong. I wonder why Karajan did that. No dramatic sense at all. It's a lovely sound, yes, but that doesn't mean everything.

[Böhm] This moves on. Marvellous ... And that's a dramatic use of the voice [Per pietà] Very difficult technically because it keeps going over the 'break' – one has to go into the chest-voice unnoticeably, and it's like walking the tightrope ... That's about right ... Fine, legato ... *Not* quite, a bit of hairpin legato there ... But it's fine.

[Böhm 'live'] That's much more dramatic ... but it's too free. [aria] [in disapproval] Oh, that's very open singing. ... The portamenti are too big for Mozart ... flat, flat ... Oh, Dio, too much chest ... all German vowels ... very German, ganz Deutsch!

[Cantelli] So far, better in tune ... G sharp! That's very flat [hears a cough] That was Walter! I'm sure coughing before it was flat. 'Very flat, my dear' ... Where did I get the idea I was a clean singer? ... We're going faster, I don't know why ... [at end] Well ... Clean singer on no account ... Sometimes, but not always. Interesting, but no, not good ... There must be singers who are always clean surely. There must be. Any orchestral player would be thrown out of the orchestra, but this damn thing [referring to the voice] ... To have to cope with vowels which have different positions, different *Spannung*, different tensions. The 'ah' vowel is one of the very worst in the middle for women, sometimes for men, because it loses tension in itself ... I'm glad I have that profession behind me!

Schubert: songs in a recital at Rome in 1952, with Giorgio Favaretto as accompanist.

'Ave Maria'
ES: Not bad is it! ... I never recorded it.

'Die Forelle'
ES: Legato! It's not too bad! ... Very good ... Well, thank you!

'Auf dem Wasser zu singen'
ES: Here come the 'h's surely ... Nicely played by Favaretto ... 'h's ... better ... Bravo, Giorgio! [second verse] Why I never recorded it, I was so afraid of those 'h's and I have not yet heard anyone sing it without 'h's ... Lovely ... ah, yes [third verse] Good! ... The sound is lovely, nicely shaded and the difference between major and minor is nice ... Thank God for that!

'Ungeduld'
ES: A man's song, but lovely ... Good for an Italian audience (they love

melody, not problems) ... You know, it's thanks to Favaretto that there
was Lieder-singing in Italy at all. Entirely due to him.

'Der Musensohn'
ES: Nice ... Consistent in mood too ... No hurry. That's one of my best
I'm sure. Yes, bravo.

'Suleika'
ES: Nice long vowels ... But the triplets should be all spaced out and
they're not, they're hurried ... Intonation [approving] Ha, that's what I
call intonation! ... Lovely, Giorgio Favaretto. Walter would have taken
his hat off to that ... Well, *everything* should be like that.

Schubert: 'Der Einsame'

ES: It's a good one ... Yes, all in place, and the mood is there. Comfortable. The only thing is that it shouldn't be sung by a woman. It just isn't
right. We did it a lot: the 'Ständchen' and all those things, but it vexes
me now. In the period of those poems, and long after that, it wouldn't
have been thinkable as a woman. It's like a woman singing 'Der heilige
Joseph singt' [Wolf's 'Nun wandre, Maria']. Many did it, but it goes
against the grain. Also with *Winterreise*: the voice should be *inside* the
piano-part: the whole lay-out of the piano-part is asking to accommodate
a man's voice: a woman's is too far outside it. And these are men's poems,
after all: Schubert's friends, who would have sung these songs first, were
men. But 'Der Einsame' is very nice: comfortable, relaxed ... A little
wistfulness shines through at one point, but not more. The many verses:
you must vary them, yet not be so free that the music suffers. The tempo
is 'mässig', in four, not two. Pears and Britten do it in two: it's a
marvellous performance, I love it, but it's not right.

Schumann: 'Die Kartenlegerin'

ES: You have to *see* the cards before you sing it. You haven't got much
time, split seconds. And even then you can't just sing on: you have to
make those 'thinking' and 'seeing' pauses filled with that thought every
time. And I didn't do that. It's nicely sung, yes ... but the real expression
of what the situation offers, that's not there. It's not significant or
picturesque enough.

Wolf: *Spanisches Liederbuch*: 'Mühvoll komm' ich und beladen'
  [This was a listening-session in ternary form, with the studio

recording of 1966 sandwiched between a first and second playing of the performance at Salzburg in 1955.]

ES: For a live performance it is quite incredible, I dare say, and I do think it does justice to the song ... But wherever you think there is enough expression it is clearly Walter, who made me aware that I could do it and should do more. He gave me *pictures* – gave me, let's say, scenic ideas of somebody sinking down under the cross and prostrating herself ... Always conjuring up ideas, what it would be like in real life, even what the scenery would be like: not just the face but the whole scene. When I'm doing the *St Matthew Passion* with students I say to them 'Well, look at the Grünewald picture of the woman under the cross, and there you have the exact expression, not just in the face but in the whole body distorted with pain.' And those pictures of people, how they walk, how they sit, how they lie, how they behave in a situation ... I have to see a situation. In Lieder-singing I have to think, and know in my mind whether it's day or night or whatever. And in performance of course it's all the theatre of the mind: there's no bodily movement, you have to stand still.

[the studio recording] Lower pitch! ... No, I don't find it as good; because I'm not doing all those crescendi and diminuendi with the piano ... It's hurried ... No, no, it's out of tempo, there's no steady rhythm ... No, it's 'made', it's not genuine ... Even Gerald hurries. [noting the elision in pronunciation of 'mich an'] Same as all the students! ... [then noting the different pronunciation in the repeat] Ah, that's better.

[Afterwards] It's not good that it is lower, and the other one is much more genuine in expression. [referring to the studio recording] I hear myself *doing* it instead of it coming genuinely as a flow of feeling and of thoughts: feeling first, then thoughts after the feeling. Also in Salzburg I made the consonants 'm' and 'n' more prominent: it makes a difference if you say '*m*ühvoll'. [commenting on the religious feeling in the song] Catholic, which I'm not, and I had to find my way in that music. I could do it, but I can't say it was innate in me ... the woman there, the Spanish Catholicism, an erotic Catholicism which is crumbling under the on-slaught of, yes, self-destruction.

Wolf: 'Wie glänzt der helle Mond'

ES: Pianissimo. Fantastic. It can be sung with a much opener, more childish voice of an old woman; here I do it with some touches of that. Fragile, yes. Perhaps it doesn't sound quite fragile enough here ... Gerald keeps the tempo beautifully steady. The only thing is, I did once sing it with longer phrases. [turning to the Salzburg recital, accompanied by Furtwängler] *Not* slower! And a tone higher than the other. Wonderful! This is much freer in tempo. Very human ... Too early, that entry – ah, he's covered it ... I think they're both valid, but I like the even tempo of the one with Moore: inexorability.

Wolf: *Eichendorff Lieder*: 'Die Zigeunerin'
  [A comparison of an early recording on Acanta (wartime) with the 1965 studio recording with Moore.]

ES: Aha! quite a lot of courage, surprising for those early days. Later I did it with a much darker voice, and I didn't *start* it with that sort of cat-voice. I don't quite like it any more; it's too much for me now. But it's amazing for a young singer with a silvery voice. In fact it's not natural for that young-sounding voice! I can't imagine that I had that chest-voice then. [starting on the later version] Yes, it *should* sound like that, Oh, ja. [as the voice goes deep] That is the sort of mature voice of the mature woman, more sensuous. And it's not a mezzo singer: it's a dark, hooded, dangerous soprano sound. And the laughs are good – and that's very hard, it takes a lot of breath, your ribs really hurt ... Both are fine, but the other is the twelve-year younger voice giving a catty expression, which it could do at that age. But [referring to the later version] That's the real thing. Thank God for that!

Strauss: *Capriccio*: Closing scene.

ES: [after a complete play-through] Well, did you hear me utter a sound? No. Everything fits together – the enharmonic changes, the feeling, elegance ... I can't say anything should be otherwise; I would if it were so, but no. And so I think perhaps I *was* sometimes a clean singer after all: in *Arabella* and this. I know that this is the main piece of all. And it is the story of my life. Because if you sing opera and Lieder all your life, everything mixed, you have to decide, not by brain but by instinct, musical instinct, when to give right to the music and when to give right to the words. Here it is sound and words together – but woe if it were not comprehensible. Then it would be nowhere ... I think this is the best in all respects: conductor, orchestra, tempo, sound, balance, diction, even expression – though it isn't an expression-opera, it's an argument-opera ... In a way, the scene is as difficult as the *Salome* last scene to sing – so that it isn't only an intellectual thing; you've got to know how to sing. And even here the sound of the *wounded* woman is much more important than the exact arguing of points, even arguing with herself. No: it's not an intellectual exercise. It is people with brains, arguing, disputing, discussing, she with herself, her heart, her brains, eternally to resolve the question. And solved it cannot be. Because you have to change the balance of the word and the sound by a hair's breadth: it was the argument of my life.

Verdi: *Otello*: 'Willow Song' and 'Ave Maria'

ES: [Willow Song] I usually take the sound of the voice in Lieder-singing in every sentence from a key-word, and here, for me, it's 'candida veste', the white wedding-dress: so it's an innocent, virginal-sounding voice. Then with 'Senti' ['Listen: if I should die before you'] you come to something quite different. ['Son mesta, tanto, tanto'] Chest, on account of the pain ... chest ... and then head-voice, but you don't hear any break of registers, not ever. [after the cry 'Ah, Emilia, addio'] You mustn't prepare it. It has to come out of nowhere, suddenly. Not prepare it vocally even with an eyelid batting, just completely forget that it is coming ...

[Ave Maria] That 'i' there ['Maria'] it's apt for the pain of it, but you wouldn't do it in German. [answering a question about the difficulty of the arpeggio on 'Ave'] No, not really as difficult as people think. The top piano note comes more easily when you have less air: if you have used a lot of air on the preceding notes then you fall much more easily into the pianissimo. Then you have to hold the A flat with your diaphragm (and it helps if you've given a little more on the third note, the E flat). It's not so difficult as the 'Salce's, the graduation of sound there, and the pianissimo F sharps ... I don't think it's half so difficult as the Countess [in *Le nozze di Figaro*]. It's written marvellously well for the voice, the feeling and the words, but the Countess ... it's a *concertante* with instruments: you have to be aware you're singing chamber music almost, as an instrument with the other instruments. With Mozart you have always to produce this mixture of instrumental singing and human feeling. The violin or clarinet may give you a sound for you to match, and in some ways your freedom is limited. There's much more freedom in Verdi.

Puccini: *La bohème*: 'Si, mi chiamano Mimì'

ES: The vowel-treatment is totally different from what we might be doing in the German language – the light-coloured 'ah' vowel. And there are not too many portamenti here ... You mustn't expect them everywhere, and you must know why you are doing them. Listen to Callas – she does everything for a purpose and she knows why it has to be there. Usually it's for the overflow of a certain sentiment, or a word that lends itself to a sentiment that is coming ... like a pot boiling over, even if only a little way. They're different in German. The German portamenti are a softening touch, a tenderising. And we have it in the German language: if you say 'Liebe', it has its own portamento, much softer, much shorter than the Italian portamento. In German it should come at the end of a note, usually on a vowel – as in 'Wonne', on the 'o'. [Going back now to the start of the record and commenting on Mimì's hesitations] Interrupting, you see ... Interrupting herself all the time. She doesn't know how to go on. [at 'mi piaccion quelle cose'] That's Walter Legge, standing in front of me, doing it and saying it. 'Mi *piacc*ion quelle cose'. He could give the expression of somebody saying it and not just singing it ... [after the high A on 'prima' in 'di primavere'] If you think I was singing 'prima', I wasn't! Women's voices[9] haven't any vowels of that kind above the F sharp, G, depending on whether it's a very light coloratura. It's an 'ah' but in a very round compartment of the mouth, and you never try to sing an 'ee' ... In this last section of the aria, for once we left the written score. It's written forte, you know, but I must apologise to Mr Puccini up in heaven, and I think he will grant me that. I thought that on the word 'perfumed' ('profumo') you shouldn't sing forte. It's not a question of first time loud, second time soft ... it's the word 'profumo'. You can't sing that loud ... [in the recit at the end, noting a little chuckle on 'narrare'] That came out by instinct. She can see out on these roofs, it's all lovely. I wanted that to sound still joyful and vivacious and tender and dainty at the same time. Smallish tender little feelings, not the consumptive dying already!

Millöcker: *Die Dubarry*: 'Ich schenk mein' Herz'

ES: I listened to records of Fritzi Massary that Walter played me – I would learn from these things but then sing in my own voice and my own way. [laughing] You won't get it like this nowadays ... Wunderbar ... 'Mannerisms'! Ja, ja ... Well, you needn't like it, but from a singer's point of view it's not bad at all ... Now I must go and look after my potatoes.

---

[9] This is a point that was made repeatedly in the course of these sessions. Conductors and critics constantly urge sopranos to sing the vowels as written, even on the high F sharp and above. If the vowel is an open one, it may be harmful to the voice (and in any case goes against German practice). The physical reasons for this can be demonstrated, but even if this were not so it is a cardinal point on which Schwarzkopf trusts the knowledge of her teacher Maria Ivogün and her own experience. The modification of vowels must be as unobtrusive as possible, but for the preservation of the vocal instrument it must be accomplished. A good technique is not demonstrated by ignoring these guidelines (even if with a temporary success) but by following them implicitly.

❊

The last sentence serves as a reminder that these were domestic occasions. The telephone rings all day, people come and go, and in the evenings there are sometimes meals to be prepared. System rules up to a point, but the point of departure from it was soon reached in our listening-sessions. Eventually, the repertoire was covered, but only by darting about here and there, seeing a space and filling it, deciding on a Brahms or Mahler session one morning, only to find that this was to be Mozart day and ending up with the operettas. The element of surprise was in fact one of the refreshing features. Not many bets, I imagine, would be placed on 'Mi chiamano Mimì' if we had been asked to speculate on which song or aria would provoke the most sustained commentary. Best of all, I dare say, were two occasions which might very easily not have arisen at all.

During the first visit we had confined the listening largely to what might be thought of as the core-repertoire. Obviously much remained unheard, but we had taken representative samples from Bach, Mozart, Schubert, Brahms, Wolf, Strauss and Mahler. By the middle of the second week it was time to look further afield. The Italian arias were encouraging; so too was the delightful collection of duets by Monteverdi, Carissimi and Dvořák with Irmgard Seefried. Sometimes a brave start would be made, as with the 'live' performances of *Pelléas et Mélisande* from La Scala and *The Rake's Progress* from the première at Venice. We did not get far with either of those. At the sound of *Pelléas* she would repeat 'Je ne suis pas heureuse ici', and with *Rake*: 'No! I don't want to hear. Take it off! ... The physical act of singing that dreadful music is quite a pleasure, but I do find it loathsome – apart from the Lullaby.'

The surprise was Walton's *Troilus and Cressida*. As is well known, the role of Cressida had been written with Schwarzkopf's voice in mind, and it was hoped that she would sing in the première. This was not to be (the first Cressida was Magda László), but excerpts were recorded with the composer conducting and Richard Lewis in his creator's role of Troilus. The original record had long disappeared from the catalogue but had recently resurfaced on CD in EMI's excellent *British Composers* series. Prospects of playing it did not seem bright, but it is an opera of which I myself had fond memories (I even croaked a few phrases by way of demonstration). Somewhat sceptically she settled to listen, and rather marvellously the record stayed its course. The music itself, which she had probably not heard from that date in 1955 to this in 1994, surprised with its warmth and its strong melodic line; and her own part in it clearly astonished her. 'It's really some of my best singing ...

Everything in place ... Expression comes out, falls into place, because the voice was obedient ... Quite incredible. I didn't know.' And (persistence rewarded) 'I wouldn't have known, you know, if you hadn't made me listen.'

The second event of this kind occurred in the third week. Here the credit was due to the third person present. By this unsystematic method we had arrived at the songs which would sometimes have a place in the second half of recital programmes – a few by Grieg and Tchaikovsky, a Rachmaninov. And then came Sibelius's 'Saf, saf, süsa' ('Sigh, sigh, sedges') in a wonderful performance which at last took the breath out of criticism's mouth. There followed an enquiry after another of the Sibelius songs, 'War det en dröm' ('Was it a dream') which appeared to have been recorded but to have remained unissued. Lily Reenvig pointed out that another recording existed, taken from a concert for Finnish Radio in 1955: not only did it exist, but it was, she believed, in the house. The origin of this lay in a request to Miss Reenvig from Walter Legge many years ago that she might ask for a copy of the tape as a favour to himself and Madame Schwarzkopf. This she did and was granted a copy on the understanding that it was for purely private use and would go no further. The tape had been preserved but apparently never played in recent years. Certainly it was new to the singer, and it contained not only this and several other songs by Sibelius, but also the major work for soprano and orchestra, *Luonnotar*, sung in Finnish and in the single performance Schwarzkopf gave of it.

What might have been an anti-climax proved the very opposite. The tape was found and played, a beautifully faithful recording of the voice at the very height of its form, used with a lyrical intensity and dramatic concentration which could only be called inspired. Again criticism was mute. Indeed one felt that finally all the bleak and mortifying rigour of self-criticism had justified itself, if only because it now conferred the right to frank enthusiasm – which was heartfelt. 'It's the best singing I have ever done,' she said; 'the best I've done in my life.' So we heard it again and opened a bottle of champagne.

These items were, as I say, retrieved from a place off-centre in Schwarzkopf's repertoire. There were various odds and ends that also deserve a brief mention. The Grieg songs are an example: 'Ich liebe dich' (or 'Jeg elsker deg') with its fine 'building' of sound towards the climax, 'Med en wandlije' ('With a water-lily') ('Ah, in my older days I learnt to sing legato at last') and four others recorded in 1970 ('I'm amazed about the middle range. I didn't even know I did it'). Adolf Jensen's sugarplum 'Murmelndes Lüftchen' pleased too, as an example of the German language musically used ('Lengthening the vowels when you want to sing on the phrase'). After Dvořák's 'Songs my mother taught me', she recalled Legge telling her that she had a Czech heart.[10] After Stravinsky's 'Vocalise' ('very "hooded" sound ... the head-voice notes, even the low ones, *sound* higher'): 'it's valid, but it isn't me.' After Tchaikovsky's 'Pimpinella': 'No, no ... Imitating a man's voice, making it bombastic ... Why did we do that, I wonder? We didn't always do it like that, God forbid!'

Then there were the operatic 'oddities'. Several have already been mentioned, and some she would probably prefer not to be mentioned at all. That curious record of 'Depuis le jour' (*Louise*), unissued in its time, caused some perplexity: 'I think Walter wanted me to fill in for somebody ... But no, I shouldn't have tried to do it, not that way. I should have done it my German way, as a Mozart singer, using the Kopfstimme.' The German repertoire itself sometimes yielded disappointing results, as she believes it did in the complete recording of Cornelius's *Der Barbier von Bagdad*: 'I was ill, I shouldn't have been singing, but the orchestra was there and I had to do it.' Of her part in Orff's *Die Kluge* she had no very high expectations, but at least 'the intonation is good, thank God for that!'. The cleanness of 'jumps' (or intervals) in the lullaby pleased her: 'Well, it's steady but it's not stiff, like they have in early music nowadays.' And a real surprise, almost comparable to that of *Troilus and Cressida* and of the Sibelius concert, was the great aria of Leonore in *Fidelio*. Not a role for Schwarzkopf on stage (where she was an outstanding Marzelline), it nevertheless fired her in the studio, and as her 'Abscheulicher!' bore down upon the villainous Pizarro in his absence, we cowered in the music-room.

Still in the category of 'oddities' – but more odd that they should be so – come the Schumann song-cycles, *Liederkreis* Op. 39 and *Frauenliebe und Leben*. Both were recorded late in Schwarzkopf's career (1974): they were coupled on two sides of an LP and did not meet with an enthusiastic press. Schwarzkopf's dislike of the *Frauenliebe* cycle is (and was then) well-known, though the precise grounds of it may not have been always understood. Her view is that Chamisso's poems are insufferable, their language embarrassing to a native German speaker, in modern times if not in the past. The last song of the cycle, 'Nun hast du mir den ersten Schmerz getan', addressed to the husband on his death, is excepted, but here another disabling factor arises, for she finds the emotion almost unbearable. So the *Frauenliebe* recording remained unplayed and rejected.

The *Liederkreis* was a different matter, and it puzzled her probably

[10] Her favourite orchestral music is Smetana's 'Vltava' from *Má Vlast*. 'It's a kind of home-coming, Heimat. My father used to sing it about the house. I don't know why it should be ... I don't know a word of Czech, but it's like a place *unruined*, and very dear to me.'

more than any other of her records. At first she disliked everything
about it apart from Geoffrey Parsons's playing. A slight mitigation came
with the haunting and evocative 'Auf einer Burg', which she agreed
caught the atmosphere well. 'Zwielicht' too was allowed, yet vocally she
found the whole thing 'painful': 'The ageing debilitates ... You can sing
while ageing but ... the weaknesses, if they are not there, can be heard
approaching ... the tone isn't there with the muscles any more.' Still it
was not this that most perplexed her. Throughout, she had been concerned with the low keys and the deep, thick quality of her voice. 'It
couldn't be right, doesn't make sense at all,' she kept saying, and we
checked that there hadn't been a power-cut that might have affected the
playing-speed. The mystery must have deepened overnight, for it pursued us the following day. Interestingly, the foretaste had prepared her
to listen afresh. On its own terms (the low keys included), the performance was now seen to have some merit after all: 'Yes, nice' she would
say to one song, 'Not bad' to another. The phenomenon of that deep
mezzo voice still teased. 'It isn't my normal voice. I can't understand ...
If you didn't *know* my normal voice ...' But no: 'I never will understand
it.'

A process at work throughout the listening-sessions was one that
might be called the delimiting of repertoire. Much was declared invalid.
A woman should not sing a man's songs (even such a song as Wolf's
'Selbstgeständnis', where an adult reflects on the wisdom of 'spare the
rod and spoil the child', was put into this category, on the grounds that
only boys got beaten). Age should not sing the songs of youth, and (but
more emphatically) *vice versa*. Music for light voices should not be
subjected to the imposition of a heavy voice, though she conceded that
a skilful technique may achieve a rare success. Dangers, sometimes
prohibitive, attend the singing of art-songs in a foreign language:
however proficient a linguist, a foreigner will have a different cultural
background and ambience, missing the overtones, the resonance, of
words and phrases (for instance, in Brahms's 'Immer leiser' comes the
phrase 'bleich und kalt', which in German, she says, is a familiar, almost
mechanical, coupling like the English 'dead and gone' and is sung that
way the first time, while the second time the literal force of the words
comes vividly to mind). Then there is the matter of temperament, of
affinity. The *Frauenliebe und Leben* cycle might be an extreme case of
the negative effect here, but to some extent the songs of Brahms were
distanced, Mahler's also. Even in Wolf there were areas which she
considered not hers by nature. In the *Spanisches Liederbuch* the religious mysticism was alien, and in the *Italienisches Liederbuch* she felt
that the character of the woman in these was something she had to work
at, whereas her contemporary Seefried could do them by instinct.

The composers with whom such misgivings arose least were Mozart and Strauss. Strauss, especially, was the one whose music provided the most reliable source of satisfaction in performance. There were reservations about the *Rosenkavalier* certainly, but none about the *Capriccio* recording, which she felt was exactly the opera for her. Arabella and Ariadne were roles she never sang on stage, though she had hoped to sing both (and Lotte Lehmann had urged her to sing Arabella at the time when she recorded excerpts – 'For God's sake sing it now, before you're too old'). The *Arabella* passages also gave her great pleasure, both in the pervasive freshness and beauty of voice and in the detail of responsiveness to enharmonic changes and the cleanness of 'take' in wide intervals. Both operas, *Arabella* and *Capriccio*, require a special sensitivity in the matter of intonation, in which a subtlety beyond mere accuracy is needed. The constant changes of harmony affect the singer as they do the orchestral player; their notes are not 'fixed' as on a keyboard, and (according to the harmonic context) a G sharp, for example, will not be the same as an A flat. Schwarzkopf's listening here brought satisfaction particularly because she found these minute adjustments in place and instinctively 'right'. In *Ariadne auf Naxos* she loved (of course) the title-role itself, but also the comical sketch of a Prima Donna in the Prologue, and its metamorphosis: 'the stupid larynx on two legs becomes a godlike creature by virtue of the music.' When the chest-voice came into play it was 'chest as it ought to be' (" "Don't go down into the cellar", Walter would say').

As with most of the records, there were cries of 'flat!', 'unclean!', 'no legato': but at least they were comparatively infrequent. With the songs (including the *Vier letzte Lieder* mentioned earlier) objections arose more often, especially with regard to the second set of orchestral songs recorded with Szell in 1968. 'This is the voice of wishful thinking on the part of Walter,' she said after 'Meinem Kinde': 'It is not there, it simply is not there.' But the Strauss songs with piano illustrated a particularly interesting point: that after all this work of perfectionism in the studio it was often the 'live' performances that came out best.

Many of these have appeared on 'pirate' labels, towards which her attitude is understandably ambivalent: she objects in principle but is (often) grateful in practice. In this instance, the 'live' recordings were of a concert given at Hannover in 1962 with Hermann Reutter as accompanist. After several versions of 'Zueignung' (which, incidentally, she new regards as essentially a man's song), the Hannover performance won: 'That's the best. The right voice for it. In the Szell it sounds emaciated.' With 'Meinem Kinde' the preference was equally marked, and probably would have been in 'Freundliche Vision' and 'Wiegenlied' had not some details of pronunciation waylaid her. After 'Ruhe, meine

Seele', with its subtle colouring and almost fierce emotional concentration, the superiority of the 'live' performance made her wonder deeply. Clearly, as she said, this was 'more projected'. Then she added: 'I think I controlled myself in a live performance, but evidently something happens in a live recital, which is technically, emotionally, more ...' The sentence remained unfinished, but we knew what she meant.

We also understood why the conclusion was a hard one for her to reach. The work on records with Walter Legge as producer aimed at perfection, and, under modern conditions of recording, had a fair chance of achieving it. 'In the flesh' there could be no retakes, and so much more was at the mercy of chance. And yet 'evidently something happens'. It was so with Wolf's *Sechs alte Weisen*. The 1962 studio recording with Gerald Moore won approval only with the fifth song ('Das Köhlerweib ist trunken'); otherwise there was a constant complaint of 'too slow'. In the Salzburg recital of 1958, the first song of the group, 'Tretet ein', lighter and quicker, was '*much* better'. In the second, 'Singt mein Schatz', where she had found the ending in the studio 'simply shrieked', here it was 'exactly right'. Similarly in a group of Wolf's Goethe-Lieder: 'I think in the hall I came to grips with it more. In the studio it's too private.'

The discovery of the Finnish Radio's Sibelius concert brought further support, and so did some chance operatic encounters. From Rome there came a concert performance of *Die Zauberflöte* under Karajan and in Italian. She liked her own part in 'Là dove prende' ('Bei Männern') and loved Giuseppe Taddei's, and 'Ah, lo so' ('Ach, ich fühl's') was found 'not too German in sound ... The Italians didn't like a non-vibrato sound, but they respected this.' It was also notable that an operatic recording in which she took as much pride as in any was of the Bayreuth 'live' 1951 *Die Meistersinger von Nürnberg*. The pleasure lay partly in an enthusiastic appreciation of her colleagues, Otto Edelmann especially, and, after the Prize Song, 'Bravo Hans Hopf'. But her own part pleased her too: the colloquial tone in the duets with Sachs (but still 'concerned with giving full value to the notes'), the radiant outburst of 'O Sachs, mein Freund', the great test of the Quintet, and (remembering the recorded voice of Meta Seinemeyer) Eva's phrases at the close of the Prize Song, 'perhaps best of all'.

The 'live' recordings are important in another respect. Walter Legge referred to his marriage with Schwarzkopf as 'the longest and happiest association of my life', and she would certainly say no less. The collaboration was nevertheless achieved at a price. One was that it incurred some resentment on the part of others, with which would sometimes go an imputation that, as the wife of the leading producer of the leading record company, Schwarzkopf had an advantage not matched by achievements in the 'real' world of performances in concert and opera. The 'live' recordings give the answer to that. They show Schwarzkopf on stage in some of the great opera houses of the world, in international company, and standing there with unquestionable distinction on her own merits. Another, and crueller, price of her work with Legge was the common, and commonplace, jibe that she played Trilby to his Svengali. Malice, ignorance or an incorrigible coarseness of mind are the only sources of this: the relationship was a complex one, but while there is no doubt at all about Legge's supreme importance as an influence and an inspiration, it is equally clear that Schwarzkopf was not an artist who could be 'drilled' or who would have valued anything that was not a genuine, free collaboration. That was not how it worked. When Legge first met her it was the combination of ability and determination that attracted his attention. She was essentially an individual, and, for that matter, already a highly accomplished and successful singer. Hence the importance of the 'live' recordings in which she was on her own, and also those early recordings made in wartime or shortly afterwards, before her meeting with Legge, and in which she can be heard not only as the possessor of an unusually beautiful and well-trained voice but also as a maturing artist.

As she listened to those records, maybe she felt a little more detached, willing to extend an indulgence towards the young singer which she could not offer the woman in her prime. As far as I could tell, she was genuinely happy to hear these young, almost impromptu performances; and they too brought their surprises. A marvellously spirited, infectious 'Schlechtes Wetter' delighted her, as did another Strauss song, 'Mein Vater hat gesagt' ('I don't think I equalled that later'). In Loewe's 'Es ist mein Herz', not too pleased with the uncovered high notes, she was happy to find 'access to the smiling voice' and already something of the other, the sad. Busoni's 'Unter den Linden' was another where, in addition to the light high voice of the Ivogün period, 'it also goes into the middle range where the sound of the later voice all comes into being'.

These and the 'live' recordings are clearly an essential part of the picture. So too are some recordings still as yet unmentioned. High in that list are the operettas. They are not, in general, a subject for critical analysis, though occasionally a remark might touch on something special. On the *Wiener Blut* waltz with Gedda she commented on the slowing down at the start of the waltz-tune: 'It's this big ritardando, like something turning in a big kettle that always comes faster. It is not, as people like to say, mannerisms; it is manners.' The large-scale choral works, such as Beethoven's *Missa solemnis* and Verdi's *Requiem* went with little comment. With others she found little satisfaction: the *St Matthew Passion* in a slow performance under Klemperer disappointed

her because there was no lamentation in the voice; and the famous
recording of the solo in Brahms's *Requiem* under Karajan (the one so
admired by Toscanini) was 'neither one thing nor the other, neither the
disembodied floating angel nor the warmer, more substantial mother-
voice'. Her best Brahms she thought very probably 'Immer leiser' in a
late recording with Geoffrey Parsons ('previously I didn't have the lower
register, so I couldn't give the expression I wanted'). And what she is
now inclined to think of as her best Schubert, also with Parsons, and
also a surprise, is 'Der Erlkönig'. It was a surprise to hear, and apparently a surprise to record: Legge sprang it on them when he thought the
time was right, and the result was a triumph of art and inspired
spontaneity.

Essentially the harvest of these three weeks is now gathered in. I
have been round picking up a few bits and pieces, and could go round
again (over there – the metaphor must have suggested it – is Mussorgsky's 'Gathering mushrooms', and there Grieg's 'Farmyard Song',
both of which she loved). But more would largely be more of the same:
the main points are made.

Legato, intonation, understanding of the voice: these are the primary
lessons. Intellectual analysis of word or music hardly enters, not at least
in the form of discursive theorising. Intellect, meaning intelligence,
clearly enters into it because in singing the whole sensibility is involved,
brain and heart. Where she senses that the assumption of a mood or a
character is false or forced, she condemns it; and however hard and
detailed the preparation for a performance, in the event the spontaneous feeling of the moment must be alive and keen or it is nothing.

For myself, the experience of those three weeks was a moving one,
impressive too in many different ways (remember, for example, that all
of this detailed talk was conducted in English, Schwarzkopf's English
being as good as my German is bad). It was also a curious business, in
that while much of the mind was occupied in following hers it still
functioned independently, forming observations and judgments that
were not infrequently at variance. We both, I think, resisted any
temptation to gossip, either about colleagues or anecdotal memories.
Yet there was no sense of inhibition. Feelings ran high and low: elation
and depression were the poles, and both were touched. There was
humour and chaff, the ever-reassuring presence of Lily Reenvig, the
prospect of a goulasch warming up in the kitchen, a champagne to be
brought from the cellar. In my sleep (I used to think) I shall hear those
cries of 'Legato! ... Sharp! ... Flat! ... *Very* flat!!', but they meld now with
the happiness, generosity and energy of an intense devotion. I also recall
that this was not a form of play. It was a time when one of the great
artists of our age risked a survey of her life's work as it stands on record,

and who spared herself neither praise nor blame. The blame, however, was in liberal supply, the praise hard-won indeed.

❄

In the list that follows, the recordings discussed above, referred to in order of appearance in the text, are related to their discography entries (discography page numbers are in **bold** type).

p. 13   Wolf: 'Elfenlied', 10 Apr. 1956, **120**; 25 Nov. 1956, **124**.

pp. 13-14 Wolf: 'Kennst du das Land?, 8 June 1957, **128-9**; 25 Nov. 1956, **124**; 20 Feb. 1967, **163**.

p. 14   Mozart: 'Un moto di gioia', 25 Nov. 1956, **124**.
Wolf: 'Elfenlied', 10 Apr. 1956, **120**.
Wolf: 'Nur wer die Sehnsucht kennt' (Mignon I), 3 Apr. 1956, **119**.
Mozart: 'Als Luise die Briefe', 13 Apr. 1955, **113**.
Mozart: 'Abendempfindung', 16 Apr. 1955, **114**; 25 Nov. 1956, **124**; 27-31 Aug. 1972, **170**.
Wolf: 'Philine', 3 Apr. 1956, **119**.

p. 15   Wolf: 'Philine', as above.
Gieseking: 'Kinderlieder', 16 Apr. 1955, **114**.
Wolf: 'Die Spröde', 11 Jan. 1958, **134**.
Wolf: 'Kennst du das Land?', 25 Nov. 1956, **124**; 8 June 1957, **128-9**; 20 Feb. 1967, **163**.

p. 16   Mozart: 'Abendempfindung', as above (p. 14) with 6 Jan. 1954, **104**.
Bach: 'Mein Herze schwimmt im Blut', 26 May 1958, **135**.
Wolf: 'Elfenlied', 10 Apr. 1956, **120**.
Bach: *Mass in B minor* 'Laudamus te', 23 Nov. 1952, **94**.

p. 17   Strauss: 'Schlagende Herzen', 'Morgen'; Verdi: 'Lo spazza-camino'; J. Strauss: 'G'schichten aus dem Wienerwald', all **61**.

p. 18   Mozart: *Le nozze di Figaro* 'Deh, vieni', 2 July 1952, **90**.
Humperdinck: *Hänsel und Gretel*, 29 June 1953, **98**; 26 Sept. 1947, **68**.
Wolf: 'Die Spröde', 11 Jan. 1958, **134**.
Mozart: *Don Giovanni* 'Non mi dir', 4 July 1952, **90**.
Wagner: *Tannhäuser* 'Dich, teure Halle', 27 Apr. 1956, **121**.
Strauss: *Ariadne auf Naxos*, 30 June 1954, **107**.
Strauss: *Der Rosenkavalier*, 12 Dec. 1956, **124**; August 1960, **143**; 31 July 1963, **152-3**.

p. 19 Strauss: 'Vier letzte Lieder', 25 Sept. 1953, **99**; 20 June 1956, **123**; 1 Sept. 1965, **159**.

Schubert: 'Die junge Nonne', 4 Oct. 1952, **92**.

Schubert: 'Wehmut', 6 Oct. 1952, **93**.

Schubert: 'Gretchen am Spinnrade', 6 Oct. 1952, **93**; 1 March 1973, **171**.

p. 20 Loewe: 'Kleiner Haushalt', 20 Oct. 1968, **166**.

Strauss: *Ariadne auf Naxos*, as above (p. 18).

Strauss: 'Waldseligkeit', 1 Sept. 1965, **159**.

p. 21 Monteverdi: Duets, 27 May 1955, **115**.

p. 22 Bach: *Mass in B minor*, as above (p. 16).

Mozart: *Die Entführung aus dem Serail*, 4 Sept. 1944, **63**; 31 Oct. 1946, **65**.

pp. 23-4 Mozart: *Don Giovanni*, 31 July 1950, **77**; 3 Aug. 1953, **98**; 7 Oct. 1959, **139**.

pp. 24-5 Mozart: *Così fan tutte* (Karajan), 13 July 1954, **107-8**; (Cantelli), 27 Jan. 1956, **119**; (Böhm 'live'), 24 Aug. 1958, **135-6**; (Böhm studio), 10 Sept. 1962, **151**.

pp. 25-6 Schubert: 'Ave Maria', 'Die Forelle', 'Auf dem Wasser zu singen', 'Ungeduld', 'Der Musensohn', 'Suleika', 16 Feb. 1952, **89**.

p. 26 Schubert: 'Die Einsame', 22 Aug. 1965, **158**.

Schumann: 'Die Kartenlegerin', 24 Oct. 1967, **164**.

pp. 26-7 Wolf: *Spanisches Liederbuch* 'Mühvoll komm' ich', 16 Dec. 1966, **162**; 27 July 1958, **135**.

pp. 27-8 Wolf: 'Wie glänzt der helle Mond', 12 Aug. 1953, **99**; 18 Jan. 1961, **146**.

Wolf: 'Die Zigeunerin', **62**; 22 August 1965, **158**.

Strauss: *Capriccio*, 2 Sept. 1957, **132**.

p. 29 Verdi: *Otello*, 24 Apr. 1959, **138**.

pp. 29-30 Puccini: *La bohème*, 24 April 1959, **138**.

Millöcker: *Die Dubarry*, 5 July 1957, **131**.

p. 31 Debussy: *Pelléas et Mélisande*, 19 Dec. 1954, **110**.

Stravinsky: *The Rake's Progress*, 11 Sept. 1951, **85**.

Walton: *Troilus and Cressida*, 18 Apr. 1955, **115**.

p. 32 Sibelius: 'Säf, säf, Susa' ('Schilf, schilf, Sausle'), 8 Apr. 1956, **120**.

Sibelius: 'War det en Dröm' ('War es ein Traum') and *Luonnotar*, unpublished.

Grieg: 'Jeg elsker deg' ('Ich liebe dich'), 12 Apr. 1956, **121**.

Grieg: 'Med en wandlije' ('Mit einer Wasserlilie'), 27 Aug. 1970, **170**.

Jensen: 'Murmelndes Lüftchen', 13 Apr. 1956, **121**.

Dvořák: 'Songs my mother taught me', 19 May 1966, **122**.

p. 33 Stravinsky: 'Vocalise' ('Pastorale'), 24 Oct. 1967, **164**.

Tchaikovsky: 'Pimpinella', 24 Oct. 1967, **164**.

Charpentier: *Louise* 'Depuis le jour', 6 May 1950, **76**.

Beethoven: *Fidelio* 'Abscheulicher', 20 Sept. 1954, **109**.

Orff: *Die Kluge*, 22 May 1956, **122**.

pp. 33-4 Schumann: *Liederkreis*; *Frauenliebe und Leben*, Jan. and Apr. 1974, **171**.

Brahms: 'Immer leiser', 27 Aug. 1972, **170**.

p. 35 Strauss: *Arabella*, 27 Sept. 1954, **109**.

Strauss: *Ariadne auf Naxos*, 30 June 1954, **107**.

Strauss: 'Meinem Kinde', 10 March 1968, **166**.

Strauss: 'Zueignung'; 'Ruhe, meine Seele', 2 March 1962, **149**.

p. 36 Wolf: *Sechs alte Weisen*, 27 June 1958, **135**; 3 Dec. 1962, **151**.

Mozart: *Die Zauberflöte*, 20 Dec. 1953, **100**.

Wagner: *Die Meistersinger von Nürnberg*, Aug. 1951, **84**.

p. 37 Strauss: 'Schlechtes Wetter'; 'Hat gesagt'; Loewe: 'Frühlings-ankunft' ('Es ist mein Herz'); Busoni: 'Unter den Linden', all **59-62**.

J. Strauss: *Wiener Blut*, 21 May 1954, **105**.

Bach: *St Matthew Passion*, 4 May 1961, **147**.

p. 38 Brahms: *Deutsches Requiem*, 21 Oct. 1947, **69**.

Schubert: 'Erlkönig', 21 Apr. 1966, **161**.

Mussorgsky: 'Gathering mushrooms' ('In dem Pilzen'), 24 Oct. 1967, **164**.

Grieg: 'Farmyard Song', 13 Apr. 1956, **121**.

Trad. arr. Weatherley: 'Danny Boy', 13 Jan. 1958, **134**.

Part II

Discography

Alan Sanders

Discography

Introduction

The period between 1949 and 1952 represented a crucial phase for record companies and artists. During 1949 tape recorders became available for use in commercial studios, and this meant that the old method of recording directly on to 78rpm wax discs could at last be abandoned. This technique had been in use for half a century and was highly restrictive, since performers could only record for periods of up to four and a half minutes, which was the maximum length of a twelve-inch 78rpm record. For an aria or any other short piece of music this was an adequate enough span, but in the case of a longer composition there was a need to slice the music into a series of 78rpm side lengths. If an artist made a mistake, it was then a question of going back and starting again, since waxes could not be edited, and it was usually the practice to record at least two takes of every side, and choose the best for publication. When magnetic tape came into use, it was possible to record in long takes and it was also possible to make as many edits as were needed.

This technological revolution gave birth to another, for it was possible to copy tape recordings on to disc lacquers which, with narrower grooves and a slower playing speed of 33rpm, could accommodate recordings lasting up to 25 minutes a side. Metal masters made from the original lacquers could in turn be the source of vinyl pressings, and so the long-playing record was born.

It was only at this point that artists were given the opportunity to make more extensive recordings of their repertoire. Some exceptionally famous singers, such as Beniamino Gigli, made several complete opera recordings, but for most vocal artists it was a question of recording selected arias and songs only.

For the first decade of her career, Elisabeth Schwarzkopf made records by the old process, with the exception of the wartime series of Lieder with Michael Raucheisen at the piano. These youthful interpretations (and also a few live recordings of wartime operatic performances in which she took part), were captured on an early form of tape recorder. It is one of the tragedies of recording history that German development of magnetic recording did not survive the end of the second world war, for in 1944 some experimental stereo recordings were even made, with startling success. We can now only imagine the possibilities lost in the immediate post-war period of a dozen of so years, when recordings were still made on wax, and then on tape, but in mono only. If the possibility of having Schwarzkopf recordings made in stereo during the late 1940s was denied us by the ravages of war, then we have every reason to be grateful for the legacy which we do have.

The long-playing record arrived just at the point when Schwarzkopf's career took on a new international dimension in 1951. This was a crucial coincidence. The new medium demanded that there should be new record-ings to satisfy a new market, and there was a rapid expansion of the recorded repertoire. Many complete works, particularly operas, were put on disc for the first time. And Schwarzkopf, in her vocal and artistic prime, and with her husband and mentor Walter Legge as producer, was given the opportunity to make many early LP mono records. She was also one of the first artists to record in the stereo medium, when it finally became available to EMI during 1955 (though stereo EMI records did not even start to appear until nearly four years later), and some of the works she had recorded in mono were re-made in stereo. Had she been born 20 years earlier, then her recorded legacy would have been much less. It is true that a few of her operatic roles, such as Violetta in Verdi's *La traviata* and Elisabeth in Wagner's *Tannhäuser*, have not been preserved in their entirety, but we can hear her on record in a large proportion of her opera and concert repertoire – as well as in some works which she only sang for the microphone. Much of that repertoire has been made available on a newer medium, compact disc, which did not exist at a time when she was still singing.

If tape recording gave performing artists new freedoms from the early 1950s onwards, then it also gave unscrupulous entrepreneurs the chance to make unauthorised recordings at live performances or, more frequently, from radio broadcasts, and to issue these for sale first on long-playing records and then rather later on compact discs. From the 1930s onwards it had been possible to record privately on disc-cutting machines, using 78rpm acetate blanks, but this was a cumbersome and expensive process. To make recordings from the radio, using a good quality reel-to-reel machine, was much easier.

Through illegitimate means there have been preserved some important examples of Schwarzkopf singing in repertoire which she did not record commercially, and it is true that the artist herself likes some of the pirated performances. But there are others which she feels do not do her art justice, and which should not have been made publicly available. She has of course had no control or say over what has been made available in the form of pirate recordings.

Layout

This discography is arranged in such a fashion that factual information is broken up, usually year by year, by a running commentary which tells the story of Schwarkopf's singing career, and how her recording sessions ran parallel to her career on the stage and in the concert hall. These narrative sections include quoted reminiscences and comments by the artist herself, taken from lengthy tape-recorded conversations between Dame Elisabeth and the author which took place in June 1994.

The data itself has been arranged chronologically session by session. In order to meet the needs of those readers who wish to refer immediately to various works there is an index of compositions at the end of the chronological listing which gives page references to the main section. An index of participating artists is also provided. Non-EMI recordings are normally listed with a reference to the issuing company; but to avoid continual repetition of EMI information there is a list of that company's and allied companies' prefixes immediately following this introduction (pp. 49-52). Unauthorised or pirate recordings and issues are given in italics.

The first part of the discography contains details of 78rpm recordings (with the exception of the recordings with Raucheisen and the live operatic recordings already noted). Each group of sessions is headed by, from left to right, the date of the recording, the location of the recording, and the names of the artists taking part. It has not been thought necessary to repeat continually the name 'Elisabeth Schwarzkopf', since her participation can obviously be taken as read: the only exceptions are where her name is included in cast lists so as to identify the part she sings. In order to show the progress of a recording as clearly as possible, particularly in those cases where a single work was recorded over more than one day, the heading details are not repeated when a new date is reached unless one or more of those details has had to be changed.

Beneath the heading, letters and numbers listed to the left show show the matrix or serial numbers of the recording waxes used. As I have already pointed out, it was customary to record more than one take of each section of music under the same matrix number, the number after the dash indicating the number of the take. (These details were stamped on the wax, and can be seen near the labels of published records.) Against each matrix and take number is shown the work or part of the work recorded. On the right side the principal UK catalogue number is set against the take selected for publication, thus showing at a glance which takes were used and which were rejected. In those cases where a recording was not issued in the UK, the principal US or continental number is set against the relevant take number.

Secondary issue numbers, non-UK issues, or transfers to other formats are listed where applicable in the centre of the page at the point where the recording was completed. The order followed in these listings is in general as follows: secondary 78rpm issues, LP reissues, seven-inch 45rpm extended play issues (EPs), seven-inch 45rpm standard play issues (SPs), reel-to-reel tape issues (denoted by the symbol T), cassette tape recordings (C), cartridge tape recordings (C8), and finally compact disc reissues (CD). In all these categories, UK numbers are in general set out first, followed by US numbers and then continental numbers. Recordings not published can obviously be identified by a lack of any issue numbers.

The layout of the second part of the discography from about 1952 onwards is simpler, for while the way in which the details of the sessions are set out remains the same, the works recorded and their issue numbers are grouped together under the name of the work. For the sake of completeness, however, 78rpm records made from tape sources are still shown with the published matrix numbers. These numbers still have some relevance in that EMI recorded in 78rpm lengths until the early 1950s, and continued to allot matrix numbers to these 78rpm tapes.

The locations of recording venues outside London are given in full when they first appear. EMI's London recordings usually took place in the EMI Studios, 3 Abbey Road, NW8, or in the Kingsway Hall, Kingsway, London WC2.

Although every effort has been made to include as many issue numbers as possible, there will be some which are not listed. Completeness is therefore not claimed.

Acknowledgements

My grateful thanks are due to Mr Charles Rodier and Mr Ken Jagger for their help in allowing me access to EMI recording information. Generous help and information has also been provided by Mrs Marie Tobin, Miss Lily Reenvig, Mr John Hunt, Dr Daphne Kerslake of the Elisabeth Schwarzkopf/Walter Legge Society, and officials of the National Sound Archive. Dame Elisabeth Schwarzkopf herself has been most generous in making various facilities available to me.

Record label prefixes:
EMI and associated companies

General symbols: LP = long-playing record; EP = seven-inch extended play 45rpm record; SP = seven-inch standard play 45rpm record; 78 = 78rpm record; T = reel-to-reel tape recording; C = cassette tape recording; C8 = cartridge tape recording; [E] = electronic stereo recording

AA	Japanese Angel LP mono and [E]
AB	Japanese Angel LP mono
AE	Japanese Angel LP mono and stereo
ALP	English HMV LP mono
AN	English EMI Angel LP mono
ASD	English HMV LP stereo
AV	Japanese Angel LP mono and stereo
BTA	English Columbia T
C	English HMV 78
C	German Electrola LP and EP mono
CAN	German Angel LP stereo
CAT	English Columbia T
CBT	English Columbia T
CC	Japanese Columbia LP mono
CCA	French HMV LP stereo
CDC	English EMI CD
CDCB	US Angel CD
CD-EMX	English EMI Eminence CD
CDHB	US Angel CD
CDM	English EMI CD
CDMB	US Angel CD
CFP	English EMI Classics for Pleasure
CFPD	English EMI Classics for Pleasure CD set
CHS	French Références CD
CMS	English EMI CD set
COLH	English HMV Great Recordings of the Century LP mono
CX	English Columbia LP mono
CZS	English EMI CD set
DB	International HMV 78
E	German Electrola LP and EP mono
EAA	Japanese Toshiba LP mono and stereo
EAC	Japanese Toshiba LP mono and stereo
EBE	German Electrola LP mono
EG	English EMI C stereo and mono
EH	English EMI LP stereo and mono
EHA	US RCA Victor EP mono
EL	US Columbia EP mono set
EMX	English EMI Eminence LP stereo
ESBF	French Columbia EP mono

ESD	English HMV LP stereo
ESL	English Columbia EP stereo
EX	English EMI LP mono and stereo
FALP	French HMV LP mono
GQ	Italian Columbia ten-inch 78
GQX	Italian Columbia 78
GR	Japanese Angel mono
H	English EMI World Records LP mono
H	Japanese Angel LP mono
HA	Japanese Angel LP mono
HB	Japanese Angel LP mono
HLM	English HMV Treasury mono
HQM	English HMV LP mono
HZE	Electrola LP mono
IB	US Angel Seraphim LP mono
LALP	Spanish HMV LP mono
LB	English Columbia ten-inch 78
LC	International Columbia ten-inch 78
LD	Danish Columbia ten-inch 78
LCT	US RCA Victor LP mono
LCX	International Columbia 78
LFX	French Columbia 78
LHMV	US RCA Victor LP mono
LM	US RCA Victor LP mono
LN	Norwegian Columbia ten-inch 78
LV	Austrian Columbia ten-inch 78
LVX	Austrian Columbia 78
LWX	German Columbia 78
LX	English Columbia 78
LZX	Swiss Columbia 78
M	US RCA Victor 78 set
M	US Columbia 78 set
ML	US Columbia LP mono
MSE	US Vox Turnabout LP set mono (licensed)
OH	English EMI World Records LP mono
OL	Japanese Columbia LP mono
OS	Japanese Columbia LP stereo
QLP	Italian HMV LP mono
REG	Spanish Regal mono
RL	Japanese Columbia LP mono
RLS	English HMV LP set mono
RO	Australian World Record Club LP mono
S-3000	US Angel LP stereo set
S-35000	US Angel LP stereo
SAN	English EMI Angel stereo
SAX	English Columbia LP stereo
SAXF	French Columbia LP stereo
SAXQ	Italian Columbia LP stereo
SCA	Japanese Columbia LP stereo
SCB	English Columbia SP mono

SCBF	French Columbia SP mono
SCBQ	Italian Columbia SP mono
SCBW	German Columbia SP mono
SCD	English Columbia SP mono
SEBQ	Italian Columbia EP mono
SEL	English Columbia EP mono
SELW	German Columbia EP mono
SEOM	English EMI LP stereo
SH	English EMI World Records LP mono and stereo
SL	French La Voix de son Maître twelve-inch 78
SLS	English LP set stereo
SMA	German Electrola LP stereo
SMAC	German Electrola LP stereo
SME	German Electrola LP stereo and [E]
SMS	German Columbia LP stereo set
SMVP	German Electrola LP stereo and [E]
SOC	English EMI World Records LP mono and stereo
SOH	English EMI World Records LP mono and stereo
ST	English EMI World Records LP mono and stereo
STC	German Electrola LP stereo
STE	German Electrola LP stereo and [E]
SVP	German Electrola LP stereo and [E]
SXDW	English HMV LP set stereo
T	English EMI World Records LP mono
TC-ALP	English HMV C mono
TC-ASD	English HMV C stereo
TC-CFPD	English EMI Classics for Pleasure CD set
TC-ESD	English HMV C stereo
TC-HLM	English HMV Treasury C mono
TC2-MOM	English EMI Miles of Music C stereo
TC-RLS	English HMV C mono set
TC-SLS	English HMV C stereo set
TC2-SXDW	English HMV C set stereo and [E]
THS	US Vox Turnabout LP mono (licensed)
TT	English EMI World Records T mono
TV	US Vox Turnabout LP mono (licensed)
XL	Japanese Columbia LP mono
WALP	German Electrola LP mono
WCT	US RCA Victor SP set mono
WF	Japanese Angel Furtwängler LP series mono
WHMV	US RCA Victor SP set mono
WL	Japanese Columbia LP mono
YKM	English EMI Your Kind of Music stereo
ZL	Japanese Columbia LP mono
1C	German Electrola LP and C mono and stereo
100000-1 series	French Pathé-Marconi LP mono
100000-4 series	French Pathé-Marconi C mono
1500000	French Pathé-Marconi LP mono
2C	French Pathé-Marconi LP and C mono and stereo
290000-3	French Pathé-Marconi LP mono

33CX	English Columbia LP mono
33FCX	French Columbia LP mono
33QCX	Italian Columbia LP mono
33VCX	Austrian Columbia LP mono
33WCX	German Columbia LP mono
33WSX	German Columbia LP mono
35000 series	US Angel LP mono
4AV	Japanese Angel C mono and stereo
4XS	US Angel C stereo
8XS	US Angel C8 stereo
567 747000-2	French Pathé-Marconi CD mono
6000 series	US Seraphim LP set
60000 series	US Seraphim LP
7RF	French La Voix de son Maître SP mono
70000-D	US Columbia 78
769.000 series	French Pathé-Marconi CD
747000-2 series	US Angel CD mono

1937-1943

Elisabeth Schwarzkopf was not even a fully professional singer when she first took part in a recording session for the gramophone. In November 1937 she was nearly twenty-three and a graduate of the Berlin Hochschule für Musik. She had already gained some experience in public performance through an occasional minor solo engagement and through membership of two small Berlin-based choral groups. One, the Rudolf Lamy Singgemein-schaft, specialised in madrigals and other early music, which was very enterprising in those days. The other, Favres Solisten Vereinigung, was more flexible, singing not only early music but later repertoire including oratorio. The choir's founder and conductor, Waldo Favre, was of Swiss origin. Many performances were given in the Berlin Singakademie. The Favres Solisten even took part in soundtracks for films. There was one occasion when they worked on an operetta film with the great tenor Leo Slezak, 'a kind and wonderful artist', but also an accomplished comedian, who pulled faces and made jokes when the chorus was trying to sing. Both groups were essentially non-professional, though they did receive fees for professional engagements. They comprised students, singers who had not quite made the grade as solo artists, and gifted amateurs.

When the Favres Solisten were invited to take part in Sir Thomas Beecham's HMV recording of Mozart's *Die Zauberflöte* they were under particular instructions to sing as a chorus with a homogenised timbre, not as a group of soloists. Sessions took place in the Beethovensaal, Berlin. Chorus members were not placed on stage with the soloists, but at a lower level on the floor next to the stage, and in a corner. One or two of the soloists were quite near the chorus, and it was a great thrill to be in the same hall as such god-like artists as Lemnitz and Roswaenge. Schwarzkopf remembers nothing of Sir Thomas's conducting, and has no recollection of the producer, Walter Legge, who would become her husband sixteen years later.

This recording was one of a number of pre-war HMV Society issues, many of them produced by Legge, and all the result of his original concept, first developed in 1931, that records could be marketed on a subscription, or 'society' basis.

In April 1938 Schwarzkopf auditioned for the Deutsches Opernhaus, Berlin, and was given a beginner's contract. Almost immediately she took the stage for the first time as one of the Flower Maidens in Wagner's

Parsifal, a work she did not know at all. She also played other minor parts – such as Wellgunde in Wagner's *Das Rheingold* and *Götterdämmerung*, and Ida in Johann Strauss's *Die Fledermaus* – and took on a number of page-boy roles, later describing this early phase of her career as 'pages for ages'. She must have made an impact, even in these lesser parts, since she was picked by the Telefunken record company to record brief single-disc selections from four operettas.

Her colleague in these ventures was the tenor Rupert Glawitsch. He was known as a radio star who rather cultivated the style of Richard Tauber and Marcel Wittrisch, and who possessed a very suitable voice for the broadcast medium, though he was also, suggests Dame Elisabeth, 'a genuine singer', not just a microphone artist. Of these sessions she has only faint recollections, though she remembers being 'totally nervous, totally awestruck' as a beginner, and grateful to the experienced Glawitsch for his help and support. One of the conductors was Walter Lütze, who worked as a staff conductor at the Berlin State Opera between 1935 and 1944, and who directed several operas in which the young soprano took minor roles – including Kienzl's *Der Evangelimann* (Eine Lumpen-sammlerin), Smetana's *Bartered Bride* (Esmeralda), Lortzing's *Der Waffenschmied* (Marie) and *Prinz Caramo* (Angela).

In September 1940 Arthur Rother gave Schwarzkopf the opportunity to play Zerbinetta in Strauss's *Ariadne auf Naxos*. One of her colleagues was the great baritone Karl Schmitt-Walter, who advised her to approach the famous soprano Maria Ivogün with a view to further study. Ivogün had seen the *Ariadne* production, and was not at all impressed with Elisabeth's singing, but she nevertheless accepted her as a pupil. The following period of study with Ivogün and her accompanist husband Michael Raucheisen constituted a turning point in her career.

In May 1941 Rother conducted a single cycle of Wagner's *Ring*, of which *Das Rheingold* was recorded from a broadcast, at least in part. Rother, who was music director of the Berlin Stadtischer Oper for over 20 years until 1958, was another great influence on Elisabeth's early career. 'We feared him greatly – a wonderful Kapellmeister really, stern to the hilt with everything which had to be done. I think he was one of the very great educators of young singers, because he didn't let them sing what they wanted to sing. He said, 'Not that, in five years you can sing it, not now'. He kept them back, back, back, and gave them things where they wouldn't hurt themselves. That was the policy then, of a great man ... of the old school'.

The Wotan in this recording of *Das Rheingold*, Wilhelm Rode, was also, somewhat curiously, the Intendant (administrative head) of the Opera House. Some of the other singers are not so well-known today, but

Schwarzkopf remembers them clearly. Constanze Nettesheim was 'our great lyrical singer', who also studied with Ivogün. Elisabeth Friedrich was 'a very good singer in the Italian style, a lovely person, very nervous', Wilhelm Schirp a 'very deep, black bass', Hans Florian the 'comic singer', Willi Worle 'our operetta tenor, a marvellous Eisenstein in *Die Fledermaus*. They were all very good singers with good voices at the time.'

Elisabeth soon gave her first recital in Berlin with Raucheisen accompanying her. There were four programmes. Tickets were given away in advance of the first, but the remaining programmes were sold out. The Opera House was not at all pleased with this success, and although Schwarzkopf now had a contract as a 'soubrette' she was still given minor roles. On Ivogün's advice she continued to sing these smaller parts, but under the pseudonym of Maria Hilfe.

A more serious setback followed. Elisabeth had been promised promotion to the part of Adele in *Die Fledermaus*, but when rehearsals began she found that the role had been alloted to someone else. She refused to sing her previous part, Ida, and in the youthful heat of the moment put the heel of her shoe through a piece of scenery. Wilhelm Rode reported her to the authorities, and she was accused of 'sabotage in wartime'. The consequences seemed serious, with the possibility that she might be sent to do forced labour in a munitions factory. Her father, a life-long humanist, was working on the Eastern front, helping to identify those who had fallen in the conflict and assisting bereaved relatives with administrative and funeral arrangements. He hurried back to Berlin. Raucheisen also interceded, informing the authorities that he needed the young singer for concerts to entertain the troops. Elisabeth kept her freedom and was allowed to continue singing.

1937

November 8. Beethovensaal, Berlin.

Tiana Lemnitz (soprano)...................................... Pamina
Erna Berger (soprano)............................Queen of the Night
Helge Roswaenge (tenor)...................................... Tamino
Gerhard Hüsch (baritone)...................................Papageno
Wilhelm Strienz (bass)...................................... Sarastro
Irma Beilke (soprano)........................... Papagena; First Boy
Hilde Scheppan (soprano)................................. First Lady
Elfriede Marherr-Wagner (soprano)..................... Second Lady
Carla Spletter (soprano)................................Second Boy
Rut Berglund (contralto)..................... Third Lady; Third Boy

Heinrich Tessmer (tenor)............... Monostatos; First Armed Man
Ernst Fabbri (tenor)..Priest
Walter Grossmann (bass)................ Speaker; Second Armed Man
Sopranos of Favres Solisten Vereinigung, Berlin Philharmonic Orchestra
conducted by Sir Thomas Beecham.

2RA2424-1 Mozart: Die Zauberflöte – Heil sei euch Geweihten! DB3483
November 9.

2RA2436-1   "   "   – Es lebe Sarastro
      -2   "   "   "   DB3473
November 12.

2RA2454-1   "   "   – Wir wandelten   DB3481
NB: The above dates and record information relate
to those items involving the chorus only. Other
sessions for the recording of the complete opera took
place on November 8, 10, 13, 15 plus February 24
and March 2 and 8, 1938.

Set DB3465-83, auto DB8475-93; Sets
M541-2; C6371-89. LP: ALP1273-5,
SH158-60, Set RLS1434653, Set LCT6101,
TV4111-3, THS65078-80, Set MSE1,
WCLP616-8, C80471-3, Set GR2115. SP:
Set WCT56, Set WCT6101. C: Set
TC-RLS1434653. CD: CHS761034-2, *Pearl
GEMMCDS9371, Nimbus NI7827-8.*

1939

September 2. Telefunken Studios, East Berlin. Rupert Glawitsch (tenor),
Deutsches Opernhaus Orchestra conducted by Hansgeorg Otto.

024618 Lehár: Paganini – selection   pt. 1 E3041
024619   "   "   "   pt. 2 E3041
E3041 is German Telefunken. Also on
Austrian Telefunken E1172, and in US
Capitol Set ECL2501. Issued on LP: US
Capitol P8033.

September 4. Telefunken Studios, East Berlin. Rupert Glawitsch (tenor),
Deutsches Opernhaus Orchestra conducted by Walter Lütze.

024622 Suppé: Boccaccio – selection   pt. 1 E3029
024623   "   "   "   pt. 2 E3029
E3029 is German Telefunken. Also on US
Capitol 89-80109.

1940

August 16. Telefunken Studios, East Berlin. Rupert Glawitsch (tenor),
   Deutsches Opernhaus Orchestra and Chorus conducted by Walter Lütze.
   025113   J. Strauss II (arr. Müller): Wiener Blut – selection   pt. 1 E3099
   025114   "   "   "   pt. 2 E3099
              E3099 is German Telefunken. Also on
              Austrian Telefunken E1160.

August 17. Telefunken Studios, East Berlin. Rupert Glawitsch (tenor),
   Deutsches Opernhaus Orchestra conducted by Walter Lütze.
   025121   Lehár: Das Land des Lächelns – selection   pt. 1 E3115
   025122   "   "   "   "   pt. 2 E3115
              E3115 is German Telefunken. Also on SP:
              Telefunken UE45-3115.

1941

May 24. Deutsches Opernhaus, Berlin.
   Wilhelm Rode (baritone)....................................Wotan
   Hans Heinz Nissen (baritone).............................Donner
   Walther Ludwig (tenor).......................................Froh
   Willi Worle (tenor)..Loge
   Wilhelm Schirp (bass).......................................Fasolt
   Wilhelm Lang (bass)..Fafner
   Eduard Kandl (bass)..Alberich
   Hans Florian (tenor)...Mime
   Carin Carlsson (contralto)...................................Fricka
   Constanze Nettesheim (soprano)............................Freia
   Else Meinhart (contralto)....................................Erda
   Elisabeth Schwarzkopf (soprano)......................Wellgunde
   Elisabeth Friedrich (soprano)...........................Woglinde
   Marie-Luise Schilp (contralto)..........................Flosshilde
   Deutsches Opernhaus Orchestra conducted by Arthur Rother.
      Wagner: Das Rheingold
      *Excerpts on LP: Acanta Set 40.23502, Melodram Set MEL082, BASF
      Set 22 21486-9, Discoreale DR10037. CD: MEL16501.*

✸

Between 1940 and 1945 Michael Raucheisen was in charge of chamber music and song programmes at the Reichsrundfunkgesellschaft. In his work for the radio station he was able to use the newly developed Magnetofon, an early form of tape recorder. The quality and comparative flexibility of this new medium enabled him to embark on a project known as 'Lied der Welt' ('Song of the World'), in which a number of singers would perform a wide-ranging repertoire of songs and Lieder from many countries for recording and broadcasting purposes. Elisabeth Schwarzkopf was one of those asked to participate. Some years before, in her student days at the Berlin Hochschule, she had taken part in experimental tape or wire recording sessions, and film sessions too, and remembers that these took place in the room where the academy kept its old instruments. But when it came to her work at the Rundfunkhaus with Raucheisen she had no idea that she was being recorded.

Although she had already studied a few of the items with Ivogün, most of the repertoire was new to her. Fortunately, however, she was an accomplished sight-reader, so the resulting performances are more in the nature of spontaneous readings caught on the wing rather than prepared studio interpretations. She would often go to the studio straight from a singing lesson, since the Raucheisens lived near the radio station. The Bach cantata with small ensemble she had already performed with a similar group at one of her Berlin recitals. She sang two groups of duets with Lea Pillti – a well-known Finnish coloratura soprano at the time, whereas 'I was a little nobody'. Their voices matched, but a slightly flat intonation gives Dame Elisabeth little pleasure now. Many of the other solo items she does like, particularly for their natural use of legato. By this time it was forbidden to sing items in English, and the Arne and Leveridge songs were sung in German translations by Hermine Mörike, the niece of the great poet. In performance this repertoire was billed merely as 'madrigals' or 'folk-songs', with no indication of its British origin.

When the recordings with Raucheisen were issued in Acanta's LP Raucheisen Edition they were allotted recording dates, but two factors suggest that these are incorrect. Schwarzkopf herself feels that the nature of her voice as recorded indicates earlier dates than those given. Moreover, some of the dates relate to a period of a whole year when she was both inactive and away from Berlin.

In November 1942 she had been invited by Karl Böhm to sing as a probationer at the Vienna State Opera. As a result she was offered a contract in Vienna, to commence the following summer. However, as a result of spending long nights in damp Berlin air raid shelters she contracted tuberculosis. Ivogün and Raucheisen came to her aid, and she was admitted to a sanitorium in the Tatra mountains, now part of Slovakia. There she had to stay for a whole year. When she was well again she travelled to Vienna in the spring of 1944 to make her delayed début at the Staatsoper. She did return to Berlin briefly during 1944, but it seems likely that all the recordings with Raucheisen were made before the end of April 1943.

Dates unknown, between 1940 and 1943

Rundfunkhaus, Berlin. Michael Raucheisen (piano).
Arne: The Lass with the Delicate Air (sung in German)
> *LP: Acanta 40.23557. CD: Acanta 42.43801.*
Bach: Cantata No. 208, Was mir behagt, ist nur die muntre Jagd – Schafe können sicher weiden
> (with Gustav Scheck, Deta Wolf, flutes, Herbert Schonecke, cello, Rudolf Schultz, violin).
> *CD: Acanta 42.43128.*
Beethoven: Das Geheimnis, WoO145
> *LP: Acanta 40.23557, Acanta 40.23535. CD: Acanta 42.43801.*
Brahms: Trennung, Op. 97 No. 6
> *LP: Acanta 40.23524, Acanta 40.23557. CD: Acanta 42.43801.*
Busoni: Unter den Linden, Op. 18 No. 2
> *LP: Acanta 40.23557. CD: Acanta 42.43128.*
Cornelius: Heimatgedenken, Op. 16 No. 1
> (with Josef Greindl, bass).
> *LP: Acanta 40.23503. CD: Acanta 42.43128.*
Cornelius: Scheiden, Op. 16 No. 4
> (with Josef Greindl, bass).
> *LP: Acanta 40.23503. CD: Acanta 42.43128.*
Gluck: La rencontre imprévue – Einem Bach der fliesst
> *LP: Acanta 40.23557. CD: Acanta 42.43801.*
Humperdinck: Winterlied
> *LP: Acanta 40.23557. CD: Acanta 42.43128.*
Leveridge: This great world is a trouble (sung in German)
> *LP: Acanta 40.23557. CD: Acanta 42.43801.*
Loewe: O süsse Mutter, Op. 62 No. 3
> *LP: Melodiya M10 41285-6, Melodiya 5289-73, Discocorp IGI385, Discocorp RR208, Acanta 40.23534.*
Loewe: Die Blume der Ergebung, Op. 62 No. 12
> *LP: Melodiya M10 41285-6, Melodiya 5289-73, Discocorp IGI385, Discocorp RR208, Acanta 40.23534.*

Loewe: Die Abendstunde
LP: Melodiya M10 41285-6, Melodiya 5289-73, Discocorp IGI385, Discocorp RR208, Acanta 40.23534, Acanta 40.23557. CD: Acanta 42.43801.
Loewe: Frühlingsankunft, Op. 130 No. 6
LP: Melodiya M10 41285-6, Melodiya 5289-73, Discocorp IGI385, Discocorp RR208, Acanta 40.23534, Melodram MEL082, Acanta 40.23557, Discoreale DR10038.
Loewe: Frühling
LP: Melodiya M10 41285-6, Melodiya 5289-73, Discocorp IGI385, Discocorp RR208, Acanta 40.23534, Melodram MEL082, Discoreale DR10038.
Loewe: Ihr Spaziergang
LP: Acanta 40.23534.
Loewe: Es ist ein Schnee gefallen
   (with Lea Piltti, soprano).
LP: Melodram MEL088.
Loewe: Vogelgesang
LP: Acanta 40.23534.
Loewe: Die verliebte Schäferin Scapine
LP: Acanta 40.23534.
Loewe: Die Sylphide, Op. 9 No. 50
LP: Acanta 40.23534, Acanta 40.23557.
Loewe: Das Glockenspiel
LP: Acanta 40.23534.
Loewe: Sonnenlicht
   (with Lea Piltti, soprano).
LP: Melodiya M10 41285-6, Melodiya 5289-73, Discocorp IGI385, Discocorp RR208.
Loewe: Liebesliedchen
   (with Lea Piltti, soprano).
LP: Melodiya M10 41285-6, Melodiya 5289-73, Discocorp IGI385, Discocorp RR208.
Loewe: März
   (with Lea Piltti, soprano).
LP: Melodiya M10 41285-6, Melodiya 5289-73, Discocorp IGI385, Discocorp RR208, Scandia SLP546, Melodram MEL088, Acanta 40.23534.
Loewe: Abschied
   (with Lea Piltti, soprano).
LP: Melodiya M10 41285-6, Melodiya 5289-73, Discocorp IGI385, Discocorp RR208.
Loewe: Die Freude
   (with Lea Piltti, soprano).
LP: Acanta 40.23534.
Loewe: An Sami
   (with Lea Piltti, soprano).
LP: Melodram MEL082, Acanta 40.23534, Discoreale DR10038.
Loewe: Zeislein
LP: Acanta 40.23534.

Loewe: Irrlichter
  LP: Acanta 40.23534.
Loewe: Kind und Mädchen
  LP: Acanta 40.23534.
Mozart: Oiseaux, si tous les ans, K307 (sung in German)
  LP: Acanta 40.23557. CD: Acanta 42.43801.
Mozart: Die Verschweigung, K518
  LP: Acanta 40.23557. CD: Acanta 42.43801.
Rameau: Hippolyte et Aricie – Rossignols amoureux (sung in German)
  LP: Acanta 40.23557. CD: Acanta 42.43801.
Reger: Ich glaub', lieber Schatz, Op. 31 No. 2
  LP: Acanta 40.23557. CD: Acanta 42.43128.
Reger: Viola d'amour, Op. 55 No. 11
  LP: Acanta 40.23565, Acanta 40.23557. CD: Acanta 42.43128.
Reger: Die Verschmähte, Op. 70 No. 8
  LP: Acanta 40.23565. CD: Acanta 42.43128.
Reger: Waldseligkeit, Op. 62 No. 2
  LP: Acanta 40.23565, Acanta 40.23557. CD: Acanta 42.43128.
Reger: Wiegenlied, Op. 142 No. 1
  LP: Acanta 40.23565, Acanta 40.23557, Discocorp IGI385, Discocorp RR208, Melodiya M10 41285-6, Melodiya LP: 5289-73. CD: Acanta 42.43801.
Rossini: Soirées musicales – No. 8, La danza
  LP: Acanta 40.23557. CD: Acanta 42.43801.
Sammartini: Weisse Schäfchen (sic)
  LP: Acanta 40.23557. CD: Acanta 42.43801.
Schubert: An den Frühling, D245
  LP: Acanta 40.23557. CD: Acanta 42.43801.
Schumann: Volksliedchen, Op. 51 No. 2
  LP: Acanta 40.23557. CD: Acanta 42.43801.
J Strauss II: G'schichten aus dem Wienerwald
  LP: Acanta 40.23557. CD: Acanta 42.43128.
Strauss: Hat gesagt, bleibt's nicht dabei, Op. 36 No. 3
  LP: Acanta 40.23557. CD: Acanta 42.43128.
Strauss: Schlagende Herzen, Op. 29 No. 2
  LP: Acanta 40.23546. LP: Acanta 40.23557. CD: Acanta 42.43801.
Strauss: Morgen, Op. 27 No. 4
  LP: Acanta 40.23546. LP: Acanta 40.23557. CD: Acanta 42.43128.
Trunk: Das Hemd, Op. 22 No. 3
  LP: Acanta 40.23557. CD: Acanta 42.43801.
Trunk: Die Allee, Op. 42 No. 9
  LP: Acanta 40.23557. CD: Acanta 42.43801.
Trunk: Vier heitere Lieder – Schlittenfahrt; Vertrag; Menuett;
    Brautwerbung
  LP: Acanta 40.23557. CD: Acanta 42.43128.
Verdi: Lo spazzacamino (sung in German)
  LP: Acanta 40.23557. CD: Acanta 42.43801.
Weber: 3 Italian Duets – 1. Mille volte mio tesoro; 2. Va ti consolo, addio;
    3. Se il mio ben
    (with Lea Piltti, soprano).

LP: *Acanta 40.23566, Melodiya M10 41285-6, Melodiya 5289-73,*
Discocorp IGI385. No. 3 only on LP: Discocorp RR208, Scandia
SLP546. No. 3 only on CD: Acanta 42.43128.
Wolf: Philine; Der Zigeunerin
   LP: *Acanta 40. 23580.*
Zilcher: Rokoko Suite
      (with Paul Richartz, vln, Adolf Steiner, cello).
   LP: Acanta 40.23557. CD: Acanta 42.43801.
Trad: Die Beruhigte
   LP: *Acanta 40.23557. CD: Acanta 42.43801.*
Trad: Gsätzli
   LP: *Acanta 40.23557. CD: Acanta 42.43801.*
Trad: O du lieb's Ängeli
   LP: *Acanta 40.23557. CD: Acanta 42.43801.*
Trad: Z'Lauterbach han i mein Strumpf verlor'n
   LP: *Acanta 40.23557. CD: Acanta 42.43801.*

1944

Schwarzkopf made her delayed début at the Vienna State Opera in April 1944 as Blondchen in Mozart's *Entführung*, conducted by Rudolf Moralt. She also sang Musetta in Puccini's *Bohème*, and Rosina in Rossini's *Barbiere*, both under Moralt, before deteriorating wartime conditions caused the opera house to be closed in June. On three days in September Moralt recorded *Entführung* for Austrian Radio, and on this occasion she took the part of Konstanze.

She continued to sing in concerts for the beleagured army units and munitions factories, giving up to a dozen performances a week. Her contributions to varied programmes, which involved all kinds of performing artists, were frequently 'Solveig's Song' from Grieg's *Peer Gynt*, and a vocal arrangement of Johann Strauss's *Frühlingsstimmen*. She made a last visit to Berlin, where she sang in a performance of Brahms's *Requiem* at Potsdam and took part in a studio recording of Weber's *Abu Hassan*. On 12 December she gave a Lieder recital in the Vienna Musikvereinsaal with Viktor Graef at the piano – her last public performance until after the war.

As the Allies advanced ever closer Schwarzkopf and her mother (who had broken her arm in an accident) were advised to make for Attersee, near Salzburg. After a perilous journey by train they stayed in somewhat primitive conditions at the house of a former Viennese colleague. When the Americans arrived they had to leave. They were rescued by the famous actress Käthe Dorsch, and stayed in quarters above her chicken run, which had just been vacated by Karl Böhm and his wife. Soon Elisabeth was singing for American rather than German troops, and after a few local engagements in St Johann, Graz and Salzburg, she and her mother returned to Vienna in November 1945. The Vienna State Opera had been bombed out of its building and had taken up residence in the Theater an der Wien. As a German citizen without a valid passport, Elisabeth could not be given a regular contract and had to go through the process of being cleared by a de-Nazification board, but she was still able to take part in a number of performances on an ad hoc basis.

September 4, 5 and 6. Mittleren Konzerthaussal, Vienna.
Elisabeth Schwarzkopf (soprano)..........................Konstanze
Emmy Loose (soprano)....................................Blondchen
Anton Dermota (tenor)...................................Belmonte
Peter Klein (tenor).......................................Pedrillo
Herbert Alsen (bass)......................................Osmin
Vienna Philharmonic Orchestra and Vienna State Opera Chorus conducted by Rudolf Moralt.
   Mozart: Die Entführung aus dem Serail
   LP: Melodram Set MEL047. Excerpts on LP: Melodram Set MEL082, Melodram Set MEL088, Rococo 5388, Acanta BB23119, Bellophon BB23.119, Discoreale DR10037. CD: Melodram Set MEL16501, Gala Set 100501. Note: Martern aller Arten, wrongly attributed to Maria Cebotari, is on Urania 7036, Saga XIG8011, Saga FDY2143, Saga STFDY2143, Saga ST7011, Saga 5911.

December 18 and 19. Reichs Rundfunk, Berlin.
Elisabeth Schwarzkopf (soprano)...........................Fatima
Erich Witte (tenor)....................................Abu Hassan
Michael Bohnen (bass)......................................Omar
Berlin Radio Symphony Orchestra and Chorus conducted by Leopold Ludwig.
   Weber: Abu Hassan
   LP: Urania URLP7029, UR7029, URLP57029, US Vox Set OPBX149, Opera Society OPS1, Classics Club 108, Saga XID5055, FDY2065, STFDY2065, Varèse-Sarabande VC81093. CD: Urania ULS5153, Forlane UCD16572. Excerpts on LP: Melodram MEL082, Discoreale DR10038. CD: Melodram MEL16501.

1946

'The happiest times of my life were in the recording studio. It was like sculpting, or painting in sound. I loved rehearsals, not only mine, but those of other artists.'

After the war EMI sent Walter Legge to the continent to make contact with established artists and seek out new talent. He heard Schwarzkopf at the Theater an der Wien as Rosina in Rossini's *Il barbiere di Siviglia*, and also at one of the private house concerts in which she was invited to participate. That such events could take place so soon after the war was largely due to the patronage of the remarkable Baron Otto Mayr. Legge asked to meet Elisabeth at the Café Mozart, and there he offered her a contract. The story of her refusal to accept terms without an audition has become something of a legend (for Walter Legge's account, see above, p. 2). At this time it was not possible for a British company to retain a German artist directly, so the actual contract had to be with an obscure EMI subsidiary in Switzerland, Turicaphon.

Herbert von Karajan was another musician then living a precarious existence in Vienna, and he too had been sought out and engaged by Legge. A ban had been placed on concerts by Karajan, but he was able to record, and he conducted Elisabeth's first Columbia recording. Another conductor who accompanied her then was Josef Krips, with whom she always enjoyed working for his art in allowing singers to phrase easily and naturally with the orchestra. She remembers how he smiled at her when things were going well in a performance: 'He beamed like a glowing sun.' In the items with piano the accompanist was Karl Hudez, one of the choral repetiteurs at the Staatsoper.

All the repertoire was familiar to her – arias from *Entführung*, the Strauss waltz (only part of which was recorded, for some unremembered reason), the Bach cantata aria once more, and English repertoire she had studied with Raucheisen and Ivogün, now actually sung in English. The Handel item she performed from a copy given to her by Ivogün.

Recording conditions in Vienna at that time were far from easy. In cold weather the heating was inadequate, the electricity voltage was variable and there were power cuts. In order not to waste precious recording time Walter Legge obtained a petrol-powered generator. Since petrol itself was a scarce commodity Legge used local influence to conjure up precious supplies, which he obtained by touring round in taxis.

October 23. Brahmssaal, Vienna. Vienna Philharmonic Orchestra conducted
   by Herbert von Karajan.

CHAX230-1	Mozart: Die Entführung aus dem Serail – Martern		
	aller Arten		pt. 1
-2	"	"	"
-3	"	"	"
231-1	"	"	pt. 2
-2	"	"	"

      Issued on LP: Set RLS763, Set RLS7714,
      Set 1546133. C: Set TC-RLS763. CD: CDH7
      63708-2, *Nota Blu 93.50923-4*.

October 26. Brahmssaal, Vienna. Karl Hudez (piano).

CHA954-1	Schubert: Seligkeit, D433	LB77
-2	" "	

also on LV5, LN9. LP: Set RLS763, Set
RLS766. C: Set TC-RLS763.

955-1	Schubert: Die Forelle, D550	LB77
-2	" "	

also on LV5, LN9. LP: Set RLS763, Set
RLS766. C: Set TC-RLS763.

956-1	Dowland: Come again! Sweet love doth now invite
-2	" " "

Issued on LP: ALP143550-1, Set 1546133.
C: TC-ALP1435504.

October 31. Musikvereinsaal, Vienna. Vienna Philharmonic Orchestra
conducted by Josef Krips.

CHAX253-1	Mozart: Die Entführung aus dem Serail – Welcher Kummer	pt. 1 LX1249
-2	" " "	"
254-1	" " "	pt. 2
-2	" " "	" LX1249

also on LZX241. LP: Set RLS763, ML4649,
Set 1546133. C: Set TC-RLS763. CD: CDH7
63708-2.

255-1	J. Strauss II: Waltz, Frühlingsstimmen, Op. 410	pt. 1
-2	" "	"

Issued on LP: ALP1435501, Set 1546133. C:
TC-ALP1435504, EG7 63654-4. CD: Set
CMS7 63790-2, CDM7 63654-2.

November 1. Brahmssaal, Vienna. Josef Niedermayer (flute), Karl Rezniček
(flute), –. Maurer (cello), Isolde Ahlgrimm (harpsichord).

CHAX256-1	Bach: Cantata No. 208, Was mir behagt, ist nur die muntre Jagd – Schafe können sicher weiden	pt. 1
-2	" " "	" LX1051
257-1	" " "	pt. 2 LX1051
-2	" " "	"

also on LCX115, GQX11325. LP:
ALP143550-1, ML4792, 60013. C:
TC-ALP143550-4. CD: CDH7 63201-2.

November 2. Brahmssaal, Vienna. Vienna Philharmonic Orchestra conducted
by Josef Krips.

CHAX259-1	Mozart: Il rè pastore – L'amerò, sarò costante	pt. 1 LX1096
-2	" " "	"
260-1	" " "	pt. 2
-2	" " "	" LX1096

(with Fritz Sedlak, violin).

also on LFX1018.
LP: Set RLS763, 290598-3. C: Set
TC-RLS763.

261-1 Handel: L'allegro, il penseroso ed il moderato
   – First and chief on golden wing   LX1010
 -2 "   "   "
262-1 " – Sweet bird, that shun'st the noise
   of folly
 -2 "   "   LX1010
   (with Josef Niedermayer, flute).
   LP: ALP143550-1, Set 1546133. EP:
   SEL1585. C: TC-ALP143550-4. CD: CDH7
   63201-2.

November 6.
 CHAX279-1 Mozart: Exsultate, jubilate, K165   pt. 1
   -2 "   "   "
  280-1 "   "   pt. 2
   -2 "   "   "
  281-1 "   "   pt. 3
   -2 "   "   "
  282-1 "   "   pt. 4
   -2 "   "   "

November 7. Brahmssaal, Vienna. Karl Hudez (piano).
 CHA967-1 T. Arne: Love's Labour's Lost – When daisies pied;
     Morley: It was a lover and his lass
   -2 "   "
   -3 "   "

1947

Schwarzkopf's August 1947 performance of the Brahms *Requiem* in Lucerne with Furtwängler was a turning point in her career, and providing her with an opening to the outside world. None of her Columbia recordings had yet been released when Walter Legge played a test pressing to Furtwängler's Swiss agent Walter Schulthess. Schulthess was not merely a businessman, but a fine musician whose judgement Furtwängler trusted completely. After hearing the recording Schulthess told Furtwängler that he should engage Elisabeth. In the normal course of events she was not allowed to leave Austria, but a Swiss diplomat made the trip possible and drove her in an open car to Lucerne via the Arlberg Pass. A slightly bedraggled Elisabeth arrived in time for the rehearsal. There she 'sang for my life'. A Swiss soprano, Sylvia Gähwiller, sat by in case of Elisabeth's non-arrival or in case she did not please Furtwängler.

Another important event for her that summer was her début at the Salzburg Festival in a single performance as Susanna in Mozart's *Le nozze di Figaro*.

Very soon after the concert with Furtwängler Schwarzkopf and her mother were summoned late one night to the office of Dr Hilbert, head of the State Opera. He wanted her for the company's forthcoming visit to London, and the only way she could obtain a visa would be to become an Austrian citizen. Her mother was unsure whether she should take this step, and so Elisabeth insisted on consulting her father. He was still obliged to live apart from his wife and daughter, and was now working for the Americans as an executive officer on the de-Nazification board at Fulda, near Frankfurt. He had no telephone, and had to be got out of bed and taken to a hotel at Gersfeld, where he was connected to his daughter. His response was characteristically generous and broadminded: he told Elisabeth that her voice was her passport, and that so far as he was concerned she could use a Chinese passport if she so wished.

So it was that Elisabeth travelled to London with the Vienna State Opera in September 1947. At the Royal Opera House she sang Don Elvira in Mozart's *Don Giovanni*, with Krips conducting, and Marzelline in Beethoven's *Fidelio*, under Clemens Krauss. Sandwiched between performances were recordings of arias from *Don Giovanni*, with Krips now conducting the Philharmonia Orchestra, and the famous duets from *Hänsel und Gretel* with Seefried. These unsurpassed recordings she much enjoys for their gaiety and rhythmical freedom. This was her first encounter with the Philharmonia Orchestra, which Walter Legge had founded two years previously, and some song recordings marked the first time that she worked with Gerald Moore as her accompanist.

On her return to Vienna she took part in more opera performances as a fully-fledged member of the State Opera's company. She sang Rosina in Rossini's *Barbiere* once more, Mimì in Puccini's *La Bohème*, and Violetta in Verdi's *La traviata*. She also took part in Karajan's Vienna Philharmonic recording of the Brahms *Requiem*. In December she recorded the 'Presentation of the Silver Rose', in the part of Sophie, from Strauss's *Der Rosenkavalier*, and she remembers that at this Musikvereinsaal session she and Irmgard Seefried were placed behind the orchestra in front of the organ at the very back of the hall, and not in the balcony. As usual, the heavy reverberation of the auditorium was damped down by the use of drapes hanging across the hall. Over the next four days Schwarzkopf was involved in Karajan's recording of Beethoven's Ninth Symphony, a part which she found particularly nerve-racking because of the high B natural, which all sopranos fear.

August 20. Lucerne Jesuitkirche. Hans Hotter (baritone), Lucerne Festival Chorus and Orchestra conducted by Wilhelm Furtwängler.
Brahms: Ein deutsches Requiem.
LP: Japan Furtwängler Series W24. CD: Wing Discs WCD1-2. Excerpts on LP: Japan Furtwängler Series W22-3.
NB: There are gaps in the music caused by the need to change over the original acetate recording discs.

September 26. EMI Studio No. 1. Philharmonia Orchestra conducted by Josef Krips.

CAX10054-1 -2	Mozart: Don Giovanni – In quali eccessi " " "	LX1210
10055-1 -2	" " – Mi tradi quell' alma ingrata " " "	LX1210
	also on 72640-D. LP: Set RLS763. EP: SEL1511. C: Set TC-RLS763.	
10056-1 -2	Humperdinck: Hänsel und Gretel – Sandman's Song; Evening Prayer " " " "	LX1037
	(with Irmgard Seefried, soprano). also on LP: RLS763. C: Set TC-RLS763. CD: CDH7 69793-2.	
10057-1 -2	Humperdinck: Hänsel und Gretel – Dance Duet " " "	pt. 1 LX1036 "
10058-1 -2	" " " " " "	pt. 2 " LX1036

September 27.

CAX10059-1 -2	" " " " " "	pt. 3 LX1037 "
	(with Irmgard Seefried, soprano). also on LP: Set RLS763, RO5417. C: Set TC-RLS763. CD: CDH7 69793-2.	

October 2. EMI Studio No. 3. Gerald Moore (piano).

CAX10050-1 -2 -3	Bach (arr. Gounod): Ave Maria " " " "	
	(with Jean Pougnet, violin).	
CA20517-1 -2	Mozart: Warnung, K433 " "	LB73
	also on LD2. LP: ML4649.	
20518-1 -2 -3	T. Arne: Love's Labour's Lost – When daisies pied; The Tempest – Where the bee sucks " " " " " "	LB73

also on LP: Set RLS763, Set 1546133. C:
Set TC-RLS763, EG7 63654-4. CD: Set
CMS7 63790-2, CDM7 63654-2.

October 21 and 22. Musikvereinsaal, Vienna. Singverein der Gesellschaft der
Musikfreunde, Vienna Philharmonic Orchestra conducted by Herbert von
Karajan.

CHAX301-1	Brahms: Ein deutsches Requiem, Op. 45 –			
	Ihr habt nun Traurigkeit			pt. 1 LX1061
-2	"	"	"	"
-3	"	"	"	"

October 22, 27 and 28.

CHAX303-1	"		"	pt. 2 LX1061
-2	"	"	"	"
-3	"	"	"	"

NB: Other sessions for the recording of the complete
work took place on the above dates and on October
20.

Set LX1055-1064, auto Set LX8595-8604;
Set SL157, Set M755. LP: Set RLS7714,
EAC30103, 2C 153 03 200-205, 2C 051 43
176. C: 2C 251 43 176. CD: CDH7 61010-2,
CDH61010.

December 9. Brahmssaal, Vienna. Erich Kunz (baritone), Vienna
Philharmonic Orchestra conducted by Herbert von Karajan.

CHA989-1	Mozart: Die Zauberflöte – Bei Männern		
-2	"	"	"
-3	"	"	"

December 9. Musikvereinsaal, Vienna. Irmgard Seefried (soprano), Vienna
Philharmonic Orchestra conducted by Herbert von Karajan.

CHAX377-1	Strauss: Der Rosenkavalier – Presentation			
	of the Silver Rose			pt. 1 LX1225
-2	"	"	"	"
378-1	"	"	"	pt. 2 LX1225
-2	"	"	"	"
379-1	"	"	"	pt. 3 LX1226
-2	"	"	"	"
-3	"	"	"	"

also on LP: SH286, Set RLS763, Set
RLS7714, ML2126, Set 1546133. C: Set
TC-RLS763. CD: CDH7 69793-2.

December 10. Musikvereinsaal, Vienna. Elisabeth Höngen (contralto), Julius
Patzak (tenor), Hans Hotter (baritone), Singverein der Gesellschaft der
Musikfreunde, Vienna Philharmonic Orchestra conducted by Herbert von
Karajan.

CHAX333-1	Beethoven: Symphony No. 9 in D		
	minor, Op. 125		mvt. 4, pt. 2 LX1103

	-2	"	"		"	"	
December 11.							
CHAX334-1		"	"	mvt. 4, pt. 3			
	-2	"	"		"	"	LX1103
335-1		"	"	mvt. 4, pt. 4			
	-2	"	"		"	"	LX1104
December 12.							
CHAX336-1		"	"	mvt. 4, pt. 5 LX1104			
	-2	"	"		"	"	
383-1		"	"	mvt. 4, pt. 6 LX1105			
	-2	"	"		"	"	
	-3	"	"		"	"	
December 14.							
CHAX384-1		"	"	mvt. 4, pt. 7 LX1105			
	-2	"	"		"	"	
	-3	"	"		"	"	
333-3		"	"	mvt. 4, pt. 2			
334-3		"	"	mvt. 4, pt. 3			
335-3		"	"	mvt. 4, pt. 4			
	-4	"	"		"	"	

NB: Other sessions for the recording of the complete work took place on November 3, 4, 5, and 6.
Set LX1097-1105, auto LX8612-20; LFX846-54; LVX32-40; GQX11250-8. LP: Set RLS7714, Set EL51, 1C 153 03 200-5, 2C 153 03 200-5. EAC30101. CD: CDH7 61076-2.

1948

Schwarzkopf's appearances in London with the Viennese company created a great impression, and almost immediately she was contracted as a member of the Royal Opera House company – though she continued to appear with the Vienna State Opera. In London she had to learn her roles in English, which was still always used at Covent Garden. Walter Legge now had the chance to record her more extensively with the Philharmonia Orchestra and Gerald Moore, but as it happened her April 1948 sessions were undertaken at short notice in place of an artist who cancelled. Her conductor was Warwick Braithwaite, a conductor with whom she worked at the Opera House, and who she felt was very competent.

In July she was back in Salzburg as the Geist in Gluck's *Orfeo ed Euridice* and as the Countess in Mozart's *Le nozze di Figaro*. In late August there was also a performance of Beethoven's Ninth with Furtwängler at the Lucerne Festival. Then in September in Vienna there were performances of *Zauberflöte, Don Giovanni, Fidelio* and two new roles – Agathe in Weber's *Der Freischütz* and Sophie in Strauss's *Der Rosenkavalier*. She returned to the Royal Opera House in September, where she repeated some of these parts in English. After this it was back and forth between Vienna and London, with the occasional concert engagement fitted in between, until late December, when the Viennese company took their production of *Le nozze di Figaro* under Karajan to La Scala, Milan. So it was that Elisabeth made her début in that theatre; and on a 'pirate' recording there is a small souvenir of her performance.

April 12. EMI Studio No. 1. Philharmonia Orchestra conducted by Warwick
    Braithwaite.
    CAX10218-1 Mozart: Die Zauberflöte – Ach, ich fühl's (sung in
                English)
        -2   "   "   "
                LP: ALP143550-1, Set 1546133. C:
                TC-ALP143550-4. CD: CDH7 63708-2.
    10219-1 Verdi: La traviata – È strano ... Ah! fors è lui (sung
                in English)   pt. 1 LX1079
        -2   "   "   "   "
    10220-1   "   "   "   pt. 2 LX1079
        -2   "   "   "   "

May 21. EMI Studio No. 3. Gerald Moore (piano).
    CA20761-1 Schubert: Die Vögel, D691; Liebhaber in allen
                Gestalten, D558
        -2   "   "   "
                Issued on LP: Set RLS766, ALP143550-1,
                Set 1546133. C: TC-ALP143550-4, EG7
                63656-4. CD: Set CMS7 63790-2, CDM7
                63656-2.
    20762-1 Mozart: Das Veilchen, K476
        -2   "   "
    CAX10257-1 Wolf: Storchenbotschaft
        -2   "   "
    10258-1 Schubert: Gretchen am Spinnrade, D118
        -2   "   "

May 26. Kingsway Hall. Philharmonia Orchestra conducted by Walter
    Susskind.
    CAX10264-1 Mozart: Exsultate, jubilate, K165   pt. 1
        -2   "   "   "
    10274-1   "   "   pt. 3 LX1197
        -2   "   "   "
    10273-1   "   "   pt. 4

-2	"	"	"
-3	"	"	"

May 28.

CAX10279-1   "   "   pt. 2

        -2   "   "   " LX1196

                Matrix CAX10264 was later transferred
                and issued as take 3 on LX1196. Matrix
                CAX10273 was transferred and issued as
                take 4 on LX1197.
                Also on LP: ML4649, 60013, C80628, Set
                1546133. CD: CDH7 63201-2.

    10280-1   Bach: Cantata No. 51, Jauchzet Gott in
                allen Landen!   pt. 1

        -2   "   "   "

May 31.

CAX10284-1	"	"	pt. 2
-2	"	"	"
10285-1	"	"	pt. 3
-2	"	"	"
10286-1	"	"	pt. 4
-2	"	"	"
10287-1	"	"	pt. 5
-2	"	"	"

November 6. Brahmssaal, Vienna. Vienna Philharmonic Orchestra conducted
by Herbert von Karajan.

    CHAX401-1   Puccini: La bohème – Si, mi chiamano Mimì
            -2   "   "   "

                Issued on LP: ALP143550-1, Set 1546133.
                C: TC-ALP143550-4. CD: CDM7 63557-2.

       402-1   "   "   – Donde lieta uscì
            -2   "   "   "

    CHA1002-1   Puccini: Gianni Schicchi – O mio babbino caro   LB85
            -2   "   "   "
            -3   "   "   "

                also on LV7, LN4, GQ7240. LP: Set
                RLS763, Set 1546133, EAC30112. EP:
                SEL1575. C: Set TC-RLS763.

November 10. Musikvereinsaal, Vienna. Vienna State Opera Orchestra,
conductor unknown.

    CHA1004-1   Puccini: Turandot – Tu che di gel sei cinta
            -2   "   "   "

December 28. La Scala Theatre, Milan.

    Elisabeth Schwarzkopf (soprano)..................Countess Almaviva
    Irmgard Seefried (soprano)...............................Susanna
    Walter Höfermeyer (baritone)....................... Count Almaviva
    Giuseppe Taddei (baritone)................................. Figaro
    Vienna State Opera Orchestra conducted by Herbert von Karajan.

Mozart: Le nozze di Figaro – Ah! La cieca gelosia
Issued on LP: Melodram Set MEL088.

1949

This was a sparse year for Schwarzkopf in terms of recording commitments, but she was kept very busy by live performances at the opera houses of Vienna and London, a series of three Beethoven's Ninths with Furtwängler in Vienna, a visit by the Vienna State Opera, first to the Champs-Elysées Theatre in Paris, where she sang Susanna in *Le nozze di Figaro* under Karl Böhm, and then to Brussels, where she appeared as Sophie in *Rosenkavalier* and Elvira in *Don Giovanni*. The Royal Opera House company went to Birmingham, where she sang Susanna once more, and also Eva in *Meistersinger* under Reginald Goodall – another English conductor for whom she had particular respect.

At the end of July there was a new departure in every sense in the shape of a three-month visit to Australia. She gave nearly 30 performances throughout the country and took part in four orchestral concerts, including three in Sydney with the Sydney Symphony Orchestra under Otto Klemperer, where she sang Bach's Cantata BWV51, *Jauchzet Gott in allen Landen*. In all the recitals she worked with the pianist Margaret Schofield.

Late in the year she returned to England for more operatic appearances and recitals. One uncharacteristic assignment was at the Royal Albert Hall in early December, when she was the soloist in Henri Sauguet's *La voyante*, with George Weldon conducting the Philharmonia Orchestra. At the end of the month she sang opera in Basel for the first time.

March 3. Musikvereinsaal, Vienna. Vienna State Opera Chorus and
    Orchestra, conductor unknown.
    CHA1056-1 Gruber: Stille Nacht
        -2   "   "   LC32
            LP: ALP143550-1. C: TC-ALP143550-4.
      1057-1 Trad: O Tannenbaum   LC32
        -2   "   "
      1058-1 Trad: O du fröhliche, O du selige   LC33
        -2   "   "   "
      1059-1 Trad: Es ist ein Ros' entsprungen   LC33
        -2   "   "   .   "

March 16. Musikvereinsaal, Vienna. Vienna Philharmonic Orchestra
    conducted by Karl Böhm.

CHA1060-1 Puccini: Turandot – Tu che di gel sei cinta
    -2   "   "   "   LB85
    -3   "   "   "
Also on LN4, GQ7240. EP: SEL1575.

1950

If 1949 had been a lean recording year, the latter part of 1950 was a busy period for Schwarzkopf in the studios. During January and February there were fifteen performances at the Royal Opera House to occupy the major part of her time – including seven performances of Butterfly in Puccini's *Madama Butterfly*. She had now left the Vienna State Opera (against Walter Legge's advice), and in March and April, between Royal Opera performances, there were concerts and recitals in Florence and Zürich and a return visit to the opera at Basel.

Her May visit to EMI's recording studios included a surprising item in the shape of 'Depuis le jour' from Charpentier's *Louise*. French repertoire did not usually come her way at this stage in her career, and she now feels that at the time she entertained a misplaced notion that a narrower than usual tone quality should be cultivated in French music. She considers the performance unidiomatic in its sound quality and in the way she responds to the French language, though some judges think highly of it.

A few days after this recording she was called upon to sing the few notes alloted to Feodor in Boris Christoff's recording of 'The Death of Boris' from Mussorgsky's *Boris Godunov*. Here is perhaps a slightly more substantial contribution than one or two other recording curiosities which have not been listed in this discography. These comprise a few top notes sung for Kirsten Flagstad, first in the 1951 recording of the Closing Scene from Act 3 of Wagner's *Siegfried* under Georges Sebastien, and then in Furt-wängler's 1952 recording of *Tristan und Isolde*; some hand-clapping in Dobrowen's complete 1952 recording of *Boris* in Paris, and Marzelline's spoken dialogue in Klemperer's 1962 recording of *Fidelio*.

In June and July Schwarzkopf joined Kathleen Ferrier and other soloists under Karajan for several performances of Bach's Mass in B minor. The work was taken to Milan, Perugia and Florence after an initial Viennese performance. Ferrier's contribution made a strong effect, and at the performance in Milan the normally self-possessed Karajan broke down in tears during the 'Agnus Dei'. This is the only occasion on which Dame Elisabeth can recall him showing his emotion to such an extent.

Also in June came the first stage of a large-scale enterprise – a recording of *Le nozze di Figaro* in Vienna under Karajan. This was Elisabeth's first experience as a soloist in an opera recording. She had sung the minor role of Barbarina, and also Susanna on one or two occasions, in her Berlin days, and she had most recently assumed the part of Susanna in a Vienna State Opera production, but she had also sung the Countess in Salzburg the previous year under Karajan, so the part was familiar to her from stage performances. Walter Legge decided that the work should be recorded without *secco* recitatives, mainly because the non-Italian cast did not pronounce Italian with sufficient accuracy – with the notable exception of the American baritone George London.

Although tape machines were now used for making master recordings, the opera was still recorded in short sections to accommodate the nearly obsolete 78rpm format. In the event it was only Electrola in Germany who issued the opera in a 78rpm set of no less than sixteen records. EMI had lagged behind other companies in issuing LPs, and this opera was in the first group of Columbia LPs to be released in the UK during October 1952.

Schwarzkopf was not artistically aware of the change from recording on wax to recording on tape. The constraints of 78rpm recording had never really troubled her, and certainly she was never asked to speed up her tempos in order to fit the music onto a 78rpm side.

In the summer of 1950 she made her greatest impact yet on the Salzburg Festival in two roles: Marzelline in Beethoven's *Fidelio*, and Elvira in *Don Giovanni*. She was experienced in both these parts, but it was her first experience of working on stage under Wilhelm Furtwängler. There were many 'fantastic' dramatic inflections in both performances, influenced by this great conductor, which she believes no one else could have conceived. His encouragement of portamento in particular went against current practice in Vienna, where very clean, neat singing was cultivated.

Immediately after Salzburg she travelled to Lucerne, where she sang in two performances as Marguerite in Berlioz's *Damnation de Faust*, sung in German. She now feels that she was ill-suited to the part, which needs a more mezzo timbre than her lighter voice was able to produce, and she has no wish to hear the 'pirate' recording – though she adds that everything Furtwängler conducted is worth hearing for the sake of his artistry.

In October she recorded the Bach cantata, *Jauchzet Gott*, which had become part of her concert repertoire. The conductor, Peter Gellhorn, was then on the Royal Opera staff and had worked with her in a number of performances of *Bohème*, *Zauberflöte* and *Fidelio*. He had also accompanied her at recitals in Oxford and Cambridge. She recalls particularly the brilliant playing by the Philharmonia's principal trumpet player, Harold

Jackson, and the fact that nobody seemed sure about the right tempo for the cantata's opening movement. In the event an over-hasty tempo was adopted, and it seems to her now that her use of *martellato* under these conditions is such that intrusive 'h' sounds are in danger of making their unwelcome presence felt.

The Medtner songs were recorded under the auspices of the Maharaja of Mysore's Musical Foundation. The repertoire was new to Schwarzkopf, and she rehearsed with Medtner at a large ground-floor studio in his Hampstead home. She remembers there being 'thousands of notes' in the accompaniments and how well the elderly composer still played them.

The sequence of aria recordings in October brought her into contact with Alceo Galliera, a 'forceful, knowledgeable conductor of the greatest integrity', who had been working with the Philharmonia almost since its formation four years earlier. Walter Legge admired him and found him an excellent orchestral trainer, and Elisabeth certainly enjoyed working with him.

May 6. EMI Studio No. 1. Philharmonia Orchestra conducted by Issay Dobrowen.

CA21438-1	Charpentier: Louise – Depuis le jour			pt. 1
-2	"	"	"	"
21439-1	"	"	"	pt. 2
-2	"	"	"	"

                Issued on LP: Set RLS763, Set 1546133. C: Set TC-RLS763.

| CAX10813-1 | Puccini: La bohème – Donde lieta uscì |
| -2 | " | " | " |

May 19. EMI Studio No. 1. Boris Christoff (bass), Philharmonia Orchestra conducted by Issay Dobrowen.

| 2EA13853-1 | Mussorgsky (orch. Rimsky-Korsakov): Boris Godunov – Hark, 'Tis the funeral bell (sung in Russian) | | | DB21097 |
| -2 | " | " | " | |

                also on LP: BLP1003, Set RLS735, WBLP1003, E70018, ORLP5002, 1C 147 03 336-7M, HB1010. EP: EHA11. C: Set TC-RLS735. SP: 7RF105, 7RF166. CD: CDH7 64252-2.

June 15. Musikvereinsaal, Vienna. Kathleen Ferrier (contralto), Walther Ludwig (tenor), Paul Schöffler (baritone), Alfred Poell (baritone), Singverein der Gesellschaft der Musikfreunde, Vienna Symphony Orchestra conducted by Herbert von Karajan.
    Bach: Mass in B minor, BWV232

CD: Hunt Set CDKAR212, Foyer Set 2CF2022, Verona Set 27073-4. C:
Verona Set 427073-4. Excerpts on C: EG7 63655-4. CD: Set CMS7
63790-2, CDM7 63655-2, *Verona 27076.*

June 17-21. Musikvereinsaal, Vienna.
Irmgard Seefried (soprano)...............................Susanna
Elisabeth Schwarzkopf (soprano)..................Countess Almaviva
Sena Jurinac (soprano)...................................Cherubino
Elisabeth Höngen (contralto)............................Marcellina
Erich Kunz (baritone).......................................Figaro
George London (baritone)...........................Count Almaviva
Marjan Rus (bass)..Bartolo
Rosl Schwaiger (soprano)..................................Barbarina
Erich Majkut (tenor)....................... Don Curzio; Don Basilio
Wilhelm Felden (bass).....................................Antonio
Vienna State Opera Chorus and Vienna Philharmonic Orchestra conducted
by Herbert von Karajan.
Mozart: Le nozze di Figaro
NB: This recording, completed in October 1950, was
made in short sections on tape.

July 31 (or August 4 or 18). Festspielhaus, Salzburg.
Tito Gobbi (baritone)..................................Don Giovanni
Ljuba Welitsch (soprano)............................. Donna Anna
Elisabeth Schwarzkopf (soprano).....................Donna Elvira
Erich Kunz (baritone)...................................... Leporello
Irmgard Seefried (soprano)...............................Zerlina
Alfred Poell (baritone)..................................... Masetto
Josef Greindl (bass).............................. Commendatore
Anton Dermota (tenor)............................... Don Ottavio
Vienna State Opera Chorus and Vienna Philharmonic Orchestra conducted
by Wilhelm Furtwängler.
Mozart: Don Giovanni
LP: Melodram Set MEL713, Olympic Set OL9109/4, Ed Smith Set
EJS419, Discocorp Set RR407, Vox Turnabout THS65154-6. T:
Discocorp Set RR658. CD: Laudis Set LDC34001, Japanese RCA Set
R30C1014-6, Priceless Set D16581. Excerpts on LP: Melodram Set
MEL082, Set MEL088, Discoreale DR10037. CD: MEL16501. NB. Some
issues mistakenly give July 27 as the date. OL9109/4 contains a section
from the 1954 performance, for which see listing.

August 5. Festspielhaus, Salzburg.
Hans Braun (baritone)..............................Don Fernando
Paul Schöffler (baritone)..............................Don Pizarro
Julius Patzak (tenor).....................................Florestan
Kirsten Flagstad (soprano)............................... Leonore
Josef Greindl (bass)... Rocco
Elisabeth Schwarzkopf (soprano)......................Marzelline
Anton Dermota (tenor)....................................Jaquino
Hermann Gallos (tenor)............................... Prisoner I

Ljubomir Pantscheff (bass)............................Prisoner II
Vienna State Opera Chorus, Vienna Philharmonic Orchestra conducted by
Wilhelm Furtwängler.
Beethoven: Fidelio
> *LP: Morgan Set MOR5001, MRF Set MRF50, BJR Set BJR112,*
> *Discocorp Set IGI328, Fonit Cetra Set FE44. C: Verona 27044-5. CD:*
> *CHS7 64901-2, Hunt CDWFE304, Hunt Set IWFE304, Verona 27044-5.*
> *Excerpts on LP: Melodram Set MEL082, Discoreale DR10037. CD:*
> *MEL16501.*

August 26. Kunsthaus, Lucerne. Franz Vroons (tenor: Faust), Hans Hotter
(baritone: Mephistofeles), Elisabeth Schwarzkopf (soprano: Marguerite),
Alois Pernerstorfer (bass-baritone: Brander), Lucerne Festival Chorus and
Orchestra conducted by Wilhelm Furtwängler.
Berlioz: La damnation de Faust (sung in German)
> *LP: Fonit Cetra Set FE21.*

October 6. Kingsway Hall. Philharmonia Orchestra conducted by Peter Gellhorn.

CAX10280-3	Bach: Cantata No. 51, Jauchzet Gott in	
	allen Landen!	pt. 1 LX1334
10284-3	" "	pt. 2 LX1334
-4	" "	"
10285-3	" "	pt. 3 LX1335
10286-3B	" "	pt. 4 LX1335
10287-3	" "	pt. 5 LX1336

> also on auto: LX8756-8. LP: ML4792,
> 60013, C80628, 33WSX578, Set 1546133.
> CD: CDH7 63201-2.

October 13. EMI Studio No. 1. Sidney Sutcliffe (oboe), Manoug Parikian
(violin), Raymond Clark (cello), Geraint Jones (organ).

CAX10925-1	Bach: Cantata No. 68, Also hat Gott die Welt	
	geliebt – Mein gläubiges Herze	LX1336
-2	" " "	
-3	" " "	

> also on auto: LX8756. LP: ML4792. CD:
> CDH7 63201-2.

October 16. EMI Studio No. 1A. Nicolai Medtner (piano).

CAX11235-1	Medtner: The Muse, Op. 29 No. 1	LX1425
	also on CD: CDC7 54839-2.	
11236-1B	Medtner: So tanzet, Op. 15 No. 5; The Waltz, Op. 32 No. 5	LX1425
	also on CD: CDC7 54839-2.	
11237-1C	Medtner: Einsamkeit, Op. 18 No. 3; Praeludium, Op. 46 No. 1	LX1426
	also on CD: CDC7 54839-2.	
11238-1	Medtner: Winternacht, Op. 46 No. 6	LX1426
	also on CD: CDC7 54839-2.	

October 18. EMI Studio No. 1. Philharmonia Orchestra conducted by Alceo
Galliera.

CA21572-1	Puccini: La bohème – Donde lieta uscì	
-2	" "	LB110
-3	" "	
	also on LW51, LN5, GQ7246. LP: Set RLS763, Set 1546133. EP: SEL1575. SP: SCD2141, SCB101, SCBQ3001, SCBF103, SCBW101. C: Set TC-RLS763.	
21573-1	Puccini: Turandot – Signore, ascolta	
-2	" "	LB110
	also on LW51, LN5. LP: Set RLS763. EP: SEL1575. SP: SCB101, SCBQ3001, SCBF108, SCBW101. C: Set TC-RLS763.	
CAX10945-1	Puccini: Madama Butterfly: Un bel dì, vedremo	
-2	" " "	LX1370
-3	" " "	
	also on GQX11456. LP: Set RLS763, Set 1546133. EP: SEL1575. SP: SCD2076, SCB102, SCBQ3004, SCBW102. C: Set TC-RLS763.	

October 19.

CAX10946-1	Beethoven: Fidelio – Ach wär'ich schon	
-2	" " "	
-3	" " "	
	The above recording was published as take 2A on LX1410. Also on LVX157. LP: Set EX7 69741-1. SP: SCD2114. CD: Set CHS7 69741-2.	
10947-1	Verdi: La traviata – Addio del passato	
-2	" " "	LX1370
	also on GQX11456. LP: Set RLS763. EP: SEL1575. SP: SCD2076, SCB102, SCBW102, SCBF107, SCBQ3004. C: Set TC-RLS763.	
10948-1	Bizet: Carmen – Je dis que rien ne m'épouvante	LX1410
-2	" " "	
	also on LVX157. LP: ALP143550-1. SP: SCD2114. C: TC-ALP143550-4.	

October 23-27, 31. Musikvereinsaal, Vienna. Artists as on June 17-21.
Schwarzkopf sang at Covent Garden on October 26, so she could only have
been present at some of the above sessions, and maybe none at all.
Available documentation is not clear on this point.

Mozart: Le nozze di Figaro

NB: Matrix numbers CHAX534-73 were assigned to
this work. The recording was made in short sections
but no allocations were made until the editing was
completed. All the recordings were made on tape.

>78: LWX410-425. LP: 33CX1007-9, Set
>SL114, C90292-4, 1C 147 01 751-3M, 1C
>197 54200-8M, 33VCX503-5, 33FCX174-6,
>2C 163 01 751-3, 33QCX10002-4,
>33WCX1007-9, WL5018-20. C: 2C 163 01
>751-3M. CD: Set CMS7 69639-2,
>CDMB69639, 769639-2. Excerpts on 78:
>LX1575 (CHAX551-3B, 552-4B). LP:
>33CX1558, Set RLS764, 35326, C80531,
>33WSX548, 33FCX30170, C70373,
>33WC518, IC 147 03 580-1, IC 063 00 839,
>RL3050. C: Set TC-RLS764, IC 263 00 839,
>EG7 63657-4. CD: Set CMS7 63790-2,
>CDM7 63657-2.

November 22. EMI Studio No. 1A. Nicolai Medtner (piano).

CAX10982-1	Medtner: The Rose, Op. 29 No. 6; When roses fade, Op. 36 No. 3	LX1423
-2	" " "	
	also on CD: CDC7 54839-2.	
10983-1	Medtner: Im Vorübergehn, Op. 6 No. 4; Elfenliedchen, Op. 6 No. 3	LX1423
	also on CD: CDC7 54839-2.	
10984-1	Medtner: Meeresstille, Op. 15 No. 7; Glückliche Fahrt, Op. 15 No. 8	
-2	" " "	LX1424
	also on CD: CDC7 54839-2.	
10985-1	Medtner: Die Quelle; Selbstbetrug, Op. 15 No. 3	
-2	" " "	LX1424
	also on CD: CDC7 54839-2.	

1951

At the end of 1950 Elisabeth Schwarzkopf could look back on a productive year, but it was during the course of 1951 that she finally became established as one of the world's leading singers. The year began well with her début as a guest artist with the La Scala company, where she sang Elisabeth in Wagner's *Tannhäuser* and Elvira in *Don Giovanni*, both under the baton of Herbert von Karajan. Less immediately striking, but auspicious in retrospect, was the beginning of her concentrated work on Wolf Lieder in the recording studio, with Legge and Gerald Moore her tireless collaborators. In May she sang in two performances of *Fidelio* at Covent Garden, and part of the first has survived in a 'pirate' recording. Here was one of those occasions when casting problems resulted in the use of two languages: the opera was sung in German but the dialogue was spoken in English. The conductor was Karl Rankl, musical director at the Opera House between 1946 and 1951. Schwarzkopf recalls him as a rather impulsive conductor with a somewhat stern personality.

In August she travelled to Bayreuth. Her first commitment was a special performance of Beethoven's Ninth Symphony under Furtwängler, played to celebrate the opening of the first Bayreuth Festival to take place after the end of the war. This was a highly important engagement for her personally, and indeed for all the soloists, who were very concerned to live up to the occasion. She recalls the atmosphere as 'incredibly moving'. The performance was recorded by EMI, but there were no plans to issue it since Furtwängler was expected to make a studio recording of the work. In the event he died three years later without having achieved this end, and so in 1955 EMI decided to issue the live Bayreuth Ninth on LP.

Elisabeth also sang Eva in *Meistersinger* at Bayreuth under Karajan. First there were piano rehearsals for the work under the direction of Max Kojetinsky, a conductor from Graz who had accompanied her in two recitals earlier that year. Then there were many more piano rehearsals supervised by Karajan himself. All were attended by Walter Legge, who was in charge of a programme of several live recordings at the Festival. Schwarzkopf knew that recordings were taking place, but like all the cast she soon forgot about it when performances were under way, and she was never aware of any intrusive microphones. All the performances plus the final rehearsal on 27 July were recorded, and the published version is an edited amalgam of the best takes. The 78rpm version of this recording has the distinction of being the largest set of shellac records ever published – it contains 34 discs.

Dame Elisabeth feels that this *Meistersinger* captures some of her best singing on record, and that the end result represents all the best aspects of performances recorded live. There were also two *Ring* cycles at this Festival, one conducted by Karajan and the other by Hans Knappertsbusch. The casts were not identical, but Elisabeth took the part of Woglinde (who appears only in *Das Rheingold* and *Götterdämmerung*) in both. Knappertsbusch was a Decca artist, and his cycle was recorded by that company (as was his famous performance of *Parsifal*). Karajan's cycle was recorded by EMI, but only the third act of *Walküre* was published on their Columbia label: *Rheingold* appeared later in a pirated edition. It is known that Decca have considered publication of the Knappertsbusch cycle. All these performances were great occasions for Schwarzkopf, and she recollects that there were 'some fantastic singers' taking part. Although Wagner was and is one of her favourite composers, she never returned to sing at Bayreuth. It was Salzburg which would henceforth claim her presence at that time of year.

When Schwarzkopf was still at Bayreuth she was invited at short notice to take the part of Anne Truelove in the first performances of Stravinsky's *The Rake's Progress* in place of another artist who had been forced to cancel. She had to learn the part in a matter of days, and even that short period of study was interrupted by two performances of Bach's Mass in B minor under Karajan at the Lucerne Festival. *The Rake* was not an easy score to master, not only because of its contemporary musical style, but also because she found Stravinsky's use of the English text by Auden and Kullman 'Russianised and cumbersome'.

Rehearsals in Venice took place under Ferdinand Leitner, who also directed two of the three scheduled performances. The première was conducted by Stravinsky himself. Although he was an experienced conductor of his own music, he had no experience of being in charge of a stage production and for the whole performance his eyes scarcely strayed away from the score. In a new work such as this more help from the conductor for those on stage was badly needed, and the performance could have been a disaster but for the fact that the singers were all 'very musical'. Leitner was sitting in the front row of the audience, and he managed to give surreptitious cues at crucial moments.

Schwarzkopf was on a brief visit to London when Ludwig Weber recorded 'Tot den Alles' from Wagner's *Tristan*, which includes a few notes from the mezzo-soprano role of Brangäne. No other singer was available, so Walter Legge asked Elisabeth to step into the breach. After engagements in Scandinavia, Amsterdam and Munich, she spent almost a month in South Africa, and then ended the year with four more performances of *The Rake* in La Scala, Milan, again with Leitner conducting. This time the opera was sung in Italian.

April 2. EMI Studio No. 3. Gerald Moore (piano).
    CAX11059-1 Wolf: Epiphanias
        -2   "   "
    11060-1 Wolf: Mein Liebster hat zu Tische; Du denkst mit
                einem Fädchen; Schweig' einmal still
        -2   "   "   "
        -3   "   "   "
        -4   "   "   "
    11061-1 Wolf: Wiegenlied
April 3.
    CA21751-1 Trad: Gsätzli; Trad: Die Beruhigte
        -2   "   "   "

```
    -3      "         "            "
    -4      "         "            "
    -5      "         "            "                        LB112
```
       LP: ALP143550-1, Set 1546133. C:
       TC-ALP143550-4.

21752-1 Trad: O du liebs Ängeli; Trad: Maria auf dem Berge LB112
       LP: ALP143550-1, Set 1546133. C:
       TC-ALP143550-4. Maria auf dem Berge is
       on C: EG7 63654-4. CD: Set CMS7 63790-2,
       CDM7 63654-2.

April 6. EMI Studio No. 3. Gerald Moore (piano).
    CAX11074-1 Wolf: Im Frühling
        -2   "   "
      11075-1 Wolf: Storchenbotschaft
        -2   "   "
        -3   "   "
April 7.
    CAX11076-1 Wolf: Elfenlied; Nixe Binsefuss
        -2   "   "   "
        -3   "   "   "
      11077-1 Wolf: Bedeckt mich mit Blumen; Mögen alle bösen
                Zungen
April 11.
    CAX11081-1 Wolf: In dem Schatten meiner Locken; Wer tat deinem
              Füsslein weh?
        -2   "   "   "
        -3   "   "   "
      11082-1 Wolf: Die Spröde; Die Bekehrte
        -2   "   "   "
        -3   "   "   "
        -4   "   "   "

May 16. Royal Opera House, Covent Garden, London.
    Kirsten Flagstad (soprano)................................. Leonore
    Elisabeth Schwarzkopf (soprano)........................Marzelline
    Howell Glynne (bass)....................................... Rocco
    Dennis Stephenson (tenor)...............................Jaquino
    Tom Williams (bass)...................................Don Pizarro
    Charles Craig (tenor)................................. Prisoner I
    Charles Morris (bass)................................. Prisoner II
    Chorus and Orchestra of the Royal Opera House, Covent Garden, conducted
    by Karl Rankl.
        Beethoven: Fidelio (sung in English)
           Excerpts on LP: Ed Smith EJS390.

June 18. EMI Studio No. 3. Gerald Moore (piano).
    CAX11059 Wolf: Epiphanias
       11060 Wolf: Mein Liebster hat zu Tische; Du denkst mit
              einem Fädchen; Schweig' einmal still

June 19.
 CAX11076   Wolf: Elfenlied; Nixe Binsefuss

July 27, August 5, 16, 19, 21 and 24. Festspielhaus, Bayreuth.
 Otto Edelmann (bass)..................................... Hans Sachs
 Friedrich Dalberg (bass)..................................... Pogner
 Erich Kunz (baritone)................................... Beckmesser
 Heinrich Pflanzl (baritone)................................ Kothner
 Hans Hopf (tenor)..Walther
 Gerhard Unger (tenor)..David
 Elisabeth Schwarzkopf (soprano)..............................Eva
 Ira Malaniuk (mezzo-soprano)......................... Magdalene
 Werner Faulhaber (bass)......................... Night Watchman
 Arnold van Mill (bass)...Foltz
 Heinz Borst (bass)... Schwarz
 Heinz Tandler (bass)..Ortel
 Gerhard Stolze (tenor).......................................Moser
 Erich Majkut (tenor)....................................Vogelgesang
 Hans Berg (bass)..Nachtigall
 Josef Janko (tenor)...Zorn
 Karl Mikurey (tenor)....................................Eisslinger
 Bayreuth Festival Chorus and Orchestra conducted by Herbert von Karajan.
  Wagner: Die Meistersinger von Nürnberg
   78: LX1465-98, also on auto LX8851-84. LP: 33CX1021-5, Set RLS7708,
   Set SL117, Set 6030, C90275-9, 33FCX128-33, Set 143390-3,
   33VCX523-7, 33WCX501-5, 1C 151 43 390-4M. C: Set TC-RLS7708.
   CD: Set CHS7 63500-2, Set CDHD63500, Set 763500-2. Excerpts: 78:
   LVX190-1. LP: IC 147 03 580-1, XL5013-7.
     NB: This issue is taken from a rehearsal and five
     live performances. The 78 rpm issues are all
     published as take 1. *A CD issue: Hunt Set
     CDKAR224, contains a broadcast of the first night.*

July 29. Festspielhaus, Bayreuth. Elisabeth Höngen (contralto); Hans Hopf
 (tenor), Otto Edelmann (bass), Bayreuth Festival Chorus and Orchestra
 conducted by Wilhelm Furtwängler.
  Beethoven: Symphony No. 9 in D minor, Op. 125
   LP: ALP1286-7, Set RLS727, Set EX290660-3, COLH78-9, Set LM6043,
   Set 6068, IF6146, Set GR4003, FALP381-2, QALP10116-7, 2C 153 00
   811-2, 1C 149 53 43 239M, E90115-6, WALP1286-7, (E) SMVP8051-2,
   (E) STE90115-6, EBE6000003-4, (E) SME90115-6, AB9403E, AA8188-9,
   AB8084-5, 1C 147 00 811-2, 1C 137 100 811-3, 1C 137 290 660-3, 2C
   151 53 678-9, 2C 153 52 540-51, 2C 281 53 678-9, 1C 149 53 432-9M,
   WF5-6, WF70020-1, WF60006-7, EAC60027, EAC47240-6, HA1012-3.
   CD: CDC7 47081-2, CDC47081, CDH7 69801-2, Set CHS7 63606-2, 555
   769 801-2, CC30-3364-9. Movement 4 is on LP: E80005S, (E)
   SME800055, WCLP508, WALPS1508.

August 11. Festspielhaus, Bayreuth.
 Sigurd Björling (baritone)...................................Wotan

Ira Malaniuk (mezzo-soprano)...............................Fricka
Werner Faulhaber (bass)....................................Donner
Robert Bernauer (tenor)...................................... Froh
Walter Fritz (tenor)... Loge
Paula Brivkalne (soprano)..................................... Freia
Ludwig Weber (bass)..Fasolt
Friedrich Dalberg (bass)......................................Fafner
Heinrich Pflanzl (baritone)................................ Alberich
Paul Kuén (tenor)..Mime
Rute Siewert (mezzo-soprano)............................... Erda
Elisabeth Schwarzkopf (soprano)...................... Woglinde
Lore Wissman (soprano).................................. Wellgunde
Herta Töpper (soprano).................................. Flosshilde
Bayreuth Festival Chorus and Orchestra conducted by Herbert von Karajan.
    Wagner: Das Rheingold
       LP: Melodram Set MEL516. CD: Melodram Set MEL26107, Hunt Set
       CDKAR216. Excerpts on LP: Melodram Set MEL088.

August 15. Festspielhaus, Bayreuth.
    Astrid Varnay (soprano)................................Brunnhilde
    Martha Mödl (soprano)....................Gutrune/Dritte Norn
    Hertha Töpper (soprano)................................ Flosshilde
    Elisabeth Schwarzkopf (soprano).......................Woglinde
    Hanna Ludwig (soprano)................................Wellgunde
    Rute Siewert (mezzo-soprano)............. Waltraute/Erste Norn
    Ira Malaniuk (mezzo-soprano)..........................Zweite Norn
    Bernd Aldenhoff (tenor).............................. Siegfried
    Hermann Uhde (baritone)..............................Gunther
    Heinrich Pflanzl (baritone)............................ Alberich
    Ludwig Weber (bass)....................................Hagen
    Bayreuth Festival Chorus and Orchestra conducted by Herbert von Karajan.
       Wagner: Götterdämmerung

September 11. La Fenice Theatre, Venice.
    Raphael Arié (bass)...................................... Truelove
    Elisabeth Schwarzkopf (soprano)...........................Anne
    Robert Rounseville (tenor)...........................Tom Rakewell
    Otakar Kraus (baritone).............................. Nick Shadow
    Nell Tangeman (mezzo-soprano)....................... Mother Goose
    Jennie Tourel (mezzo-soprano).......................Baba the Turk
    Hugues Cuenod (tenor)................................. Sellem
    Emanuel Menkes (bass)..................................Keeper
    La Scala Chorus and Orchestra conducted by Igor Stravinsky.
       Stravinsky: The Rake's Progress
             LP: Fonit Cetra Set DOC29.

September 16. EMI Studio No. 1. Ludwig Weber (bass), Philharmonia Orchestra
    conducted by Wilhelm Schüchter.
    CAX11390-4B Wagner: Tristan und Isolde – Tot denn Alles!   LX8892
          LP: 1C 177 0093-4M.

October 5. Universität, Munich. Bavarian Radio Symphony Orchestra conducted
by Eugen Jochum.
  Bach: Cantata No. 51, Jauchzet Gott in allen Landen!
    LP: Melodram Set MEL082, Discoreale
    DR10038. CD: Melodram MEL16501.

November 25. EMI Studio No. 1. Gerald Moore (piano).
  CA21982   Gluck: La rencontre imprévue – Einem Bach der fliesst
  CAX11518   Strauss: Hat gesagt bleibt's nicht dabei, Op. 36 No. 3;
             Schlechtes Wetter, Op. 69 No. 5
November 29.
  CA21990-3 Schumann: Der Nussbaum, Op. 25 No. 3   LB122
             also on LW58, LV16, LD6.
  21991-3A   Schumann: Aufträge, Op. 77 No. 5   LB122
             also on LW58, LV16. LP: Set RLS154700-3.
  21992-2   Mozart: Der Zauberer, K472   LB118
             also on LW59, LD2.
  21993   Trad. (arr. Brahms): Deutsche Volkslieder – No. 6, Da
             unten im Tale
December 2.
  CA21993-4   "   "   "   LB118
             also on LV59, LD6.
  21996   Schubert: Der Musensohn, D764

1952

During January 1952 Schwarzkopf sang in six performances of *Rosenkavalier* at La Scala, Milan, with Karajan conducting. In London and elsewhere
she had sung the part of Sophie: now for the first time she assumed a role
for which she would become famous, that of the Marschallin.

In February came a recording assignment with a most unusual background. The actor Bernard Miles was renowned for a sketch in which he
told the story of *Tristan and Isolde* in the manner of an old army bandsman.
His performance of this monologue at a private party once reduced Kirsten
Flagstad to helpless laughter, and the incident not only sparked a friendship between the actor and the soprano but ultimately led to the creation
of the little Mermaid Theatre in the garden of Miles's home in Hampstead.
The theatre was opened in September 1951 with a production of *Dido and
Aeneas.* Flagstad took the part of Dido, and was paid at the rate of one pint
of stout per performance. Elisabeth Schwarzkopf and Walter Legge lived
very near by, and Elisabeth was originally going to take the part of Belinda
in the production. In the end she was unable to do so, but she did

participate in the recording which Legge arranged six months later. She recalls that the style of the opera was very foreign to her – she had sung one or two Purcell songs in recital, but that was all. She is not clear why Walter Legge asked her to make the recording, but she found it 'an incredible honour' to sing with Flagstad. The record cover and labels suggest that the Mermaid Orchestra took part in the recording, but the musicians were in fact members of the Philharmonia. The conductor and the other cast members were the same as in the original production.

Even when recording took up a significant portion of Schwarzkopf's time there were many other engagements for her to fulfil. In the month of the *Dido* recording, for example, she sang Beethoven's Ninth in Florence under Knappertsbusch, Bach's *St John Passion* in Basel, and excerpts from *The Rake* plus a Bach cantata in Geneva with Ernest Ansermet conducting. There was a BBC Third Programme broadcast, a recital in Milan, and two Philharmonia concerts at the Royal Festival Hall. She also appeared in recitals and concerts at such diverse English centres as Cambridge, Liverpool, Bolton, Chelsea, Brighton, Woking and Southall. All this plus the recording sessions in one calendar month!

By now she was making regular visits to Abbey Road for concentrated recording sessions with Gerald Moore. At this time there was a regular programme which she and Legge approached from all manner of angles. There was the Gluck 'Einem Bach der fliesst', Wolf's *Mausfallen Sprüchlein*, Beethoven's *Wonne der Wehmut*, and a dozen or so other items. These songs and arias were tried in different keys and at different tempi. No interpretation was ever static. They were recorded time and time again, with second, third, fourth and fifth thoughts, though sometimes the first 'takes' turned out to be the best. Elisabeth was never particularly enamoured with EMI Studio No. 3, and sometimes she and Moore were able to use what was descibed as 'Studio No. 1A' – this was the large Studio No. 1 with two-thirds of the auditorium curtained off. Even this arrangement presented difficulties, since the curtaining caused two different lengths of reverberation from either side of the singer. The main Studio No. 1 presented her with no difficulties, but in Kingsway Hall she found that she tended to 'underlight' her singing. She was always happiest in large halls, where 'the pronunciation gets ever so much sharper, the expression gets better and more concise and more projected'.

This concentrated recording activity with Walter Legge and Gerald Moore was never queried by EMI, and the artists stopped working only when the studio was required for another project. Dame Elisabeth remarks wryly that there were no trade unions for soloists, but in fact the technicians were glad to be involved and never objected, for they enjoyed the

work. And there was the ever-dependable Gerald Moore at hand, whose
work had total constancy. He had a wonderful keyboard touch, with what
Legge described as 'soft-padded fingers', and what Schwarzkopf now
describes as a 'very warm, soft, fleshy, and human' tone colour, though he
possessed a superlative technique and was capable of brilliance when it
was needed. He did not speak German very well, but he knew the words
of each song intimately, and when there was a piano postlude 'You thought,
"here's the man who really explains the German words". It was always as
if he would now show you what was really meant in the song, every time',
even if it were just four notes for him to play. 'Listen to the Schubert with
Fischer-Dieskau, where Gerald sums it all up – and that is a high compli-
ment – to match even Fischer-Dieskau with a few notes.'

On 5 June Schwarzkopf sang in Mahler's Fourth Symphony at the
Amsterdam Concertgebouw, with Bruno Walter conducting. Later that
month she sang Mimì in three performances of *Bohème* at Covent Garden,
with Franco Capuana as conductor. Her commitments to the Opera House
had been much reduced since 1950, but after a Verdi *Requiem* in the Royal
Festival Hall under Victor de Sabata on 29 June she returned to the Royal
Opera in early July for four performances as Eva in *Meistersinger*. This
was with a conductor she admired greatly, Clemens Krauss. Sandwiched
between rehearsals and appearances were recording sessions in which she
sang Mozart arias with John Pritchard. These she regards as 'quite good'.
In August she returned to Salzburg to sing in just one opera production,
as the Countess in *Le nozze di Figaro* under Rudolf Moralt, and also in two
more performances of the Verdi *Requiem* with De Sabata.

September appears to have been free of public engagements, but there
were several recording sessions leading up to a highly important studio
engagement in early October. This was a programme of Schubert songs
with Edwin Fischer. Years before, as a student in Berlin, Schwarzkopf had
made pilgrimages to Fischer's concerts, hearing him mainly in the music
of Beethoven, and sometimes in partnership with Wilhelm Furtwängler
as conductor. Fischer was not a very experienced accompanist, she relates,
although he enjoyed the role. She feels now that the opportunity to record
with him came perhaps too early in her career. 'I was in terrible awe,
because he was a romantic accompanist, and I had not a romantic-sound-
ing voice – that means I had not much of a middle register. I was very
terrified that I should not be able to match him. I think in the end some
valid performances came out of the two of us. I hope so, I think so, but when
I hear the recordings I still have my misgivings, not that I hear anything
wrong, but I know what I felt at the time – I shall never be able to match
the pianistic colours of that man.' He wasn't in any way authoritative. 'Not

Elisabeth Schwarzkopf recording Strauss's *Capriccio* at Kingsway Hall in September 1957 with the baritone Karl Schmitt-Walter, who was instrumental in recommending her to Maria Ivogün for study.

Michael Raucheisen and Elisabeth Schwarzkopf at the time of their second recital at the Beethovensaal, Berlin, in December 1941.

Maria Ivogün, Schwarzkopf's teacher and mentor in the early 1940s. Photo: Lebrecht Collection.

Bruno Walter's farewell concert with the Vienna Philharmonic in the Musikvereinsaal, Vienna, 29 May 1960. Elisabeth Schwarzkopf was the soloist in Mahler's Fourth Symphony and three of his songs with orchestra.

Douglas Larter, who worked as balance engineer on many early Schwarzkopf recordings.

Elisabeth Schwarzkopf sings the solo part in Verdi's *Requiem* under the baton of Victor de Sabata. They recorded the work together in June 1954.

Walter Legge with Schwarzkopf, making some notes in her score during an early 1960s recording session.

Herbert von Karajan, who conducted many Schwarzkopf recordings and performances, discusses an interpretative point with Walter Legge.

Gerald Moore *(left)* accompanied Schwarzkopf more often on record and in recital than any other pianist. Here he discusses the performance of a Wolf song with the singer and Walter Legge at a recording session in the EMI studios in St John's Wood, London.

The great German pianist Walter Gieseking accompanied Schwarzkopf in recordings of some Mozart songs and his own *Kinderlieder* in April 1955.

The Austrian conductor Karl Böhm, pictured here at a Kingsway Hall recording session for Mozart's *Così fan tutte* in September 1962, was an important influence on Schwarzkopf's career and conducted many of her operatic performances.

Recording Mozart's *Così fan tutte* at Kingsway Hall in September 1962: *(from left)* Christa Ludwig, Elisabeth Schwarzkopf, Walter Berry, Hanny Steffek, Giuseppe Taddei and Alfredo Kraus.

Carlo Maria Giulini discusses a point in the score with two of his soloists, Elisabeth Schwarzkopf and Christa Ludwig, during the 1963/4 recording of Verdi's *Requiem* in Kingsway Hall.

Elisabeth Schwarzkopf, surrounded by *(from left)* Nicolai Gedda, Hanny Steffek, Walter Legge, Lovro von Matačić and Douglas Larter, listen to a playback at the July 1962 recording of Lehár's *Die lustige Witwe* at Kingsway Hall.

Below Elisabeth Schwarzkopf, Dietrich Fischer-Dieskau and Gerald Moore rehearse for their Berlin recording of Brahms's *Deutsche Volkslieder* in August/September 1965 in Fischer-Dieskau's music salon.

Above Elisabeth Schwarzkopf recording Strauss Lieder with George Szell conducting the London Symphony Orchestra at Kingsway Hall in March 1968.

Schwarzkopf with Walter Legge and Geoffrey Parsons, her accompanist, Bordeaux 1967.

Johann Matthes was the admired sound engineer for Schwarzkopf's recording sessions at the Evangelisches Gemeindhaus, Berlin, between 1965 and 1975, responsible for what she now considers her best Lied-rendition: Schubert's 'Der Erlkönig' with Geoffrey Parsons.

at all. He was the sweetest man possible – something enchanting – he was a good man, and that was all we knew. The goodness comes out in his playing. We called him Mr Music. A grand pianist, not in the virtuoso manner – we know all about that, but oh dear, for expression and all those things ... ' In *Auf dem Wasser*, for instance, 'It's very good, and you listen more to him than to me.'

A few days after these sessions Elisabeth was giving the first of several recitals in Brazil. Her South American visit lasted three weeks, and she came back in November to a curiously hybrid enterprise. Herbert von Karajan recorded the Bach *Mass in B minor*, with the solo parts of the work taped in London with the Philharmonia Orchestra, and the choral parts in Vienna with the Chorus and Orchestra of the Gesellschaft der Musikfreunde. The 'Laudamus' does not please Dame Elisabeth now, for she finds there, if not not quite the intrusive 'h' which she so dislikes (and which Walter Legge also hated), then certainly some 'jerks in the musical line'.

The items with Schüchter she has heard in re-broadcasts. The Korngold item she likes, but she finds the *Butterfly* entrance 'rather screeching on top'.

February 16. RAI Studios, Rome. Giorgio Favaretto (piano).
    Schubert: Die schöne Müllerin, D795 – No. 7, Ungeduld; Der Musensohn,
        D764; Suleika 1, D720; Auf dem Wasser zu singen, D774; Die
        Forelle, D550; Ave Maria, D839
        CD: Hunt CD535.

March 15, 27 and 28. EMI Studio No. 1.
    Kirsten Flagstad (soprano)....................................Dido
    Thomas Hemsley (baritone)................................Aeneas
    Elisabeth Schwarzkopf (soprano)............Belinda/Second Attendant
                                        Woman/Spirit
    Eilidh McNab (soprano).....................First Attendant Woman
    Arda Mandikian (soprano)................................Sorceress
    Sheila Rex (mezzo-soprano)............................First Witch
    David Lloyd (tenor)...Sailor
    Mermaid Singers and Orchestra conducted by Geraint Jones.
                  (NB: Recording ledgers suggest that the orchestra was
                  in fact the Philharmonia.)
    Purcell: Dido and Aeneas
        LP: ALP1026, H117, SH117, LHMV1007, 60346, FALP200, WALP1026,
        E90031, 2C 051 03 613, HA1084. SP: Set WHMV1007. C: 2C 251 03
        613. CD: CDH7 61006-2. Excerpts on LP: IC 147 01 491-2. EP: EHA13.

April 9. EMI Studio No. 1A. Gerald Moore (piano).
        CA22163 Gluck: La rencontre imprévue – Einem Bach der fliesst
        22164 Wolf: Mausfallen Sprüchlein

22165 Beethoven: Wonne der Wehmut, Op. 83 No. 1
22166 Strauss: Schlechtes Wetter, Op. 69 No. 5
22167 Strauss: Hat gesagt, bleibt's nicht dabei, Op. 36 No. 3

May 30. RAI Studios, Turin.
Cesare Valletti (tenor), Miriam Pirazzini (mezzo-soprano), Boris Christoff (bass), Luigia Vincenti (soprano), Turin Radio Symphony Chorus and Orchestra conducted by Mario Rossi.
Mozart: La betulia liberata, K118
LP: Melodram Set MEL211. CD: Nuova Era Set CD2377, Memories HR4222. Excerpts on LP: Ed Smith EJS276.

July 1. Kingsway Hall. Philharmonia Orchestra conducted by John Pritchard.
Mozart: Don Giovanni – Batti, batti
LP: 33CX1069, T583, 35021, 33QCX10058, 33FCX183, 143222-1, C90321, 2C 051 43222, 33WCX1069. EAC40151. EP: SEL1511. T: CAT281. CD: CDC7 47950-2, CDH7 63708-2, 747950-2, 567 747 950-2, *Nota Blu 93.50911-2.* 78: LB145 (CA22823-3E), GQ7260.
Mozart: Le nozze di Figaro – Voi che sapete
LP: 33CX1069, T583, 35021, 33QCX10058, 33FCX183, 143222-1, C90321, 2C 051 43222, 33WCX1069, EAC40151, EAC70130, EAC43085-6. T: CAT281. CD: CDC7 47950-2, CDH7 63708-2, 747950-2, 567 747 950-2.
Mozart: Le nozze di Figaro – Porgi amor
July 2.
Mozart: Don Giovanni – Vedrai, carino
LP: 33CX1069, T583, 35021, 33QCX10058, 33FCX183, 143222-1, C90321, 2C 051 43222, 33WCX1069, XL5032, OL3124, ZL38, EAC40151. EP: SEL1511, SEBQ124, ESBF122. T: CAT281. CD: CDC7 47950-2, CDH7 63708-2. 78: LB145 (CA22824-5D), GQ7260.
Mozart: Le nozze di Figaro – Non si più
LP: 33CX1069, T583, 35021, 33QCX10058, 33FCX183, 143222-1, C90321, 2C 051 43222, 33WCX1069, XL5032, OL3124, ZL38, EAC40151. T: CAT281. CD: CDC7 47950-2, CDH7 63708-2, *Nota Blu 93.50911-2.*
Mozart: Le nozze di Figaro – Giunse alfin … Deh, vieni
LP: 33CX1069, T583, Set RLS763, 35021, 33QCX10058, 33FCX183, 143222-1, C90321, 2C 051 43222, 33WCX1069, XL5032, OL3124, ZL38, EAC40151. T: CAT281. C: Set TC-RLS763. CD: CDC7 47950-2, CDH7 63708-2, *Nota Blu 93.50911-2.*
July 4.
Mozart: Le nozze di Figaro – Giunse alfin … Deh, vieni
Mozart: Le nozze di Figaro – Porgi amor
LP: 33CX1069, T583, Set RLS763, 35021, 33QCX10058, 33FCX183, 143222-1, C90321, 2C 051 43222, 33WCX1069, XL5032, OL3124, ZL38, EAC40151. T: CAT281. C: Set TC-RLS763. CD: CDH7 63708-2, *Nota Blu 93.50911-2.*
Mozart: Don Giovanni – Crudele … Non mi dir
LP: 33CX1069, T583, Set RLS763, 35021, 33QCX10058, 33FCX183, 143222-1, C90321, 2C 051 43222, 33WCX1069, XL5032, OL3124, ZL38,

EAC40151. EP: SEL1515, SEBQ124, ESBF122. T: CAT281. CD: CDC7
47950-2, CDH7 63708-2, *Nota Blu 93.50911-2.*
July 5.
    Mozart: Don Giovanni – Crudele ... Non mi dir
    Mozart: Die Zauberflöte – Ach, ich fühl's
September 9.
    Mozart: Le nozze di Figaro – Dove sono
        LP: 33CX1069, T583, Set RLS763, 35021, 33QCX10058, 33FCX183,
        143222-1, C90321, 2C 051 43222, 33WCX1069, XL5032, OL3124, ZL38,
        EAC40151. T: CAT281. C: Set TC-RLS763. CD: CDH7 63708-2.
    Mozart: Don Giovanni – In quali eccessi ... Mi tradi
September 10.
    Mozart: Don Giovanni – In quali eccessi ... Mi tradi
    Mozart: Idomeneo – Zeffiretti lusinghieri

September 11. EMI Studio No. 1A. Gerald Moore (piano).

CAX11823-4B	Bach: Anna Magdalena Notenbuch – No. 25, Bist du bei mir, BWV508	LX1580
11743-2A	Mozart: Abendempfindung, K523	LX1580
CA22311	Schubert: Die Forelle, D550	
CAX11748	Schubert: Litanei, D343	

September 12.
    CA22313   arr. Brahms: Deutsche Volkslieder – No. 33, Och
                    Mod'r ich well en Ding han
                    LP: Set RLS154700-3.
       22314   Brahms: Vergebliches Ständchen, Op. 84 No. 4
                    LP: Set RLS154700-3.
       22315   Schubert: Wiegenlied, D498
    CAX11748   Schubert: Litanei, D343
September 13.
    CA22311   Schubert: Die Forelle, D550

September 15-16. Kingsway Hall. Philharmonia Orchestra conducted by John
    Pritchard.
    Mozart: Exsultate, jubilate, K165
            (with Geraint Jones, organ).
September 16.
    Mozart: Don Giovanni – In quali eccessi ... Mi tradi
    Mozart: Idomeneo – Zeffiretti lusinghieri
        LP: 33CX1069, T583, 35021, 33FCX183, 143222-1, 33QCX10058,
        C90321, 2C 051 43222, 33WCX1069, XL5032, OL3124, ZL38,
        EAC40151. EP: SEL1515, SEBQ124, ESBF122. T: CAT281. CD: CDC7
        47950-2, CDH7 63708-2, 747950-2, 567 747 950-2, *Nota Blu 93.50911-2.*

September 21. EMI Studio No. 1. Gerald Moore (piano).
    CA22320   Beethoven: Wonne der Wehmut, Op. 83 No. 1
       22321   Gluck: La rencontre imprévue – Einem Bach der fliesst
       22322   Schubert: Die schöne Müllerin, D795 – No. 7, Ungeduld
       22323   Wolf: Mausfallen Sprüchlein

22324   Strauss: Hat gesagt, bleibt's nicht dabei, Op. 36 No. 3
22325   Strauss: Schlechtes Wetter, Op. 69 No. 5
September 27.
   CAX11748   Schubert: Litanei, D343
   11749   Wolf: Wiegenlied im Sommer; Mausfallen Sprüchlein

October 3. Kingsway Hall. Chorus of the Royal Opera House, Covent Garden,
Hampstead Parish Church Choir, Philharmonia Orchestra conducted by
John Pritchard.
   CA22344-5D   Gruber (arr. Salter): Silent Night, Holy Night   LB131
               also on SP: SCD2112.
   22346   Trad. (arr. Salter): O come all ye faithful
   22347-2C   Trad. (arr. Salter): The First Nowell   LB131
               also on SP: SCD2112.

October 4. EMI Studio No. 1A. Edwin Fischer (piano).
   Schubert: Auf dem Wasser zu singen, D774
      LP: 33CX1040, ALP3843, 35022, 33FCX181, 33FCX30307,
      33QCX10214, C90305, 2C 053 00 404, 33WCX1040, ZL38, 1C 137 53
      032-6M, AB8068, XL5029, OL3108, EAC70145, EAC47149-50,
      EAC47083-4, Set AA930258. EP: SEL1582. C: 2C 269 00 404. CD:
      CDC7 47326-2, CDC47326, CDH7 64026-2, 747326-2, 567 747 326-2.
   Schubert: An Sylvia, D891
      LP: 33CX1040, ALP3843, 35022, 33FCX181, 33FCX30307,
      33QCX10214, C90305, 2C 053 00 404, 33WCX1040, ZL38, 1C 137 53
      032-6M, AB8068, XL5029, OL3108, EAC70223, EAC47149-50, EAA176,
      AA8589, Set AA930258. EP: SEL1564, C50581, E50157. C: 2C 269 00
      404. CD: CDC7 47326-2, CDC47326, CDH7 64026-2, 747326-2, 567 747
      326-2.
   Schubert: An die Musik, D547
      LP: 33CX1040, ALP3843, 35022, 33FCX181, 33FCX30307,
      33QCX10214, C90305, 2C 053 00 404, 33WCX1040, ZL38, 1C 137 53
      032-6M, AB8068, XL5029, OL3108, EAC47149-50. EP: SEL1564,
      C50581, E50157. C: 2C 269 00 404. CD: CDC7 47326-2, CDC47326,
      CDH7 64026-2, 747326-2, 567 747 326-2.
   Schubert: An die Musik, D547
   Schubert: Nachtviolen, D752
      LP: 33CX1040, ALP3843, 35022, 33FCX181, 33FCX30307,
      33QCX10214, C90305, 2C 053 00 404, 33WCX1040, 1C 137 53 032-6M,
      AB8068, XL5029, OL3108, EAC47149-50. EP: SEL1582. C: 2C 269 00
      404. CD: CDC7 47326-2, CDC47326, CDH7 64026-2, 747326-2, 567 747
      326-2.
   Schubert: Die junge Nonne, D828
      LP: 33CX1040, ALP3843, 35022, 33FCX181, 33FCX30307,
      33QCX10214, C90305, 2C 053 00 404, 33WCX1040, 1C 137 53 032-6M,
      AB8068, XL5029, OL3108, EAC47149-50. EP: SEL1570. C: 2C 269 00
      404. CD: CDC7 47326-2, CDC47326, CDH7 64026-2, 747326-2, 567 747
      326-2.
   Schubert: Nähe des Geliebten, D162

LP: 33CX1040, ALP3843, 35022, 33FCX181, 33FCX30307,
33QCX10214, C90305, 2C 053 00 404, 33WCX1040, 1C 137 53 032-6M,
AB8068, XL5029, OL3108, EAC47149-50. EP: SEL1570, C50581. C: 2C
269 00 404. CD: CDC7 47326-2, CDC47326, CDH7 64026-2, 747326-2,
567 747 326-2.
Schubert: Das Lied im Grünen, D917
LP: 33CX1040, ALP3843, 35022, 33FCX181, 33FCX30307,
33QCX10214, C90305, 2C 053 00 404, 33WCX1040, 1C 137 53 032-6M,
AB8068, XL5029, OL3108, ZL38, EAC47149-50. EP: SEL1564, E50157.
C: 2C 269 00 404. CD: CDC7 47326-2, CDC47326, CDH7 64026-2,
747326-2, 567 747 326-2.

October 6.
Schubert: Der Musensohn, D764
LP: 33CX1040, ALP3843, 35022, 33FCX181, 33FCX30307,
33QCX10214, C90305, 2C 053 00 404, 33WCX1040, 1C 137 53 032-6M,
AB8068, XL5029, OL3108, ZL38, EAC70223, EAC47149-50, EAA176,
AA8589, Set AA930258. EP: SEL1582, C50581. C: 2C 269 00 404. CD:
CDC7 47326-2, CDC47326, CDH7 64026-2, 747326-2, 567 747 326-2.
Schubert: Gretchen am Spinnrade, D118
LP: 33CX1040, ALP3843, 35022, 33FCX181, 33FCX30307,
33QCX10214, C90305, 2C 053 00 404, 33WCX1040, 1C 137 53 032-6M,
AB8068, XL5029, OL3108, ZL38, EAC70145, EAC47149-50, Set
AA930258. EP: SEL1564, E50157, C50581. C: 2C 269 00 404. CD:
CDC7 47326-2, CDC47326, CDH7 64026-2, 747326-2, 567 747 326-2.
Schubert: Wehmut, D772
LP: 33CX1040, ALP3843, 35022, 33FCX181, 33FCX30307,
33QCX10214, C90305, 2C 053 00 404, 33WCX1040, 1C 137 53 032-6M,
AB8068, XL5029, OL3108, ZL38. EAC47149-50. EP: SEL1570. C: 2C
269 00 404. CD: CDC7 47326-2, CDC47326, CDH7 64026-2, 747326-2,
567 747 326-2.

October 7.
Schubert: Ganymed, D544
LP: 33CX1040, ALP3843, 35022, 33FCX181, 33FCX30307,
33QCX10214, C90305, 2C 053 00 404, 33WCX1040, 1C 137 53 032-6M,
AB8068, XL5029, OL3108, EAC47149-50. C: 2C 269 00 404. CD: CDC7
47326-2, CDC47326, CDH7 64026-2, 747326-2, 567 747 326-2.
Schubert: Im Frühling, D882
LP: 33CX1040, ALP3843, 35022, 33FCX181, 33FCX30307, 33QCX10214,
C90305, 2C 053 00 404, 33WCX1040, 1C 137 53 032-6M, AB8068, XL5029,
OL3108. EAC47149-50. EP: SEL1582. C: 2C 269 00 404. CD: CDC7
47326-2, CDC47326, CDH7 64026-2, 747326-2, 567 747 326-2.

October 8. EMI Studio No. 1A. Gerald Moore (piano).
CAX11749-5E Wolf: Wiegenlied in Sommer; Mausfallen
             Sprüchlein   LX1577
CA22321 Gluck: La rencontre imprévue – Einem Bach der fliesst

November 23, 28-30. EMI Studio No. 1. Marga Höffgen (contralto), Nicolai
Gedda (tenor), Heinz Rehfuss (baritone), Philharmonia Orchestra
conducted by Herbert von Karajan.

Bach: Mass in B minor, BWV232
> NB: Schwarzkopf was present at the sessions held
> on November 23 and 29. She may have taken part in
> the session on 28 November, but she did not attend
> the session on 30 November, or a final session on 16
> July 1953.
> LP: 33CX1121-3, T854-6, Set RLS746, Set 3500, 33FCX291-3,
> 290974-3, 33QCX10055-7, C90337-9, 33WCX1121-3, 1C 181 01 791-2M,
> 1C 153 01 312-5, XL5095-7. T: TT854-6. CD: Set CHS7 63505-2, Set
> CDHB63505, 653 763 058-2. Excerpts on C80527, 33WSX544.

December 1. Turin Radio Studios. Turin Radio Symphony Orchestra conducted
by Mario Rossi.
> Mozart: Die Zauberflöte – Ach, ich fühl's (sung in Italian)
> *LP: Discocorp Set RR208, Fonit Cetra LMR5018, Melodram Set*
> *MEL047, Melodram Set MEL088. CD: Gala GL100501.*
> Mozart: Idomeneo – Zeffiretti lusinghieri
> *LP: Discocorp Set RR208, Fonit Cetra LMR5018, Melodram Set*
> *MEL088. CD: Melodram CDM16529.*
> Mozart: Don Giovanni – In quali eccessi
> *LP: Discocorp Set RR208, Fonit Cetra LMR5018.*
> Mozart: Don Giovanni – Mi tradi
> *LP: Melodram Set MEL047. CD: Melodram CDM16529.*
> Mozart: Le nozze di Figaro – Deh, vieni, non tardar
> *CD: Melodram CDM16529.*

December 6. Norddeutsche Rundfunk Studios, Hamburg. North German Radio
Symphony Chorus and Orchestra conducted by Wilhelm Schüchter.
> Handel: Messiah – He shall feed his flock (sung in German)
> *LP: Melodram Set MEL082, Discocorp Set RR208, Discocorp Set*
> *RR537, Discoreale DR10037. CD: MEL16501.*
> Puccini: Madama Butterfly: Ancora un passo (sung in German); Un bel dì,
> vedremo (sung in German); Con onor muore (sung in German)
> *LP: Melodram Set MEL088.*
> Korngold: Die tote Stadt – Glück, das mir verblieb
> *LP: Melodram Set MEL088.*
> Strauss: Der Rosenkavalier – Da geht er hin
> *LP: Melodram Set MEL088.*
> Mozart: Le nozze di Figaro – Porgi amor
> *LP: Melodram Set MEL082, Discoreale DR10037.*

December 10. EMI Studio No. 1A. Gerald Moore (piano).
> Gluck: La rencontre imprévue – Einem Bach der fliesst
December 19.
> Wolf: Wiegenlied im Sommer; Mausfallen Sprüchlein

1953

The first two months of 1953 were largely taken up with performances at La Scala. There were three stage works involved – Wagner's *Lohengrin* (Schwarzkopf took the part of Elsa), *Don Giovanni* (Elvira) and an unusual item in the shape of Orff's *Trionfi*, a triptych which comprised 'Carmina Burana' (in which she did not sing), 'Catulli Carmina' and 'Trionfo di Afrodite'. All three productions were conducted by Karajan, who moreover ventured for the first and only time into the music of Tippett, conducting an RAI broadcast of *A Child of our Time*, with Elisabeth also making her only acquaintance with this composer and his work in the soprano part. There were two more performances of *Trionfi* in Munich, with Eugen Jochum conducting. On 10 March Schwarzkopf sang Wolf's *Italienisches Liederbuch* at the Festival Hall with Fischer-Dieskau and Hermann Reutter at the piano, and another notable occasion in the following month was her only appearance at Glyndebourne, where she sang Bach and Mozart in a concert conducted by John Pritchard, who was then the Sussex opera house's musical director.

In April she returned to the recording arena for the first two of her operetta recordings. The conductor was Otto Ackermann, whom she admired very much in this kind of repertoire: she feels in fact that the standards of performance they achieved could not have been reached without him. 'To perform operetta is much more difficult than opera. The rules are not so strict, seemingly. For the knowing person they are, but not in the way that Beethoven is strict, or Mozart – in tempo and what have you. You have seemingly a lot of freedom, but you have to know which freedom to take and which not.' Some of the the roles were unfamiliar to her, and some of the operettas she had never even seen. She had sung Adele, but not Rosalinde in *Die Fledermaus*. In *Zigeunerbaron* she had sung the part of Arsena, but not Saffi.

After the initial operetta sessions Schwarzkopf sang Mélisande in a La Scala production of Debussy's *Pelléas et Mélisande* conducted by Victor de Sabata. This was in May, when her engagements also included a performance of Conrad Beck's *Der Tod zu Basel*, which took place in Basel under the direction of Paul Sacher. In June there were three Viennese concert performances of *Fidelio* under Karajan.

At the end of June she returned to London to take part in the recording of *Hänsel und Gretel*. This was a labour of love for everybody, even the normally unbending Karajan. The fairy-tale opera by Humperdinck is part of a particular German tradition associated with the memory and experience of innocence and childhood. Thus the artists were all in a relaxed frame of mind when they undertook the project. The sessions took place at the same time as Elisabeth rehearsed the part of Eva for four Covent Garden performances of *Meistersinger* under Clemens Krauss. The change of voice needed from Gretel in the morning to Eva later in the day was 'quite something'.

Salzburg was once more dominated by Furtwängler. Elisabeth sang Donna Elvira in *Don Giovanni* again, and the Countess in a German language production of *Le nozze di Figaro*. Then on 12 August Furtwängler accompanied her in a Wolf recital. It had been his suggestion, after a Beethoven's Ninth in Turin, that he should undertake this role, and he practised hard for the occasion. 'The Wolf songs are so fiendish that perhaps he hadn't reckoned that they would be so difficult to play. I was in very good voice, considering the slow tempi. I'm amazed how I coped, how I managed to keep the Wolf sounds intact, breathing every five words.' Furtwängler loved the songs, and his was 'a symphonic approach, a composer's approach, since he was a romantic composer, as well as a conductor, and so when he played wrong notes he immediately did something to put another harmonic change in to make them seem right. We had some right and wrong entries here and there, but it doesn't matter. Furtwängler accompanying was an event, and so one had to do what one could to make it possible. It was a service to Wolf, and to music, and a labour of love, that recital. With any other accompanist it matters if he cannot achieve the right tempi, but with Furtwängler it didn't matter.'

In September Watford Town Hall was the unlikely setting for recordings of Strauss's *Vier letzte Lieder* and the Closing Scene from *Capriccio*. In fact it was a very good venue acoustically; the oblong town hall auditorium shape always suited Schwarzkopf well. This first recording of Strauss's late song cycle proved to be her 'passport to America'. The remainder of the year was mainly taken up with a busy round of recitals and concerts. On 8 October she even took the soprano part in Delius's *Mass of Life*, given in Leeds under Sir Malcolm Sargent. In late October she sang in six consecutive Swiss performances of *Fidelio*, with Karajan conducting. Here she took the part of Leonore for the only time in her life. She did not really possess the vocal power for the role, but the conductor wanted a more 'vulnerable' interpretation of the part, and Elisabeth somehow managed to negotiate its demands without hurting her voice. In December she gave three performances in Rome of Elvira in *Don Giovanni* under Karajan, and also in Rome was a single radio performance of Pamina in Zauberflöte, sung in Italian.

Years later she heard a recording of this performance late one night on the radio, without knowing what it was. 'I listened through to Pamina's aria. I knew it was Gedda in his young years, I knew it was Taddei in his young years, and there were actors used for the dialogue. I heard the soprano, and I thought this is incredible because I know all the singers of that time in Italy and there was not such a good Mozart singer as I hear here as Pamina – until the aria when I recognised myself. It is so good, very Italian and very Mozart at the same time.'

April 16-19, 21. Kingsway Hall.
    Erich Kunz (baritone)...Danilo
    Elisabeth Schwarzkopf (soprano)...........................Hanna
    Nicolai Gedda (tenor)..Camille
    Anton Niessner (baritone).......................Baron Mirko Zita
    Emmy Loose (soprano)....................................Valencienne
    Otakar Kraus (baritone)....................................Cascada
    Josef Schmidinger (bass)..................................St Brioche
BBC Chorus, Philharmonia Orchestra conducted by Otto Ackermann.
    Lehár: Die lustige Witwe
        LP: 33CX1051-2, Set (E) SXDW3045, Set 3501, 33FCX237-8,
        33QCX10050-1, 33VCX515-6, C80516-7, 33WSX537-8, 1C 149 03
        116-7M, 1C 153 00 001-2, XL5077-8. T: CAT262-3. C: Set (E)
        TC2-SXDW3045. CD: CDH7 69520-2, CDH69520, 555 769 520-2, Set
        CZS5 68058-2. Excerpts on LP: 33CX1712, Set RLS763, C80587,
        33WSX563, 1C 147 03 580-1, EG7 63657-4. EP: SEL1559. SP: SCB113,
        SCD2083, SCBQ3019. 78: LX1597 (CAX11984-1A, 85-3A). CD: Set
        CMS7 63790-2, CDM7 63657-2.

April 17, 19-21. Kingsway Hall.
    Elisabeth Schwarzkopf (soprano)..............................Lisa
    Nicolai Gedda (tenor)...................................Sou-chong
    Emmy Loose (soprano)..Mi
    Erich Kunz (baritone).....................................Gustav
    Otakar Kraus (baritone)..................................Tschang
    Felix Kent (speaker)..Fu-Li
    André Mattoni (speaker)...................................Servant
BBC Chorus, Philharmonia Orchestra conducted by Otto Ackermann.
    Lehár: Das Land des Lächelns
                NB: Schwarzkopf did not attend a session for this
                work on April 17, when the overture only was
                recorded.

June 27. Kingsway Hall.
    Elisabeth Grümmer (soprano) .... Hänsel
    Elisabeth Schwarzkopf (soprano). .... .Gretel
    Josef Metternich (baritone). .... Father
    Maria von Ilosvay (contralto). .... Mother
    Else Schürhoff (contralto). .... Witch
    Anny Felbermayer (soprano). .... .Sandman/Dew Fairy
    Loughton High School for Girls' Choir, Bancrofts' School Choir, Philharmonia
    Orchestra conducted by Herbert von Karajan.
    Humperdinck: Hänsel und Gretel

June 28. Kingsway Hall. Artists as on April 17.
    Lehár: Das Land des Lächelns
        LP: 33CX1114-5, Set (E) SXDW3044, Set 3507, 33FCX288-9,
        33WSX535-6, C80514-5, 1C 149 03 047-8, 1C 147 03 580-1, 1C 137 103
        047-3. C: Set (E) TC2-SXDW3044. CD: Set CHS7 69523-2, Set
        CDH69523, 655 769 523-2, Set CZS5 68058-2. Excerpts on LP:
        33CX1712, Set (E) SLS5250, Set RLS763, C80587, 33WSX563. EP:
        SEL1556. C: Set (E) TC-SLS5250.

June 29-30, July 1-2. Kingsway Hall. Artists as on June 27.
    Humperdinck: Hänsel und Gretel
        LP: 33CX1096-7, OC187-8, Set (E) SLS5145, Set EX7 69293-1, Set
        3506, 33FCX286-7, 33QCX10048-9, LALP207-8, C90327-8,
        33WCX1096-7, 1C 153 769 293-1, XL5044-5. T: CAT276-7. C: Set (E)
        TC-SLS5145, Set EX7 69293-4. CD: Set CMS7 69293-2, CDMB69293,
        655 769 295-2. Excerpts on LP: 33CX1819, OH189, C80528,
        33WSX545. EP: SEL1694. C: EG7 63657-4. CD: Set CMS7 63790-2,
        CDM7 63657-2.

July 4. EMI Studio No. 1. Gerald Moore (piano).
    Mozart: Abendempfindung, K523
    Mozart: Der Zauberer, K472
    Schumann: Aufträge, Op. 77 No. 5
July 7.
    Wolf: Mausfallen Sprüchlein
    Beethoven: Wonne der Wehmut, Op. 83 No. 1
    Bach: Anna Magdalena Notenbuch – No. 25, Bist du bei mir
    Trad. (arr. Brahms): Deutsche Volkslieder – No. 6, Da unten im Tale

August 3. Felsenreitschule, Salzburg.
    Cesar Siepi (bass). .... Don Giovanni
    Elisabeth Schwarzkopf (soprano). .... .Donna Elvira
    Raphael Arié (bass). .... Commendatore
    Elisabeth Grümmer (soprano). .... Donna Anna
    Anton Dermota (tenor). .... Don Ottavio
    Otto Edelmann (bass). .... .Leporello
    Erna Berger (soprano). .... .Zerlina
    Walter Berry (bass). .... .Masetto

Vienna State Opera Chorus and Vienna Philharmonic Orchestra conducted
by Wilhelm Furtwängler.
　　Mozart: Don Giovanni
　　　　CD: Rodolphe Set RPC32527-30, Virtuoso Set 269.9052, Gala Set
　　　　100.602. Excerpts on CD: Virtuoso 269.7152.

August 11. Festspielhaus, Salzburg.
　　Paul Schöffler (baritone)............................ Count Almaviva
　　Elisabeth Schwarzkopf (soprano)...................Countess Almaviva
　　Irmgard Seefried (soprano)................................Susanna
　　Erich Kunz (baritone)......................................Figaro
　　Hilde Güden (soprano)...................................Cherubino
　　Peter Klein (tenor)..................................... Don Basilio
　　Endre Koréh (bass)...................................... Bartolo
　　Sieglinde Wagner (mezzo-soprano)......................Marcellina
　　Alois Pernerstorfer (bass-baritone)....................... Antonio
　　Liselotte Maikl (soprano)................................Barbarina
　　Erich Majkut (tenor)...................................Don Curzio
　　Vienna State Opera Chorus, Vienna Philharmonic Orchestra conducted by
　　Wilhelm Furtwängler.
　　Mozart: Le nozze di Figaro (sung in German)
　　　　LP: Cetra Set LO8, Discocorp Set IGI343, Ed Smith Set GMR999, Fonit
　　　　Cetra Set FE27. CD: Rodolphe RPC32527-30. Excerpts on LP:
　　　　Melodram Set MEL082. CD: Melodram MEL16501.

August 12. Mozarteum, Salzburg. Wilhelm Furtwängler (piano).
　　Wolf: (a) Im Frühling; (b) Elfenlied; (c) Lebewohl; (d) Schlafendes
　　　　Jesuskind; (e) Phänomen; (f) Die Spröde; (g) Die Bekehrte; (h)
　　　　Anakreons Grab; (i) Blumengruss; (j) Epiphanias; (k) Wie lange
　　　　schon war immer; (l) Was soll der Zorn; (m) Nein, junger Herr; (n)
　　　　Mein Liebster hat zu Tische; (o) Bedeckt mich mit Blumen; (p) Herr,
　　　　was trägt der Boden hier; (q) In dem Schatten meiner Locken; (r)
　　　　Mögen alle bösen Zungen; (s) Wie glänzt der helle Mond; (t)
　　　　Wiegenlied im Sommer; (u) Nachtzauber; (v) Die Zigeunerin
　　　　LP: Fonit Cetra Set FE30, 143549-1, 1C 053 143 549-1. CD: Fonit Cetra
　　　　Set CDC21, Virtuoso 269.7312. Excerpts: (a) to (j), and (o) to (r) on CD:
　　　　Priceless D18355; (a) to (j) on CD: Virtuoso 269.7152; (b) to (g), (i), (j),
　　　　(l), (p), (t), (u) and (v) on LP: ALP 2114, 1C 063 01915M, 60179, WF36,
　　　　WF60033, AB8301; (a), (h), (k), (m), (n), (o), (q), (r) and (v) are on LP:
　　　　Melodram Set MEL088; (a), (h), (o), (q), (r) and (v) are on LP: Discocorp
　　　　IGI382 and Nippon Columbia OZ7603; (a), (h), (k), (m), (n), (o), (q), (r),
　　　　(v) are on LP: Discocorp Set RR208.

September 25. Town Hall, Watford, Hertfordshire. Philharmonia Orchestra
　　conducted by Otto Ackermann.
　　Strauss: Vier letzte Lieder, Op. posth.
　　　　LP: 33CX1107, Set RLS751, 35084, 38266, 33FCX294, 103865-1, 100
　　　　8651, 33WCX1107, 2C 061 01 208, EAC40119. T: CBT554. C:
　　　　4XS-38266, 103865-4. CD: CDH7 61001-2, CDH61001, 761001-2, 555
　　　　761 001-2, *Nota Blu 93.50923-4.*

September 26.
> Strauss: Capriccio – Closing Scene
> LP: 33CX1107, Set RLS751, 35084, 38266, 33FCX294, 103865-1. T:
> CBT554. C: 4XS-38266, 103865-4. CD: CDH7 61001-2, CDH61001,
> 761001-2, *Nota Blu 93.50923-4.*

October 1. Kingsway Hall. Rolando Panerai (baritone), Philharmonia Orchestra
conducted by Alceo Galliera.
> Verdi: La traviata – Madamigella Valery? Pura siccome un angelo
> LP: 291075-3.

October 5. Kingsway Hall. Philharmonia Orchestra conducted by Alceo Galliera.
> Verdi: Otello – Ave Maria

December 20. RAI Studios, Rome.
> Elisabeth Schwarzkopf (soprano)............................ Pamina
> Rita Streich (soprano)............................ Queen of the Night
> Alda Noni (soprano)................................Papagena
> Nicolai Gedda (tenor).. Tamino
> Giuseppe Taddei (baritone)..............................Papageno
> Mario Petri (bass-baritone) .... Sarastro
> Carla Schlehan (soprano)................................ First Lady
> Ester Orelli (mezzo-soprano)............................Second Lady
> Anna Maria Rota (contralto).................... Third Lady/Third Boy
> Antonio Pirino (tenor).......................................Monostatos
> Nino del Sole (bass)................................First Armed Man
> Plinio Clabassi (bass)............................ Second Armed Man
> Bruno Rizzoli (treble)...............................First Boy
> Gilda Capozzi (soprano)................................ Second Boy
> RAI Chorus and Symphony Orchestra conducted by Herbert von Karajan.
> > Mozart: Die Zauberflöte (sung in Italian)
> > *CD: Hunt MCD890.07. Excerpts on LP: Gala 317. CD: Hunt CD535.*

1954

After a Royal Festival Hall recital on 3 January Schwarzkopf and Moore
returned to the studios to make the final versions of the LP song recital
they had worked on for so long. In February Karajan conducted five
performances of *Le nozze di Figaro* at La Scala – 'by that time we were a
little more Italianate, I hope!' – and there were five performances of
Gounod's *Faust* under Artur Rodzinski, with Schwarzkopf as Marguerite.
Edwin Fischer accompanied her in two Brahms recitals, one of which was
recorded and later issued on a 'pirate' CD. On several occasions between
May and September of that year there were attempts to record Wolf's

Italienisches Liederbuch in the Wigmore Hall after Schwarzkopf and Moore had performed the collection there in a live recital. But the project eventually came to nothing owing to a persistent problem with a glass insert in the roof resonating around middle C. During the latter part of May there was much concentrated work on operetta recordings, and then in June Elisabeth made her commercial recording début at La Scala in the Verdi *Requiem* under De Sabata. At the time of this recording she was far from well. She also had to insert herself quietly among the chorus sopranos, who were tending to sing flat, to help them keep to the correct pitch. This was a practical function which was by no means unfamiliar to her.

Later in June it was back to London for the recording of *Ariadne auf Naxos*. Elisabeth felt that she didn't have the right kind of voice for Ariadne (she had never sung the role on stage), but Karajan wanted her kind of voice, and a more poetic, less powerful approach. The Composer was Irmgard Seefried, who in Elisabeth's view was never surpassed in this role. Walter Legge waged a battle with his superiors in order to get the project confirmed, for the general opinion was that it would take years for the set to sell enough copies to offset recording costs.

After *Ariadne* came the first *Così fan tutte* recording – 'a strange sequence'. Although she was already a highly experienced Mozartian, Schwarzkopf had not sung this work on stage, nor had Merriman or Panerai. She particularly admired Léopold Simoneau's performance as Ferrando. 'It was incredible singing, of tonal beauty, of expression in everything, really of the utmost elegance and knowledge. I don't think there was anybody to match him – perhaps Wunderlich would have later, but otherwise, no. Dermota, when he had good days, sang beautifully – entirely different from Simoneau – it was a southern voice, dark, creamy, always covered, never open, and Simoneau was a lighter tenor, more in the Bjørling style of singing.'

Then there was the song recital at Aix-en-Provence with Rosbaud, and in August came the last *Don Giovanni* with Furtwängler. It had been apparent for some time that the great conductor's hearing was failing. In the Felsenreitschule he was comparatively distant from the performers, and he would continually complain that the singers were dragging, there being a gap between the actual moment of a sung note and his assimilation of that sound. He held rehearsals even on the mornings after performances of the opera. Singers were used to singing just slightly ahead of the beat, but here they had to anticipate even further, and it was very disconcerting.

Furtwängler's baton technique was never a problem. 'Not really, we knew perfectly well what he wanted – no, no, no, that's a myth, you know

– you could follow him easily.' He didn't give cues. 'We knew our parts, you don't have to get cues, we were not beginners, and you tried to anticipate and be before the beat, a little bit, so that the sound was already there so he could register.'

After Salzburg Elisabeth sang in Furtwängler's last Beethoven's Ninth Symphony at Lucerne. 'I remember travelling with him, maybe from Lucerne, where we stood in the gangway of the train, when he said, "By the way, I must tell you, please watch your voice, because you won't sing the Ninth Symphony for ever – watch out that you know the time when you have to give up that particular part – it is still fine now, but it will come and I hear already that it will come soon".'

In September Schwarzkopf returned to Watford to record two Beethoven items. Both were unusually and enterprisingly used as fill-ups to Karajan's recordings of Beethoven's Fourth and Fifth Symphonies. In the 'Abscheulicher' from *Fidelio* she took the role of Leonore once more, and with superb horn playing from Dennis Brain the result was felt to be highly successful. This was the celebrated red-letter day for Watford, when Callas recorded Italian arias with Serafin in the morning, and Schwarzkopf recorded with Karajan in the afternoon.

A few days later she was in the Kingsway Hall to record excerpts from Strauss's *Arabella*. Lotte Lehmann had told her that she should sing the role of Arabella, but she had only seen the opera once in Vienna. As ever she was quick and efficient in assimilating a new score, and she had the part well in hand before piano rehearsals, which were held at the Legge home in Hampstead. Heinrich Schmidt was the pianist. He knew the score and indeed all the Strauss operas from the time when he had worked with Clemens Krauss at the Munich Opera, and his presence was 'an incredible help' to the singers and to the conductor, Matačić.

'After a while, maybe half a year later, I'd come back from some great tour somewhere [it was in fact in North America], and Walter was playing some music in the music room. "Whatever is that, and who is it? Why do you make me sing if somebody can sing so much better?" He said, "Don't you know who it is?" I said, "No". "Well", he said, "it's you." And I thought, my goodness, that is such good singing, I could never have been able to do it. I had, in half a year, already forgotten what I had done. I have often forgotten things which I learned quickly. I could now not ever produce a note of *Faust* or many things, even *Butterfly*, though I could do the aria.'

The American tour took place between mid-October and early December. Notable engagements included three performances of Strauss works with Fritz Reiner and the Chicago Symphony Orchestra, and a Houston

Symphony Orchestra concert under Ferenc Fricsay. At recitals her accompanist throughout the tour was Arpad Sándor.

At the end of the year she took part in a RAI broadcast of *Pelléas et Mélisande* under Karajan. As noted earlier, she had first taken the role of Mélisande in May of the previous year under Victor de Sabata. For that production she studied the part with a Belgian actress who had worked with the librettist Maurice Maeterlinck. 'So to my astonishment my French became quite well done, in that piece; not otherwise, but there it did, really – and De Sabata maintained that for him it was the most beautiful event he had in his life. And I think by the time we did the broadcast [December 1954], I wasn't afraid of anything any more, because I knew it quite well ... De Sabata could be very disappointed and then become very tempestuous, which never happened to me, thank God, but it did happen.'

January 4. EMI Studio No. 1. Gerald Moore (piano).
> Bach: Anna Magdalena Notenbuch, BWV508 – No. 25, Bist du bei mir
> > LP: 33CX1044, Set RLS763, 35023, 33FCX182, 33WCX1044, C90306.
> > C: Set TC-RLS763, EG7 63654-4. CD: Set CMS7 63790-2, CDM7 63654-2.
> Gluck: La rencontre imprévue – Einem Bach der fliesst
> > LP: 33CX1044, Set RLS763, 35023, 33FCX182, 33WCX1044, C90306.
> > C: Set TC-RLS763, EG7 63654-4. CD: Set CMS7 63790-2, CDM7 63654-2.

January 5.
> Trad. (arr. Brahms): Deutsche Volkslieder – No. 33, Och Mod'r ich well en Ding han
> > LP: 33CX1044, Set RLS763, 35023, 33FCX182, 33WCX1044, C90306.
> > C: Set TC-RLS763, EG7 63654-4. CD: Set CMS7 63790-2, CDM7 63654-2.
> Wolf: Mausfallen Sprüchlein
> arr. Brahms: Deutsche Volkslieder – No. 6, Da unten im Tale
> > LP: 33CX1044, Set RLS763, 35023, 33FCX182, Set 1546133, 33WCX1044, C90306. C: Set TC-RLS763, EG7 63654-4. CD: Set CMS7 63790-2, CDM7 63654-2.
> Strauss: Schlechtes Wetter, Op. 69 No. 5
> > LP: 33CX1044, Set RLS763, 35023, 33FCX182, Set 1546133, 33WCX1044, C90306, EAC40119, EAC70223, EAA176, AA8589, Set AA930258. C: Set TC-RLS763, EG7 63656-4. CD: Set CMS7 63790-2, CDM7 63656-2. 78: LX1577 [CAX11795-1D].
> Mozart: Der Zauberer, K472
> > LP: 33CX1044, Set RLS763, 35023, 33FCX182, 33WCX1044, C90306, EAC40119, EAC70223. C: Set TC-RLS763.
> Strauss: Hat gesagt, bleibt's nicht dabei, Op. 36 No. 3

January 6.
    Strauss: Hat gesagt, bleibt's nicht dabei, Op. 36 No. 3
        LP: 33CX1044, Set RLS763, 35023, 33FCX182, Set 1546133,
        33WCX1044, C90306, EAC40119. C: Set TC-RLS763, EG7 63656-4. CD:
        Set CMS7 63790-2, CDM7 63656-2. 78: LX1577 [CAX11795-1D].
    Mozart: Abendempfindung, K523
        LP: 33CX1044, HQM1072, Set RLS763, 35023, 60044, 33FCX182,
        33WCX1044, C90306, EAC40119. C: Set TC-RLS763.
    Brahms: Vergebliches Ständchen, Op. 84 No. 4
        LP: 33CX1044, Set RLS763, 35023, 33FCX182, 33WCX1044, C90306,
        EAC70223, EAC47083-4, EAC47031-41, EAA176, AA8589, Set
        AA930258. C: Set TC-RLS763.
January 7.
    Schumann: Aufträge, Op. 77 No. 5
January 9.
    Schubert: Litanei, D343
        LP: 33CX1044, Set RLS763, 35023, 33FCX182, Set 1546133,
        33WCX1044, C90306, EAC70223, EAC47149-50, EAA176, AA8589, Set
        AA93028. C: Set TC-RLS763.
    Schumann: Der Nussbaum, Op. 25 No. 3
        LP: 33CX1044, Set RLS763, 35023, 33FCX182, Set 1546133,
        33WCX1044, C90306, EAC40119, EAC70223, EAC47083-4,
        EAC47031-41, EAA176, AA8589, Set AA930258. C: Set TC-RLS763.
January 10.
    Schumann: Aufträge, Op. 77 No. 5
        LP: 33CX1044, Set RLS763, 35023, 33FCX182, 33WCX1044, C90306,
        EAC40119. C: Set TC-RLS763, EG7 63656-4. CD: Set CMS7 63790-2,
        CDM7 63656-2.
    Beethoven: Wonne der Wehmut, Op. 83 No. 1
        LP: 33CX1044, 35023, 33FCX182, Set 1546133, 33WCX1044, C90306.
        C: EG7 63654-4. CD: Set CMS7 63790-2, CDM7 63654-2.
    Schubert: Die schöne Müllerin, D795 – No. 7, Ungeduld
        LP: 33CX1044, Set RLS763, 35023, 33FCX182, 33WCX1044, C90306,
        EAC47149-50. C: Set TC-RLS763.
    Wolf: Wiegenlied im Sommer
January 11.
    Wolf: Wiegenlied im Sommer
        LP: 33CX1044, Set RLS763, 35023, 33FCX182, Set 1546133,
        33WCX1044, C90306, EAC40119. C: Set TC-RLS763.
    Wolf: Mausfallen Sprüchlein
        LP: 33CX1044, Set RLS763, 35023, 33FCX182, Set 1546133,
        33WCX1044, C90306, EAC40119, EAC70223, EAA176, AA8589. EP:
        SELW1805, C50202. C: Set TC-RLS763.

February 2. La Scala Theatre, Milan.
    Mario Petri (bass-baritone) . . . . .Count Almaviva
    Elisabeth Schwarzkopf (soprano). . . . . .Countess Almaviva
    Rolando Panerai (baritone). . . . . Figaro
    Irmgard Seefried (soprano). . . . . .Susanna
    Mariella Adani (soprano). . . . . Barbarina

Sena Jurinac (soprano)................................. Cherubino
Silvio Maionica (bass)...................................... Bartolo
Luisa Villa (mezzo-soprano)............................ Marcellina
Antonio Pirino (tenor)..................................Don Basilio
Franco Calabrese (bass)..................................... Antonio
Giuseppe Nessi (tenor)................................. Don Curzio
La Scala Chorus and Orchestra conducted by Herbert von Karajan.
  Mozart: Le nozze di Figaro
    LP: Fonit Cetra Set LO70. CD: Hunt Set CDKAR225, Melodram
    MEL37075. Excerpts are on LP: Gioielli della lirica GML30, Priceless
    C70565.

February 21. RAI Studios, Rome. Edwin Fischer (piano).
  Brahms: Feldeinsamkeit, Op. 86 No. 2; Therese, Op. 86 No. 1; Der Tod,
    das ist die kühle Nacht, Op. 96 No. 1; Von ewiger Liebe, Op. 43 No.
    1; Wie Melodien zieht es mir, Op. 105 No. 1; Meine Liebe ist grün,
    Op. 63 No. 5; Liebestreu, Op. 3 No. 1; Vergebliches Ständchen, Op.
    84 No. 4; Wiegenlied, Op. 49 No. 4
  Trad. (arr. Brahms): Deutsche Volkslieder – No. 6, Da unten im Tale; No.
    42, In stiller Nacht
    CD: Hunt CD535.

April 12-13, 15, 20-21. Wigmore Hall, London W1. Gerald Moore (piano).
  Wolf: Italienisches Liederbuch

May 18-21. Kingsway Hall.
  Hermann Prey (baritone)............................... Homonay
  Willy Ferenz (bass)......................................Carnero
  Nicolai Gedda (tenor)...................................Barinkay
  Erich Kunz (baritone)..................................... Zsupan
  Erika Köth (soprano)....................................... Arsena
  Monica Sinclair (contralto)............................... Mirabella
  Josef Schmidinger (bass)................................. Ottokar
  Gertrud Burgsthaler-Schuster (contralto)..................... Czipra
  Elisabeth Schwarzkopf (soprano)............................ Saffi
  Erich Paulik (bass)... Pali
  Karel Stepanek (speaker)................................. Carnero
  Lea Seidl (speaker)....................................... Mirabella
Chorus and Philharmonia Orchestra conducted by Otto Ackermann.
  J. Strauss II: Der Zigeunerbaron

May 21-22. Kingsway Hall.
  Karl Dönch (baritone)............................... Prime Minister
  Nicolai Gedda (tenor)...................................Graf Zedlau
  Elisabeth Schwarzkopf (soprano)...........................Gabriele
  Erika Köth (soprano)....................................... Franzi
  Alois Pernerstorfer (bass-baritone)........................Kagler
  Erich Kunz (baritone)....................................... Josef
  Emmy Loose (soprano)...........................Pepi Pleininger
  Hanna Norgerd (speaker)....................................Franzi

1954

Karel Stepanek (speaker)...................................Bitowski
Chorus and Philharmonia Orchestra conducted by Otto Ackermann.
   J. Strauss II (arr Müller): Wiener Blut

May 25-26. Kingsway Hall.
   Elisabeth Schwarzkopf (soprano)...........................Annina
   Nicolai Gedda (tenor)......................................Herzog
   Peter Klein (tenor)......................................Pappacoda
   Erich Kunz (baritone)....................................Caramello
   Karl Dönch (baritone)......................................Delacque
   Hanna Ludwig (soprano)........................... Barbara/Agricola
   Emmy Loose (soprano).....................................Ciboletta
   Karel Stepanek (speaker).............................. Barbaruccio
   Hanna Norgerd (speaker)................................. Barbara
   Lea Seidl (speaker)..Agricola
Chorus and Philharmonia Orchestra conducted by Otto Ackermann.
   J. Strauss II: Eine Nacht in Venedig

May 26. Kingsway Hall. Artists as on May 18-21.
   J. Strauss II: Der Zigeunerbaron

May 26. Kingsway Hall. Artists as on May 21-22.
   J. Strauss II (arr. Müller): Wiener Blut

May 27. Kingsway Hall. Artists as on May 25-26.
   J. Strauss II: Eine Nacht in Venedig

May 27. Kingsway Hall. Artists as on May 21-22.
   J. Strauss II (arr. Müller): Wiener Blut

May 28. Kingsway Hall. Artists as on May 18-21.
   J. Strauss II: Der Zigeunerbaron

May 28. Kingsway Hall. Artists as on May 21-22.
   J. Strauss II (arr. Müller): Wiener Blut

May 28. Kingsway Hall. Artists as on May 25-26.
   J. Strauss II: Eine Nacht in Venedig

May 31. Kingsway Hall. Artists as on May 18-21.
   J. Strauss II: Der Zigeunerbaron

May 31. Kingsway Hall. Artists as on May 25-26.
   J. Strauss II: Eine Nacht in Venedig

May 31. Kingsway Hall. Artists as on May 21-22.
   J. Strauss II (arr. Müller): Wiener Blut
      LP: 33CX1186-7, Set (E) SXDW3042, Set 3519, C80518-9,
      33WSX539-40, 1C 149 03 180-1. CD: CDH7 69529-2. CDH69529,
      769529-2, 555 769 529-2, Set CZS5 68058-2. Excerpts on LP: Set

RLS763, C80113, 33WSX608, 1C 047 01 954, 1C 147 03 580-1, (E)
SMVP6075, Set 1546133.

June 1. Wigmore Hall. Gerald Moore (piano).
  Wolf: Italienisches Liederbuch

June 18-22, 25-27. La Scala Theatre, Milan. Oralia Dominquez (mezzo-soprano),
  Giuseppe di Stefano (tenor), Cesare Siepi (bass), La Scala Chorus and
  Orchestra conducted by Victor de Sabata.
  Verdi: Messa da Requiem
    LP: 33CX1195-6, Set 3520, 33FCX361-2, 33QCX10104-5,
    33WCX1195-6, C90387-8, 1C 137 100 937-3, 1C 147 00 937-8, 2C 147
    00 937-8, 100 937-3. C: 2C 295 00 937-8, XL5070-1. *CD: Set Theorema
    TH121.123-4.* Excerpts on LP: RO6085, 1C 187 28 985-6M. C: EG7
    63657-4. CD: Set CMS7 63790-2, CDM7 63657-2.

June 30, July 1-2, 5-7. Kingsway Hall.
  Elisabeth Schwarzkopf (soprano)..........................Ariadne
  Rita Streich (soprano)................................Zerbinetta
  Irmgard Seefried (soprano)..............................Composer
  Rudolf Schock (tenor)....................................Bacchus
  Alfred Neugebauer (speaker).........................Major-Domo
  Karl Dönch (baritone)................................Music Master
  Hugues Cuenod (tenor)............................Dancing Master
  Erich Strauss (baritone)...............................Wigmaker
  Otakar Kraus (baritone)..................................Lackey
  Lisa Otto (soprano)......................................Naiade
  Grace Hoffman (mezzo-soprano).............................Dryad
  Anny Felbermayer (soprano)................................Echo
  Hermann Prey (baritone)...............................Harlequin
  Gerhard Unger (tenor)...............................Scaramuchio
  Fritz Ollendorff (bass)..............................Truffaldino
  Helmut Krebs (tenor)...................................Brighella
  Philharmonia Orchestra conducted by Herbert von Karajan.
    Strauss: Ariadne auf Naxos
      LP: 33CX1292-4, Set RLS760, Set EX7 69296-1, Set 3532, 33FCX506-8,
      C90458-60, 33WCX1292-4, 33QCX10168-70, Set 1C 153 769 296-1, Set
      2C 153 03 520-2. C: Set EX7 69296-4. CD: Set CMS7 69296-2,
      CDMB69296. Excerpts on C: EG7 63657-4. CD: Set CMS7 63790-2, Set
      CDM7 63657-2, Set 769 296-2, Set 655 769 296-2.

July 12. Wigmore Hall. Gerald Moore (piano).
  Wolf: Italienisches Liederbuch

July 13. Kingsway Hall. July 14-16, 19-20, EMI Studio No. 1. July 14, 17, 19,
  EMI Studio No. 3.
  Elisabeth Schwarzkopf (soprano).........................Fiordiligi
  Nan Merriman (mezzo-soprano)...........................Dorabella
  Lisa Otto (soprano)......................................Despina
  Léopold Simoneau (tenor)................................Ferrando

Rolando Panerai (baritone). . . . . Guglielmo
Sesto Bruscantini (baritone). . . . . .Don Alfonso
Chorus and Philharmonia Orchestra conducted by Herbert von Karajan.
  Mozart: Così fan tutte
              NB: Schwarzkopf was not present at a session for
              this work on July 21, when the overture only was
              recorded.

July 23. Théâtre de la Cour de l'Archevêché, Aix-en-Provence, France. Hans
  Rosbaud (piano).
    Bach: Anna Magdelena Notenbuch – No. 25, Bist du bei mir, BWV508
    Gluck: La rencontre imprévue – Einem Bach der fliesst
    Beethoven: Wonne der Wehmut, Op. 83 No. 1
    Mozart: Abendempfindung, K523; Warnung, K433
    Parisotti: Se tu m'ami
    Handel: Atalanta – Care selve
    Martini: Plaisir d'amour
    Schubert: Die Liebe hat gelogen, D751; Der Einsame, D800; Die schöne
        Müllerin, D795 – No. 7, Ungeduld; An Sylvia, D891; Die Vögel, D691
    Schumann: Der Nussbaum, Op. 25 No. 3; Aufträge, Op. 77 No. 5
    Brahms: Von ewige Liebe, Op. 43 No. 1
    Wolf: Kennst du das Land?; Wir haben beide lange Zeit geschwiegen; In
        den Schatten meiner Locken; Sohn der Jungfrau; Lebewohl; Nein,
        junger Herr; Nachtzauber; Die Zigeunerin
    Trad. (arr. Brahms): Deutsche Volkslieder – No. 6, Da unten im Tale
    Trad: Gsätzli
      CD: Melodram Set CDM26524.

August 6. Felsenreitschule, Salzburg.
    Cesare Siepi (bass). . . . . Don Giovanni
    Elisabeth Grümmer (soprano). . . . . Donna Anna
    Anton Dermota (tenor). . . . . Don Ottavio
    Elisabeth Schwarzkopf (soprano). .Donna Elvira
    Erna Berger (soprano). . . . . .Zerlina
    Otto Edelmann (bass). . . . . .Leporello
    Walter Berry (bass). . . . . .Masetto
    Desző Ernster (bass). . . . . Commendatore
  Vienna State Opera Chorus, Vienna Philharmonic Orchestra conducted by
    Wilhelm Furtwängler.
    Mozart: Don Giovanni.
      *LP: Morgan Set MOR5302, Fonit Cetra Set FE23, Discocorp Set
      MORG003, Cetra Set LO7, Foyer Set FO1017, Nippon Columbia
      OZ7568-71, Set EX290667-3, Set IC1645, 1C 153 290 667-3. CD: Music
      and Arts Set CD003, Hunt Set CD509, Nippon Columbia 9OC37-7313.
      Excerpts on LP: Gioielli della lirica GML05, Rodolphe RP12707. C:
      EG7 63657-4. CD: Set CMS7 60790-2, CDM7 63657-2, 269716-2.* The
      final scene is missing from the above recordings, and a recording of this
      scene from the 1953 performance has been included.

August 22. Kunsthaus, Lucerne. Elsa Cavelti (mezzo-soprano), Ernst Häfliger (tenor), Otto Edelmann (bass), Lucerne Festival Chorus, Philharmonia Orchestra conducted by Wilhelm Furtwängler.
Beethoven: Symphony No. 9 in D minor, Op. 125
LP: Japan Furtwängler Series MF18862-3, Cetra LO530, Japanese Cetra K19C-21-2, Discocorp RR390. CD: Seven Seas K35Y-41, Hunt CDLSMH34006, Rodolphe RPC32522-4, Music and Arts CD790, Tahra FURT1003. Last movement on LP: French Wilhelm Furtwängler Society SWF7701.

September 16-17. Wigmore Hall. Gerald Moore (piano).
Wolf: Italienisches Liederbuch

September 20. Town Hall, Watford. Philharmonia Orchestra conducted by Herbert von Karajan.
Beethoven: Fidelio – Abscheulicher! Wo eilst du hin?
LP: 33CX1266, Set RLS7715, 35231, 33FCX454, 33FCX30093, Set 1546133, 33QCX10186, XL5117, EAC37001-19. CD: CDH7 63201-2.
Beethoven: Ah! perfido – Concert Aria, Op. 65
LP: 33CX1278, Set RLS7715, 35203, Set 1546133, C90447, 33WCX1278, 33QCX10149, XL5202, EAC37001-19. CD: CDH7 63201-2.

September 25. Kingsway Hall. Artists as on May 18-21.
J. Strauss II: Der Zigeunerbaron
LP: 33CX1329-30, Set (E) SXDW3046, Set 3566, C80520-21, 33WSX541-2, 1C 137 103 051-3, 2C 149 03 151-2, 5C 181 03 051-2, XL5127-8. C: Set (E) TC2-SXDW3046. CD: Set CHS7 69526-2, Set CDH69526, Set 769 526-2, Set 555 769 526-2, Set CZS5 68058-2. Excerpts on LP: Set (E) SLS5250, Set RLS763. C: Set (E) TC-SLS5250.

September 25. Kingsway Hall. Artists as on May 25-26.
J. Strauss II: Eine Nacht in Venedig
LP: 33CX1224-5, Set (E) SXDW3043, Set 3530, C80510-1, 33WSX531-2, 1C 149 03 171-2, 5C 181 03 149-50. C: Set (E) TC2-SXDW3043. CD: Set CDH7 69530-2, Set769530-2, Set 555 769 530-2, Set CZS5 68058-2. Excerpts on LP: Set RLS763, (E) SMVP6075, 2C 053 00 478, 1C 047 01 954.

September 27-29, October 6. Kingsway Hall.
Elisabeth Schwarzkopf (soprano)...........................Arabella
Josef Metternich (baritone)..............................Mandryka
Nicolai Gedda (tenor).....................................Matteo
Anny Felbermayer (soprano)................................Zdenka
Walter Berry (bass)......................................Lamoral
Harald Pröglhöf (baritone)...............................Dominik
Murray Dickie (tenor)....................Elemer/Zimmerkellner
Theodor Schlott (bass)...................................Waldner
Philharmonia Orchestra conducted by Lovro von Matačić.
Strauss: Arabella – excerpts

LP: 33CX1226, 33CX1897, OH199, Set RLS751, 35094, 33FCX385, Set 1546133, 33WSX571, C80619, C90406, 1C 037 03 297. EP: SEL1579, SCBW802, C30166. T: CAT271. C: 1C 237 03 297. CD: CDH7 61001-2, CDH61001, 761001-2, 555 761 001-2, *Nota Blu 93.50923-4.*

November 6. EMI Studio No. 1. Artists as on July 13.
    Mozart: Così fan tutte
        LP: 33CX1262-4, SOC195-7, Set RLS7709, Set 3522, 33FCX484-6, C90432-4, 1C 147 01 748-50M, 1C 197 54 200-8M, 2C 153 01 748-50, 33WCX1262-4, 33QCX10146-8. C: Set TC-RLS7709, 2C 163 01 748-50M. CD: Set CHS7 69635-2, Set CDHC69635, Set 769635-2, Set 653 269 635-2. Excerpts on LP: OH198, SOH198, C80574, 33WSX557, 1C 063 00 838, XL5114-6. C: EG7 63657-4. 1C 243 00 838, TC-EMX2211. CD: Set CMS7 63790-2, CDM7 63657-2, EMX2211.

December 19. RAI Studios, Rome.
    Ernst Häfliger (tenor)....................................... Pelléas
    Michel Roux (tenor).. Golaud
    Mario Petri (bass-baritone)................................. Arkel
    Elisabeth Schwarzkopf (soprano)........................ Mélisande
    Graziella Sciutti (soprano)................................. Yniold
    Franco Calabrese (bass)................................. A Shepherd
    Christiane Gayraud (mezzo-soprano) .... Geneviève
    RAI Symphony Orchestra and Chorus conducted by Herbert von Karajan.
        Debussy: Pelléas et Mélisande
            LP: Fonit Cetra Set ARK6, Rodolphe RP12393-5. CD: Hunt Set CDKAR218.

1955

In the first three months of 1955 Schwarzkopf was absent from the recording studios, but as usual she was busy with platform and stage performances. In January she gave several recitals in France and Switzerland with Dinu Lipatti's widow Madeleine at the piano. There was a production of *Le nozze di Figaro* in Monte Carlo under Otto Ackermann, and a number of engagements in Britain, including two concerts with Sir John Barbirolli and the Hallé Orchestra.

April was very much a recording month. The first assignment was a Mozart Lieder record with Walter Gieseking. Schwarzkopf had been apprehensive about recording Schubert with Edwin Fischer, and she was similarly worried about the prospect of recording Mozart with Gieseking. They rehearsed thoroughly in Studio No. 1. 'I was very terrified when he started playing. It was all without pedal, and I had to match the timing and sonority of his playing. To hear the first bars of *Das Veilchen* – you know you can't match it. He was very vulnerable in his musical impressions. I know one day after we had recorded *Falstaff* [in June 1956] Walter played bits of it, and he [Gieseking] broke into tears, and he said, "Why have I never heard this piece before?" He was quite beside himself. "How can a piece of music like that escape my attention?" You knew that he would be wounded with every wrong inflection, and something a bit out of style. If you had to match something without pedal when singing you knew that all the embellishments, the slides and whatever, that creep in by fault, were completely out.' In this context the strophic verses in Mozart's songs posed particular problems. On the one hand it was important to bring out the poetic and dramatic content of the words, yet there was also a need for consistency in matters of tempo, rhythm and phrasing.

At the end of the Mozart programme there was some recording time left, and Gieseking asked Elisabeth whether she would record his own *Kinderlieder*. This exercise was intended only for the pianist's personal pleasure, and there was no question at the time that the recordings should be released. Schwarzkopf had an evening to look through the German settings of verses for children, and though the music was composed in a French style – not normally her home ground – the words were in German, and she found herself very much at ease with both words and music: 'Some of the most charming things I have ever done.' Thirty-five years later the original tapes were recovered from EMI's archives, and Schwarzkopf approved publication of the recordings as part of the edition issued to celebrate her 75th birthday.

A few days after the sessions with Gieseking there was a very different recording assignment in the shape of excerpts from Walton's *Troilus and Cressida*. The composer had written the part of Cressida with Schwarzkopf in mind, but in the event she did not sing the role on stage. Her recording of scenes from the opera under the baton of the composer has obvious historical importance, and she herself feels it to be very successful artistically. The part, she says, is for a lyric soprano, but the voice needs to be substantial, to have a good 'kernel'.

Soon afterwards came the *Fledermaus* recording under Karajan. Schwarzkopf remembers that the conductor was just as demanding in this work as in a more serious opera, and brought great elegance to a score which he respected greatly.

Then in May 1955 Elisabeth was joined by Irmgard Seefried in a Festival Hall concert followed by a recording of duets by Dvořák, Monteverdi and Carissimi. This order of events was in itself unusual, for recording sessions usually preceded an associated concert. The enterprise was 'a labour of love' for both singers, who had performed together for many years. They did not sing early music in 'faceless madrigal voices', where it is a question of 'woe if something personal comes over', but in 'very individual, expressive voices'. When the recordings were reissued on compact disc a well-known expert in older music told Schwarzkopf how surprised he was that she and Seefried sang Monteverdi with the degree of expression which was then coming to be regarded as authentic. Schwarzkopf says that she and Seefried knew how to breathe together, and pronounce consonants together, and how long a note should be. Some of this knowledge had been gleaned from their stage performances together, when they were accustomed to listening to one another, 'and sometimes with great envy if the other one could do some phrase better than one could – one wanted to do it just as well, at least. We had some problems with intonation, I believe. It's very hard in these texts – some vowels don't lend themselves to very clean pitch, the "aah" vowels especially in women's voices in the middle of the range are always dangerous. We weathered that problem, I hope. The voices matched so well that sometimes I cannot make out who is singing which five notes now. We were of course from the same *Fach* – she was the Susanna *Fach* to the hilt, and I still had something of the Susanna *Fach* to the end of my career.'

After the recording of Beethoven's Ninth in Vienna – for the second time under Karajan – there were no more commercial sessions until April the following year. But Schwarzkopf was busy enough with live performances. A tour of Scandinavia in June took her to Helsinki, where there was a very successful recital of Sibelius songs and a performance of the same composer's *Luonnotar*, for which she learned the Finnish text. In late July she returned to North America for a tour which was interrupted by a number of appearances in Europe. This was one of the few years when she did not appear at Salzburg, but in September she made her début with the San Francisco Opera in *Rosenkavalier* and *Don Giovanni*. There were also two more concerts with Reiner and the Chicago Symphony Orchestra. It was not until early December that she finally returned from the USA and went almost straight to Milan for a performance of Pamina in *Zauberflöte* under Karajan, sung in Italian.

April 4. EMI Studio No. 1A. Gerald Moore (piano).
    Wolf: Blumengruss
    Wolf: Frühling übers Jahr
    Wolf: Phänomen
    Wolf: Epiphanias

April 10. EMI Studio No. 1. Philharmonia Orchestra conducted by Alceo
Galliera.
  Mozart: Nehmt meinen Dank, K383
    C: EG7 63655-4. CD: Set CMS7 63790-2, CDM7 63655-2.

April 13. EMI Studio No. 1A. Walter Gieseking (piano).
  Mozart: Der Zauberer, K472
    LP: 33CX1321, ASD3858, 35270, C90478, 33FCX30116, 33QCX10303,
    33WCX1321, 2C 061 01 578, 101578-1, XL5149, OL3140, EAC70168. C:
    TC-ASD3858. CD: CDC7 47326-2, CDH7 63702-2, CDC47326.
  Mozart: Als Luise die Briefe, K520
    LP: 33CX1321, ASD3858, 35270, C90478, 33FCX30116, 33QCX10303,
    33WCX1321, 2C 061 01 578, 101578-1, XL5149, OL3140, EAC70168,
    EAC81060. C: TC-ASD3858. CD: CDC7 47326-2, CDH7 63702-2,
    CDC47236.
  Mozart: Das Veilchen, K476
    LP: 33CX1321, ASD3858, 35270, C90478, 33FCX30116, 33QCX10303,
    33WCX1321, 2C 061 01 578, 101578-1, XL5149, OL3140, EAC70145,
    EAC81060, EAC70168, EAC47031-41, Set AA930258. C: TC-ASD3858,
    CDH7 63702-2.
  Mozart: Un moto di gioia, K579
  Mozart: Die Verschweigung, K518
  Mozart: An Chloë, K524
  Mozart: Abendempfindung, K523
April 14.
  Mozart: Ridente la calma, K152
    LP: 33CX1321, ASD3858, 35270, C90478, 33FCX30116, 33QCX10303,
    33WCX1321, 2C 061 01 578, 101578-1, XL5149, OL3140, EAC70168,
    EAC81060. C: TC-ASD3858. CD: CDC7 47326-2, CDH7 63702-2,
    CDC47326, 747326-2, 567 747 326-2.
  Mozart: Die Zufriedenheit, K473
    LP: 33CX1321, ASD3858, 35270, C90478, 33FCX30116, 33QCX10303,
    33WCX1321, 2C 061 01 578, 101578-1, XL5149, OL3140, EAC70168,
    EAC81060. C: TC-ASD3858. CD: CDC7 47326-2, CDH7 63702-2,
    CDC47326, 747326-2, 567 747 326-2.
  Mozart: Im Frühlingsanfange, K597
    LP: 33CX1321, ASD3858, 35270, C90478, 33FCX30116, 33QCX10303,
    33WCX1321, 2C 061 01 578, 101578-1, XL5149, OL3140, EAC70168,
    EAC81060. C: TC-ASD3858. CD: CDC7 47326-2, CDH7 63702-2,
    CDC47326, 747326-2, 567 747 326-2.
  Mozart: Die kleine Spinnerin, K531
    LP: 33CX1321, ASD3858, 35270, C90478, 33FCX30116, 33QCX10303,
    33WCX1321, 2C 061 01 578, 101578-1, XL5149, OL3140, EAC70168,
    EAC81060. C: TC-ASD3858. CD: CDC7 47326-2, CDH7 63702-2,
    CDC47326, 747326-2, 567 747 326-2.
  Mozart: Das Traumbild, K530
    LP: 33CX1321, ASD3858, 35270, C90478, 33FCX30116, 33QCX10303,
    33WCX1321, 2C 061 01 578, 101578-1, XL5149, OL3140, EAC70168,
    EAC81060. C: TC-ASD3858. CD: CDC7 47326-2, CDH7 63702-2,
    CDC47326, 747326-2, 567 747 326-2.

Mozart: Die Alte, K517
LP: 33CX1321, ASD3858, 35270, C90478, 33FCX30116, 33QCX10303,
33WCX1321, 2C 061 01 578, 101578-1, XL5149, OL3140, EAC70168,
EAC81060. C: TC-ASD3858. CD: CDH7 63702-2.

Mozart: Das Kinderspiel, K598
LP: 33CX1321, ASD3858, 35270, C90478, 33FCX30116, 33QCX10303,
33WCX1321, 2C 061 01 578, 101578-1, XL5149, OL3140, EAC70168,
EAC81060. C: TC-ASD3858. CD: CDC7 47326-2, CDH7 63702-2,
CDC47326, 747326-2, 567 747 326-2.

Mozart: Das Lied der Trennung, K519
LP: 33CX1321, ASD3858, 35270, C90478, 33FCX30116, 33QCX10303,
33WCX1321, 101578-1, 2C 061 01 578, XL5149, OL3140, EAC70168,
EAC81060. C: TC-ASD3858, CDH7 63702-2.

Mozart: Oiseaux, si tous les ans, K307
LP: 33CX1321, ASD3858, 35270, C90478, 33FCX30116, 33QCX10303,
33WCX1321, 2C 061 01 578, 101578-1, XL5149, OL3140, EAC70168,
EAC81060. C: TC-ASD3858. CD: CDC7 47326-2, CDH7 63702-2,
CDC47326, 747326-2, 567 747 326-2.

Mozart: Dans un bois solitaire, K308
LP: 33CX1321, ASD3858, 35270, C90478, 3FCX30116, 33QCX10303,
33WCX1321, 101578-1, 2C 061 01 578, XL5149, OL3140, EAC70168,
EAC81060. EP: ESBF17122. C: TC-ASD3858. CD: CDH7 63702-2.

Mozart: Sehnsucht nach dem Frühling, K576

Mozart: Warnung, K433

April 16.

Mozart: An Chloë, K524
LP: 33CX1321, ASD3858, 35270, C90478, 33FCX30116, 33QCX10303,
33WCX1321, 2C 061 01 578, XL5149, OL3140, EAC70168,
EAC47031-41, EAC70223, EAC81060, EAC47031-41, EAA176, AA8589,
Set AA930258. C: TC-ASD3858. CD: CDC7 47326-2, CDH7 63702-2,
CDC47236, 747326-2, 567 747 326-2.

Mozart: Sehnsucht nach dem Frühling, K596
LP: 33CX1321, ASD3858, 35270, C90478, 33FCX30116, 33QCX10303,
33WCX1321, 2C 061 01 578, 101578-1, XL5149, OL3140, EAC70168,
EAC70145, EAC40034, EAC47031-41, EAC47083-4, EAC81060,
EAC47083-4, EAC47031-41, Set AA930258. C: TC-ASD3858. CD: CDC7
47326-2, CDH7 63702-2, CDC47326, 747326-2, 567 747 326-2.

Mozart: Abendempfindung, K523
LP: 33CX1321, ASD3858, 35270, C090478, 33FCX30116, 33QCX10303,
33WCX1321, 101578-1, 2C 061 10 578, XL5149, OL3140, EAC70168,
EAC70223, EAC47083-4, EAC81060, EAC47031-41, EAA176, AA8589,
Set AA930258. C: TC-ASD3858. CD: CDC7 47326-2, CDH7 63702-2,
CDC47326, 747326-2, 567 747 326-2.

Mozart: Die Verschweigung, K518
LP: EAC70168, EAC81060.

Gieseking: Kinderlieder, Nos. 1-21
C: EG7 63655-4. CD: Set CMS7 63790-2, CDM7 63655-2.

April 18-20. Kingsway Hall.
 Richard Lewis (tenor)......................................Troilus
 Elisabeth Schwarzkopf (soprano).........................Cressida
 Monica Sinclair (contralto)................................Evadne
 Geoffrey Walls (tenor)................................. Watchman
 John Hauxvell (baritone)...............................Watchman
 Lewis Thomas (tenor).................................. Watchman
 Philharmonia Orchestra conducted by Sir William Walton.
  Walton: Troilus and Cressida – excerpts

April 26-30. Kingsway Hall.
 Elisabeth Schwarzkopf (soprano).........................Rosalinde
 Nicolai Gedda (tenor)....................................Eisenstein
 Helmut Krebs (tenor)...................................... Alfred
 Rita Streich (soprano).....................................Adele
 Karl Dönch (baritone)...................................... Frank
 Erich Kunz (baritone)......................................Falke
 Rudolf Christ (tenor)......................................Orlovsky
 Erich Majkut (tenor)..Blind
 Franz Boheim (baritone)................................... Frosch
 Luise Martini (soprano)..Ida
 Chorus and Philharmonia Orchestra conducted by Herbert von Karajan.
  J. Strauss II: Die Fledermaus
   LP: 33CX1309-10, Set RLS728, Set 3539, C80512-3, 33WSX533-4,
   33QCX10183-4, 1C 149 00 427-8M, 2C 181 00 427-8, 291044-3. T:
   CAT286-7. C: Set TC-RLS728. CD: Set CHS7 69531-2, Set
   CDHB69531, Set 769531-2, Set 655 769 531-2, Set CDS5 68058-2.
   Excerpts on LP: 33CX1516, Set RLS763, C80110, 1C 047 01 953, 1C
   147 03 580-1, 33WSX602, XL5127-8. EP: SEL1557. C: EG7 63657-4.
   CD: Set CMS7 63790-2, CDM7 63657-2.

May 9. EMI Studio No. 1. Géza Anda (piano), Philharmonia Orchestra
 conducted by Otto Ackermann.
  Mozart: Ch'io mi scordi di te? ... Non temer, K505

May 16. Kingsway Hall. Artists as on April 18-20.
  Walton: Troilus and Cressida – excerpts
   LP: 33CX1313, OH217, 35278, 3QCX10173. T: CAT283. CD: CDM7
   64199-2.

May 25-27. EMI Studio No. 1A. Irmgard Seefried (soprano), Gerald Moore
 (piano).
  Dvořák: Moravian Duets, Op. 32
   LP: 33CX1331, HLM7267, 35290, 60376, 33FCX515, 2C 251 43 240. C:
   TC-HLM7267, 2C 051 43 240. CD: CDH7 69793-2, 769793-2, 555 769
   793-2.
May 27.
  Carissimi: Lungi omai; Il mio core; A pie d'un verde alloro; Detesta la
   cattiva sorte in amore

LP: 33CX1331, HLM7267, 35290, 60376, 33FCX515, 2C 251 43 240. C:
TC-HLM7267, 2C 051 43 240. CD: CDH7 69793-2, 769793-2, 555 769
793-2.
Monteverdi: Io son pur vezzoseta pastorella; Ardo e scoprir; O bel pastor;
    Baci cari
    LP: 33CX1331, HLM7267, 35290, 60376, 33FCX515. C: TC-HLM7267.
    CD: CDH7 69793-2, 769793-2, 555 769 793-2.

July 26-27. Musivereinsaal, Vienna. Marga Höffgen (contralto), Ernst Häfliger
    (tenor), Otto Edelmann (bass), Singverein der Gesellschaft der Musikfreunde,
    Philharmonia Orchestra conducted by Herbert von Karajan.
    Beethoven: Symphony No. 9 in D minor, Op. 125
              NB: Schwarzkopf did not attend the purely
              orchestral sessions which took place on July 24-25,
              and 28-29.
    LP: 33CX1391-2, T536-7, SH143-9, Set (E) SLS5053, Set 3544,
    33FCX448-9, C90515-6, 33QCX10190-1, 33WCX1391-2, HZE107, 1C
    181 01 830-6Y, 1C 063 01 200M, 1C 065 101 200-1, XL5164-5,
    EAC37001-19. EAC47121-2, EAC40002, EAC30216. C: Set (E)
    TC-SLS5053, 1C 263 01 200M. CD: CMS7 63310-2, 555 761 076-2.

August 3. Festival Concert Hall, Stratford, Ontario. Hart House Orchestra
    conducted by Boyd Neel.
    Bach: Cantata No. 202, Weichet nur, betrübte Schatten (without final
        recitative and aria)
        LP: Rococo 5374.
    Mozart: Exsultate, jubilate, K165
        LP: Rococo 5388.

September 20. War Memorial Opera House, San Francisco.
    Elisabeth Schwarzkopf (soprano)................. Die Feldmarschallin
    Frances Bible (mezzo-soprano)..........................Octavian
    San Francisco Opera Orchestra conducted by Erich Leinsdorf.
    Strauss: Der Rosenkavalier – Da geht er hin ... to end of Act I
        LP: Rococo 5388.

1956

At the end of January 1956 Schwarzkopf made her stage début in a role
for which she would become famous, Fiordiligi in *Così fan tutte*. There were
seven performances under Guido Cantelli. Contrary to some assertions,
this was not Cantelli's only appearance as an opera conductor at the Piccola
Scala, but it was certainly his last and most important. Merriman,
Simoneau and Panerai sung the roles they had assumed in the commercial

recording a year and a half previously, and Walter Legge attended most of the stage rehearsals with orchestra. Cantelli was an HMV artist, and by this time Legge only recorded repertoire for the Columbia label, so the two never worked together in the recording studio. Legge admired Cantelli greatly, however, and thought his *Così* the finest he had ever heard.

During one rehearsal Legge went up to Cantelli and pointed out that one of the singers was allowing intrusive 'h' sounds to enter his phrasing. Cantelli reacted very strongly against the suggestion that he had over-looked a technical blemish, but he still asked the singer concerned to repeat the aria he had just sung. The 'h' sounds were indeed there, and the hyper-sensitive Italian realised that he had been guilty of an oversight. He rushed to his dressing room, cursing himself as he went. Victor de Sabata was present at the session and went round to see what had happened. He became equally heated when he learned the cause of the trouble and, like Cantelli, had to be calmed down before the rehearsal could continue. There were no more intrusive 'h' sounds from any singer. 'Walter made Callas aware of it at one session, early on. He said, "Maria, you are making 'h' sounds." She said, "Me?, no, never! – that's not true." He played it to her – this was in the afternoon. She said, "Cancel the session, and I'll come back at 7 o'clock and I won't have 'h' sounds any more" – and she didn't. That was incredible, since it is one of the most fiendish things to eliminate.'

Interspersed with the *Così* production and concert appearances were four performances of *Don Giovanni* under Ackermann, and then another two with the same conductor in Monte Carlo. In early April Schwarzkopf and Moore began a double recording project, one a Wolf recital containing Goethe Lieder, and the second a mixed recital with the title 'Songs You Love'. Then a record of arias with Walter Susskind as conductor entitled 'Romantic Heroines' was successfully completed – Dame Elisabeth now finds the Weber items the most satisfactory part of this collection.

In May she recorded the part of Margiana in Cornelius's *Der Barbier von Bagdad*. The score as a whole was new to her, and at the time of the recording she was not in good health and had to husband her resources as best she could. The music itself presented her with problems too, since she found that it was awkwardly written for the voice. A more enjoyable assignment was Orff's *Der Kluge* later in the month, even though she was virtually sight-reading her part and some of the music went almost beyond the lowest part of her range. Here, using a Bavarian manner of pronun-ciation, particularly the soft 'ig', she cultivated a different sound from her norm, with 'those clean, virgin-like sounds on one note', each placed precisely like a 'good oboe'. The composer was present at the sessions and evidently approved.

The role of Alice Ford in *Falstaff* was also new to her at the time of recording, but would later become part of her stage repertoire. The recording sessions were naturally preceded by some intense rehearsal. Almost immediately she was involved with more Verdi, the *Requiem*, in two Festival Hall performances under Cantelli. She then went to Salzburg and sang in a Festival production of *Le nozze di Figaro* under Böhm. She also gave a Lieder recital with Gerald Moore in the Mozarteum.

From mid-September until early December Schwarzkopf was once more in North America. She gave her first stage performance as Alice in *Falstaff*, in a production mounted by the San Francisco Opera, with William Steinberg conducting. She also sang Fiordiligi in *Così fan tutte* at San Francisco, Los Angeles and San Diego, under Hans Schweiger. At all her recitals the accompanist was George Reeves.

The Carnegie Hall recital of 25 November is a rare case in which rights to a live recording not originally intended for issue were acquired by EMI. At the time of the performance Elisabeth did not know that it was being recorded. 'I would have been more terrified than ever if I had known, but I would have kept more to one direction when singing, whereas I turned away from the forward position quite a lot as you can hear, since the voice suddenly vanishes from the presence. I'm quite glad that recital is there, all the more since people say that with that small voice one could not fill Carnegie Hall. I have heard it and seen it written that that small voice was all produced by Walter Legge. Well, I'm glad that other proofs are there, although I am very much against this pirating business, because we don't earn a penny from it, and it's really very bad. But as a proof of how one did sing it is irreplaceable, and this is one of my very best recitals. I didn't work much with George Reeves, and I don't know why he was engaged, but he was a very considerable pianist. Apart from Gerald [Moore], Geoffrey [Parsons] and Raucheisen I would single him out for the particular excellence of his playing. Listen to the piano part in *Un moto di gioia*. Walter knew him, and he knew that Reeves played for Elisabeth Schumann in America, where he lived. He was a Scotsman, very stiff looking, with reddish hair, pale, very erect and lean, and you would think that no romantic sound could come out of that man, but it did. Yes, it was really very good playing, I find and found. A very wonderful accompanist, one of the best.'

On her return to Europe Elisabeth sang the Strauss *Vier letzte Lieder* in three Berlin performances, with Karajan conducting the Berlin Philharmonic. By the time of the *Rosenkavalier* recording, which commenced a few days later, she had sung the Marschallin on stage in three productions since 1952, but she feels that she still needed more stage experience before making the recording, since the interpretation does not sound experienced. She wishes that she had recorded the role again, and for that reason she is glad that the 1960 film exists, where her portrayal is more mature. She feels that the film is better vocally too, for in the recording there are passages, particularly at the beginning of the opera, where there is a certain 'fragility', and the interpretation is not 'double-bedded', as Walter Legge once memorably described Lotte Lehmann's assumption of the role. 'Sometimes in a recording I did not give the voice that I would have been giving in an opera house.' On the other hand, she feels that the 'French' aspect of the Marschallin is brought out successfully in this portrayal.

January 27. Piccola Scala Theatre, Milan.
    Elisabeth Schwarzkopf (soprano)...........................Fiordiligi
    Nan Merriman (mezzo-soprano)..........................Dorabella
    Graziella Sciutti (soprano)..................................Despina
    Luigi Alva (tenor)..Ferrando
    Rolando Panerai (baritone) ....Guglielmo
    Franco Calabrese (bass)................................Don Alfonso
Piccola Scala Chorus and Orchestra conducted by Guido Cantelli.
    Mozart: Così fan tutte
        LP: Estro Armonico Set EA029, Cetra Set LO13, Pantheon Set C87662, Stradivarius STR13597-9, Discocorp IGI326. CD: Stradivarius STR73597-9.

April 3. EMI Studio No. 1. Gerald Moore (piano).
    Wolf: Philine; Mignon 1
        LP: 33CX1657, SAX2333, Set SLS5197, 35909, 33FCX837, SAXF256, Set 1546133, 1C 037 03 725, EAC40089, AA8292. C: EG7 63653-4, 1C 237 03 725. CD: Set CMS7 63790-2, CDM7 63653-2. Philine is on LP: Set S-3754.
    Wolf: Kennst du das Land?
    Wolf: Mignon 2
April 4.
    Wolf: Mignon 2; Frühling übers Jahr; Gleich und Gleich
        LP: 33CX1657, SAX2333, Set SLS5197, 35909, 33FCX837, SAXF256, 1C 037 03 725, EAC40089, AA8292. C: 1C 237 03 725. Mignon 2 is on LP: Set 1546133. C: EG7 63653-4. CD: Set CMS7 63790-2, CDM7 63653-2.
    Wolf: Blumengruss; Mignon 3; Epiphanias; Phänomen
April 5.
    Wolf: Epiphanias; Phänomen; Die Bekehrte; Die Spröde
April 6.
    Wolf: Epiphanias; Phänomen; Anakreons Grab; Blumengruss; Ganymed
April 7.
    Wolf: St Nepomuks Vorabend; Epiphanias
        LP: 33CX1657, SAX2333, Set SLS5197, 35909, 33FCX837, SAXF256, 1C 037 03 725, EAC40089, AA8292. C: 1C 237 03 725.

Wolf: Phänomen; Anakreons Grab; Ganymed
April 8.
> Wolf: Ganymed
>> LP: 33CX1657, SAX2333, Set SLS5197, 35909, 33FCX837, SAXF256,
>> 1C 037 03 725, EAC40089, AA8292. C: EG7 63653-4, 1C 237 03 725.
>> CD: Set CMS7 63790-2, CDM7 63653-2, Nota Blu 93.50911-2.
> Sibelius: Schwarze Rosen, Op. 36 No. 1
>> LP: 33CX1404, SAX2265, 35383, 33FCX664, SAXF145, Set 1546133,
>> C90545, 33WCX1404, EAC80016. EP: SEL1600, ESL6274.
> Sibelius: Schilf, schilf, Sausle, Op. 36 No. 4
>> LP: 33CX1404, 35383, 33FCX664, Set 1546133, C90545, 33WCX1404.
>> EP: SEL1600.
> Sibelius: War es ein Traum?, Op. 37 No. 4
> Strauss: Wiegenlied, Op. 41 No. 1; Ruhe, meine Seele, Op. 27 No. 1
April 9.
> Schubert: Seligkeit, D433
> Dvořák: Gipsy Songs, Op. 55 – No. 4, Songs my mother taught me
April 10.
> Wolf: Elfenlied; In dem Schatten meiner Locken
>> LP: 33CX1404, SAX2265, 35383, 33FCX664, SAXF145, C90545,
>> 33WCX1404, EAC80016, EAC70223, EAA176, AA8589, Set AA930258.
>> EP: SEL1588, C50502, SELW1805. Elfenlied is on C: EG7 63653-4. CD:
>> Set CMS7 63790-2, CDM7 63653-2. In dem Schatten is on LP: Set
>> AA9539-42.
> Wolf: Die Zigeunerin
> Hahn: Si mes vers avait des ailes
>> LP: 33CX1404, SAX2265, 35383, 33FCX664, SAXF145, Set 1546133,
>> C90545, 33WCX1404. EAC80016, EAC70145, Set 930258. EP:
>> SEL1589. ESL6255, ESBF17122. C: EG7 63653-4. CD: Set CMS7
>> 63790-2, CDM7 63654-2.
April 11.
> Tchaikovsky: Nur wer die Sehnsucht kennt, Op. 6 No. 6
>> LP: 33CX1404, SAX2265, 35383, 33FCX664, SAXF145, C90545,
>> 33WCX1404, EAC80016, EAC47083-4, EAC47031-41, EAC70145, Set
>> AA930258. EP: SEL1600, ESL6274.
> Mendelssohn: Auf Flügeln des Gesanges, Op. 34 No. 2
>> LP: 33CX1404, SAX2265, 35383, 33FCX664, SAXF145, C90545,
>> 33WCX1404, EAC80016, EAC70145, EAC40034, EAC47031-41,
>> EAC47083-4, Set AA930258. EP: SEL1589, ESL6255. SP: SCD2149.
> Trad: Gsätzli
April 12.
> Martini: Plaisir d'amour
>> LP: 33CX1404, SAX2265, 35383, 33FCX664, SAXF145, Set 1546133,
>> C90545, 33WCX1404. EAC80016, EAC70145, EAC47083-4, EAC40034,
>> EAC47031-41, Set AA930258. EP: SEL1589, ESL6255. C: EG7 63654-4.
>> CD: Set CMS7 63790-2, CDM7 63654-2.
> Trad. (arr. Gund): O du lieb's Ängeli
>> LP: 33CX1404, SAX2265, 35383, 33FCX664, SAXF145, C90545,
>> 33WCX1404, EAC80016. EP: SEL1588. C: EG7 63653-4. CD: Set CMS7
>> 63790-2, CDM7 63654-2.

Grieg: Ich liebe dich, Op. 5 No. 3
    LP: 33CX1404, SAX2265, 35383, 33FCX664, SAXF145, C90545,
    33WCX1404, EAC80016. EP: SEL1600, ESL6274.
Trad: Gsätzli
Parisotti: Se tu m'ami
Trad (arr. Quilter): Drink to me only with thine eyes
April 13.
    Trad. (arr. Woodman): The Vesper Hymn
    Trad. (arr. O'Connor Morris): Alleluia
    Jensen: Murmelndes Lüftchen, Op. 21
        LP: 33CX1404, SAX2265, 35383, 33FCX664, SAXF145, C90545,
        33WCX1404, EAC80016, Set AA9528-31. EP: SEL1600, ESL6274.
    Grieg: The Farmyard Song, Op. 61 No. 3
        LP: 33CX1404, SAX2265, 35383, 33FCX664, SAXF145, C90545,
        33WCX1404, EAC80016. EP: SEL1600, ESL6274.
April 14.
    Flies: Wiegenlied
    Trad. (arr. O'Connor Morris): Alleluia
April 15.
    Wolf: Kennst du das Land?; Mignon 3

April 27. Kingsway Hall. Philharmonia Orchestra conducted by Walter
    Susskind.
    Weber: Oberon – Ozean, du Ungeheuer
    Wagner: Tannhäuser – Dich, teure Halle
        LP: 33CX1658, SAX2300, T520, ST520, Set SXDW3049, 35806,
        S-35806, 33FCX821, 2C 181 52 291-2, 152291-3, 1C 181 52 291-2,
        EAC47085-6. C: TC-SXDW3049, EG7 69501-4, 245 769 501-4. CD:
        CDM7 69501-2, CDM69501, 795012, 545 769 501-2.
    Wagner: Tannhäuser – Allmächt'ge Jungfrau
        LP: 33CX1658, SAX2300, T520, ST520, Set SXDW3049, 35806,
        S-35806, 33FCX821, 2C 181 52 291-2, 152291-3, 1C 181 52 291-2, C:
        TC-SXDW3049, EG7 69501-4, 245 769 501-4. CD: CDM7 69501-2,
        CDM69501, 795012, 545 769 501-2.
    Weber: Der Freischütz – Und ob die Wolke
        LP: 33CX1658, SAX2300, T520, ST520, Set SXDW3049, 35806,
        S-35806, 33FCX821, 2C 181 52 291-2, 152291-3, 1C 181 52 291-2, Set
        S-3754. C: TC-SXDW3049, EG7 69501-4, 245 769 501-4. CD: CDM7
        69501-2, CDM69501, 795012, 545 769 501-2.
April 28.
    Weber: Der Freischütz – Wie nahte mir der Schlummer ... Leise, leise
        LP: 33CX1658, SAX2300, T520, ST520, Set SXDW3049, 35806,
        S-35806, 33FCX821, 2C 181 52 291-2, 152291-3, 1C 181 52 291-2. C:
        TC-SXDW3049, EG7 69501-4, 245 769 501-4. CD: CDM7 69501-2,
        CDM69501, 795012, 545 769 501-2.
    Wagner: Lohengrin – Einsam in trüben Tagen
        LP: 33CX1658, SAX2300, T520, ST520, Set SXDW3049, 35806,
        S-35806, 33FCX821, 2C 181 52 291-2, 152291-3, 1C 181 52 291-2. C:
        TC-SXDW3049, EG7 69501-4, 245 769 501-4. CD: CDM7 69501-2,
        CDM69501, 795012, 545 769 501-2.

May 9. Kingsway Hall. Grace Hoffman (mezzo-soprano), Otto von Czerwenka
(bass), Philharmonia Orchestra conducted by Walter Susskind.
Wagner: Lohengrin – Euch Lüften, die mein Klagen

May 11-12, 14. Town Hall, Watford.
Otto von Czerwenka (bass)............................Abu Hassan
Elisabeth Schwarzkopf (soprano)......................Margiana
Nicolai Gedda (tenor)...................................Nureddin
Hermann Prey (baritone)...................................Kalif
Gerhard Unger (tenor)......................................Kadi
Grace Hoffman (mezzo-soprano)..........................Bostana
Eberhard Wächter (baritone).............................Muezzin
August Jaresch (tenor)..................................Muezzin 2
Rudolf Christ (tenor)...................................Muezzin 3
Chorus and Philharmonia Orchestra conducted by Erich Leinsdorf.
Cornelius: Der Barbier von Bagdad

May 15. EMI Studio No. 1. Artists as on May 11-12, 14.
Cornelius: Der Barbier von Bagdad
LP: 33CX1400-1, Set 3553, C90885-6, 33WCX1400-1, 1C 147 01
448-9M, REG2047-8. CD: Set CMS5 56284-2.

May 18. EMI Studio No. 1. Gerald Moore (piano).
Strauss: Wiegenlied, Op. 41 No. 1
LP: 33CX1404, SAX2265, 35383, 33FCX664, SAXF145, Set 1546133,
C90545, 33WCX1404, 1C 147 01 448-9M, EAC80016, EAC70145,
AA93058. EP: SEL1588. C: EG7 63656-4. CD: Set CMS7 63790-2,
CDM7 63656-2.
Trad: Gsätzli
May 19.
Trad: Gsätzli
LP: 33CX1404, SAX2265, 35383, 33FCX664, SAXF145, C90545,
33WCX1404, EAC80016. EP: SEL1588. C: EG7 63654-2. CD: Set CMS7
63790-2, CDM7 63654-2.
Trad (arr. Quilter): Drink to me only with thine eyes
LP: 33CX1404, SAX2265, 35383, 33FCX664, SAXF145, Set 1546133,
C90545, 33WCX1404, EAC80016. EP: SEL1589, ESL6255. SP:
SCD2149. C: EG7 63654-4. CD: Set CMS7 63790-2, CDM7 63654-2.
Dvořák: Gipsy Songs, Op. 55 – No. 4, Songs my mother taught me
LP: 33CX1404, SAX2265, 35383, 33FCX664, SAXF145, C90545,
33WCX1404, EAC80016, EAC70145, EAC47031-41, EAC47083-4,
AA930258. EP: SEL1589, ESL6255.
Trad. (arr. O'Connor Morris): Alleluia

May 22-26. EMI Studio No. 1.
Marcel Cordes (baritone)................................. The King
Gottlob Frick (bass)...................................The Peasant
Elisabeth Schwarzkopf (soprano)..................Peasant's Daughter
Georg Wieter (bass)......................................The Jailer
Rudolf Christ (tenor).........................Man with the Donkey

Benno Kusche (baritone)........................Man with the Mule
Paul Kuén (tenor)...................................First Vagabond
Hermann Prey (baritone)..........................Second Vagabond
Gustav Neidlinger (bass)............................ Third Vagabond
Philharmonia Orchestra conducted by Wolfgang Sawallisch.
    Orff: Die Kluge
            NB: Schwarzkopf only attended one day at these
            sessions, but documentation does not suggest which
            one this might have been.
        LP: 33CX1446-7, SAX2257-8, Set 3551, Set S-3551, Arabesque 8021-2,
        C90284-5, STC90284-5, 33WCX510-1, 1C 137 43 291-3. T: BTA124-5.
        CD: CMS7 63712-2. Excerpts on LP: 33CX1810, SAX2456, 1C 063 00
        719.

June 20. Royal Festival Hall, London. Philharmonia Orchestra conducted by
    Herbert von Karajan.
    Strauss: Vier letzte Lieder, Op. posth.
        C: EG7 63655-4. CD: Set CMS7 63790-2, CDM7 63655-2.

June 21-23, 25-29. Kingsway Hall.
    Tito Gobbi (baritone)......................................Falstaff
    Luigi Alva (tenor)...Fenton
    Rolando Panerai (baritone)....................................Ford
    Tomaso Spataro (tenor)..................................Dr Caius
    Renato Ercolani (tenor)................................... Bardolph
    Nicola Zaccaria (bass).......................................Pistol
    Elisabeth Schwarzkopf (soprano)..................... Mistress Ford
    Anna Moffo (soprano)....................................Nannetta
    Nan Merriman (mezzo-soprano)...........................Meg Page
    Fedora Barbieri (mezzo-soprano)...................Mistress Quickly
Chorus and Philharmonia Orchestra conducted by Herbert von Karajan.
    Verdi: Falstaff
        LP: 33CX1410-2, SAX2254-6, Set SMS1001, Set SLS5037, Set
        SLS5211, Set EX7 49668-1. Set 3552, Set S-3552, C90524-6,
        33WCX1410-2, 33QCX10244-6, 1C 153 00 442-4, 1C 165 02 125-7, 1C
        149 668-1, 2C 167 03 951-2, RL3031-3. T: BTA115-7. C: Set
        TC-SLS5037, Set TC-SLS5211, Set EX7 49668-4, Set 4X2X3552. CD:
        Set CDS7 49668-2, Set CDCB49668, 749668-2, 667 749 668-2. Excerpts
        on LP: 33CX1939, SAX2579, 1C 027 03 903, C80615, 33WSX568. C: IC
        243 02 209.

July 3. EMI Studio No. 1. Gerald Moore (piano).
    Wolf: Kennst du das Land?; Mignon 3
July 4.
    Wolf: Anakreons Grab

August 7. Mozarteum, Salzburg. Gerald Moore (piano).
    Schumann: Der Nussbaum, Op. 25 No. 3; Strauss: Schlechtes Wetter, Op.
        69 No. 5
        CD: Stradivarius STR10009.

November 25. Carnegie Hall, New York. George Reeves (piano).

    Mozart: *Abendempfindung, K523; *Als Luise die Briefe, K520; Dans un
bois solitaire, K308; Un moto di gioia, K579; *Così fan tutte –
Temerare! ... Come scoglio

    Schubert: *An Sylvia, D891; *Der Einsame, D800; *Romanze zum Drama
Rosamunde, D797 – Der Vollmond strahlt; *Die Vögel, D691;
*Gretchen am Spinnrade, D118; *Seligkeit, D433

    Schumann: *Der Nussbaum, Op. 25 No. 3

    Gluck: *La rencontre imprévue – Einem Bach der fliesst

    Strauss: †Ruhe, meine Seele, Op. 27 No. 1; Schlechtes Wetter, Op. 69 No.
5; †Hat gesagt, Op. 36 No. 3; †Wiegenlied, Op. 41 No. 1

    Brahms: *Vergebliches Ständchen, Op. 84 No. 4

    Wolf: †Herr, was trägt der Boden hier; †Bedeckt mich mit Blumen; †In
dem Schatten meiner Locken; †Zum neuen Jahr; †Philine; *Kennst
du das Land?; †Wir haben beide lange Zeit geschwiegen; †Was soll
der Zorn; †Wiegenlied im Sommer; †Elfenlied; †Nachtzauber; †Die
Zigeunerin; Ich hab' in Penna

    Handel: *Atalanta – Care selve

    Traditional: Gsätzli.

    All the above items are on CD: Set CHS7 61043-2, Set CDHB61043, Set
653 761 043-2. *Items marked * are on CD: Nota Blu 9350911-2. Items
marked + are on CD: Nota Blu 93.50923-4.*

December 12-14. Kingsway Hall.

    Elisabeth Schwarzkopf (soprano).........Die Feldmarschallin/Orphan I
    Otto Edelmann (bass)................................Baron Ochs
    Christa Ludwig (mezzo-soprano)..................Octavian/Orphan II
    Eberhard Wächter (baritone)...........Faninal/Footman III/Waiter III
    Teresa Stich-Randall (soprano)............................Sophie
    Ljuba Welitsch (soprano).............................Leitmetzerin
    Paul Kuén (tenor)......................................Valzacchi
    Kerstin Meyer (contralto).......................Annina/Orphan III
    Franz Bierbach (bass)...............Police Commissioner/Waiter IV
    Erich Majkut (tenor)......Marschallin's Majordomo/Footman II/Waiter II
    Gerhard Unger (tenor)..................Faninal's Majordomo/Animal
                                     Seller/Footman I/Waiter I
    Harald Pröglhöf (bass)..........................Notary/Footman IV
    Karl Friedrich (tenor)....................................Landlord
    Nicolai Gedda (tenor)................................Italian Tenor
    Anny Felbermayer (soprano)..............................Milliner
    Loughton High School for Girls' Choir, Bancroft School Boys' Choir, Chorus
and Philharmonia Orchestra conducted by Herbert von Karajan.

    Strauss: Der Rosenkavalier

December 14. Kingsway Hall. Philharmonia Orchestra conducted by Heinrich
Schmidt.

    Smetana: Die verkaufte Braut – Endlich allein; Wie fremd und tot
        LP: CX5286, SAX5286, Set SXDW3049, 36434, S-36434, AV34009, 1C
181 52 291-2, 2C 181 52 291-2, 152291-3. C: Set TC-SXDW3049, EG7

69501-4, 4AV34009, 1C 245 769 501-4. CD: CDM7 69501-2, CDM69501,
79501-2, 545 769 501-2.
Wagner: Die Meistersinger von Nürnberg – Was duftet doch der Flieder;
　　also unspecified excerpt from Act 3
　　(with Otto Edelmann, bass).

December 15, 17-22. Kingsway Hall. Artists as on December 12-14.
　　Strauss: Der Rosenkavalier
　　　LP: 33CX1492-5, SAX2269-72, Set SLS810, Set EX290045-3, Set EX7
　　　49354-1, Set 3563, Set S-3563, Set SDX3970, 33FCX750-3, 290045-3,
　　　C90566-9, STC90566-9, 33WCX1492-5, 1C 191 00 459-62, Set 1C 151
　　　290 045-3, Set 1C 153 749 354-1, 2C 165 00 459-62. T: BTA126-9. C: Set
　　　TC-SLS810, Set EX290045-9, Set EX7 49354-4, Set 4CDX3970. CD: Set
　　　CDS7 49354-2, Set CDCC49354, Set 667 749 354-2, Excerpts on LP:
　　　33CX1777, SAX2423, 35645, S-35645, Set S-3754, 30507, 130507, 1C
　　　063 00 720. C: 1C 243 00 720, 2C 261 00720, EG7 63657-4. CD: CDM7
　　　69338-2, CDM7 63452-2, Set CMS7 63790-2, CDM7 63657-2, Set CMS7
　　　69131-2, 763452-2, 061 100 720-1.

1957

In the early part of 1957 Schwarzkopf gave concerts and recitals in France,
Switzerland, Holland and Germany. On 6 February she sang Bach's
cantata, *Weichet nur, betrübte Schatten* with the Concertgebouw Orchestra
under Otto Klemperer. This performance was recorded and issued on
'pirate' labels, and she feels that it represents her best ever singing of Bach.
In March she sang in four performamces of *Falstaff* at La Scala under
Karajan, and in mid-May she sang in two performances of Beethoven's
Missa solemnis, again with the Concertgebouw under Klemperer. Later in
the month she made her first recordings of the year when she and the
conductor Charles Mackerras started work together on her Christmas
record. In *Stille Nacht* she sang a duet with herself, recording a second
part on top of a recording of the first. 'I sang to my own voice. It was a
gimmick, and Walter was very ashamed of it really, but he had thought
of it and said, "Oh well, for Christmas we can do a special little thing"
– it was nothing serious. I think it was meant mainly for the American
market to do something extraordinary. A terrible experience, I never
did anything of the sort again. Not a success; besides, one was a bit
ashamed of it.' After an initial release, the 'duet' item was dropped for
reissues.

In between the unseasonal work on Christmas songs there was sterner
fare in the shape of Bach cantatas – a Festival Hall concert and recording
sessions with the Philharmonia directed by the early music specialist,
Thurston Dart. None of the recordings was issued. The Cantata No. 199,
Mein Herze schwimmt im Blut, gave her particular problems. 'I had sung
it several times in concerts, but it was very difficult because it goes very
low down, and you have at all times to be very sure to use exemplary
technique in applying *Übergang* to the lower voice register.' Then it was
back to work on the Wolf Lieder record, and the start of a new collection,
'The Elisabeth Schwarzkopf Song Book'. At the end of June she returned
briefly to a part she had first sung seven years before, Marguerite in
Berlioz's *Damnation de Faust*, at a Festival Hall performance with the
Philharmonia under Massimo Freccia. This time the work was sung in
French. At the beginning of July the expert operetta conductor Otto
Ackermann was called upon once more, this time to accompany
Schwarzkopf in excerpts from various lighter stage works. 'I could only do
it with Ackermann, because he was so closely connected to the singer. It
was uncanny how he knew what was happening.' He also knew how to
tread the path between allowing expression and keeping the reins tight
enough so that the music did not lapse into 'kitsch'.

In July Schwarzkopf made her only operatic recording at La Scala, with
Maria Callas, in Puccini's *Turandot*, with Tullio Serafin conducting. She
had sung the part of Liù eight years previously in Vienna, and doesn't
remember having to re-study the role. 'I had not sung before with Callas,
but they were very amicable sessions. I tried to be as Italianate as I could;
some people like it and some don't. I find it quite good, quite decent singing,
it didn't sound too German to Italian ears.' As was by now her custom she
took part in the Salzburg Festival, singing in *Le nozze di Figaro* under
Böhm, and in *Falstaff* under Karajan. She also gave a Wolf recital with
Gerald Moore.

Then in September she recorded the Countess in Strauss's *Capriccio*.
She had not yet sung the part on stage, but she had already recorded the
closing scene from the opera with Ackermann in 1953, and she had also
sung excerpts in concert performances. It became her favourite operatic
part, not only because it is 'the most gorgeous music, and beautiful to sing,
even if there is one scene which was very feared – though if you could sing
well you could cope with it', but because it contains a very elegantly
phrased discussion about words and music – about stagecraft. The argument takes place clearly and with little emotional expression. There is no
final resolution to the discussion, which is left for each individual to solve.
'Every time you sing a Lied should the voice win, or language? One had to

decide that on the spur of the moment, not by brains but by instinct.' It was for her the most significant music she ever sang.

The recording of this opera was attended by misfortune in more than one respect. On the eve of the first session Dennis Brain, the incomparable and enormously popular first horn player in the Philharmonia, was killed in a car accident. This was a devastating blow to the Orchestra and to Walter Legge. The opera needed virtuoso horn playing, but fortunately another excellent player, Alan Civil, was able to step into the breach. Then there was a problem over microphone placement. One of the leading singers complained that some of his colleagues were being given advantageous positions on the sound stage. Legge could only respond by inviting the artist to take Schwarzkopf's position. This destroyed the arrangement which had been set up for stereo recording, and so the recording was issued only in mono.

Walter Legge was initially sceptical about stereo. He had been very proud of the echo effects in *Hänsel und Gretel,* and the far-away placements of Naiade, Dryade and Echo in *Ariadne auf Naxos,* both of which were in mono recordings and achieved through natural spacing of the singers, not by 'knob-twiddling'. He felt strongly that music should be heard from a single, homogenised source, and not from right and left. When stereo came in Schwarzkopf was not artistically aware of the new process except in so far as there were early and quickly abandoned attempts to mark up singing stages for positional effects.

A few days after the *Capriccio* recording Elisabeth was in Vienna to sing in four performances of *Falstaff.* Then she returned to America. There were three performances of *Rosenkavalier* at San Francisco and Los Angeles, and also performances of *Così fan tutte,* both with Erich Leinsdorf conducting. There was the usual round of concerts and recitals (George Reeves was once more the accompanist) until mid-December, when she returned to Europe.

February 6. Concertgebouw, Amsterdam. Concertgebouw Orchestra conducted
    by Otto Klemperer.
       Bach: Cantata No. 202, Weichet nur, betrübte Schatten
        LP: Discocorp RR537, Discocorp Set RR208. CD: Hunt Set HN727,
        AS-Disc AS533.

May 25. EMI Studio No. 1. Chorus, Philharmonia Orchestra conducted by
    Charles Mackerras.
       Silcher (orch. Mackerras): Die Lorelei
       Trad. (orch. Mackerras): I saw three ships
        LP: 33CX1482, ASD3798, 35530, S-36750, 100453-1. C: TC-ASD3798,
        EG7 63574-4, 100453-4. CD: CDM7 63574-2, CDM63574, 763574-2.

Franck: Panis angelicus
    LP: 33CX1482, ASD3798, 35530, S-36750, 100453-1. C: TC-ASD3798,
    EG7 63574-4, 100453-4. CD: CDM7 63574-2, CDM63574, 763574-2.
Trad: O du fröhliche
    LP: 33CX1482, ASD3798, 35530, S-36750, 100453-1. C: TC-ASD3798,
    EG7 63574-4, 100453-4. CD: CDM7 63574-2, CDM63574, 763574-2.
Gruber: Stille Nacht
May 26.
Silcher (orch. Mackerras): Die Lorelei
Humperdinck (arr. Mackerras): Weihnachten
    LP: 33CX1482, ASD3798, 35530, S-36750, 100453-1. C: TC-ASD3798,
    EG7 63574-4, 100453-4. CD: CDM7 63574-2, CDM63574, 763574-2.
Trad: Von Himmel hoch; In dulci jubilo
    LP: 33CX1482, ASD3798, 35530, S-36750, 100453-1. C: TC-ASD3798,
    EG7 63574-4, 100453-4. CD: CDM7 63574-2, CDM63574, 763574-2.
Trad. (orch. Mackerras): The First Nowell; Easter Alleluia
    LP: 33CX1482, ASD3798, 35530, S-36750, 100453-1. C: TC-ASD3798,
    EG7 63574-4, 100453-4. CD: CDM7 63574-2, CDM63574, 763574-2.
Bach (arr. Gounod and Mackerras): Ave Maria

**May 29-30. EMI Studio No. 1. Philharmonia Orchestra conducted by Thurston
Dart.**
Bach: Cantata No. 199, Mein Herze schwimmt im Blut
May 31.
Bach: Cantata No. 202, Weichet nur, betrübte Schatten – Weichet nur,
    betrübte Schatten

**June 1. EMI Studio No. 1. Chorus and Philharmonia Orchestra conducted by
Charles Mackerras.**
Trad. (arr. Brahms): Volkskinderlieder – No. 4, Sandmännchen
    LP: 33CX1482, ASD3798, 35530, S-36750, 100453-1. C: TC-ASD3798,
    EG7 63574-4, 100453-4. CD: CDM7 63574-2, CDM63574, 763574-2.
Trad: Maria auf dem Berge
    LP: 33CX1482, ASD3798, 35530, S-36750, 100453-1. C: TC-ASD3798,
    EG7 63574-4, 100453-4. CD: CDM7 63574-2, CDM63574, 763574-2.
Gluck: In einem kühlen Grunde
    LP: 33CX1482, ASD3798, 35530, S-36750, 100453-1. C: TC-ASD3798,
    EG7 63574-4, 100453-4. CD: CDM7 63574-2, CDM63574, 763574-2.
Trad. (arr. Fiske): O Tannenbaum

June 2. EMI Studio No. 1. Philharmonia Orchestra conducted by Thurston Dart.
Bach: Cantata No. 202, Weichet nur, betrübte Schatten – Weichet nur,
    betrübte Schatten
Bach: Cantata No. 68, Also hat Gott die Welt geliebt – Mein gläubiges Herz
Bach: Cantata No. 208, Was mir behagt, ist nur die muntre Jagd – Schafe
    können sicher weiden

June 8. EMI Studio No. 1. Gerald Moore (piano).
Wolf: Kennst du das Land?

LP: 33CX1657, SAX2333, Set SLS5197, 35909, Set S-3754, 33FCX837, SAXF256, Set 1546133, 1C 037 03 725, EAC40089, EAC70223, EAA176, AA8589, AA8292, Set AA930258. C: 1C 237 03 725, EG7 63653-4. CD: Set CMS7 63790-2, CDM7 63653-2.

June 9.
> Wolf: Die Bekehrte; Die Spröde; Als ich auf dem Euphrat schiffte; Nimmer will ich dich verlieren; Mignon 3; Der Schäfer

June 10.
> Wolf: Die Bekehrte
>> LP: 33CX1657, SAX2333, Set SLS5197, 35909, 33FCX837, SAXF256, 1C 037 03 725, EAC40089, AA8292. C: 1C 237 03 725, EG7 63653-4. CD: Set CMS7 63790-2, CDM7 63653-2.
>
> Wolf: Anakreons Grab
>> LP: 33CX1657, SAX2333, Set SLS5197, 35909, 33FCX837, SAXF256, 1C 037 03 725, EAC40089, EAC70223, EAA176, AA8589, AA8292, Set AA930258. C: 1C 237 03 725.
>
> Wolf: Hochbeglückt in deiner Liebe
> Bohm: Was i hab'

June 11.
> Bohm: Was i hab'
> Schubert: Seligkeit, D433
> Strauss: Zueignung, Op. 10 No. 1
> Schumann: Widmung, Op. 25 No. 1
> Giordani: Caro mio ben
> Schubert: Heidenröslein, D257
>> LP: CX5268, SAX5268, S-36345, 1C 187 01 307-8, Set 1546133, EAC80012, AA8070, EAC60167, Set AA930258, EAC70145, EAC47031-41, EAC47083-4, EAC47149-50, EAC40034. C: EG7 63656-4. CD: Set CMS7 63790-2, CDM7 63656-2.

June 21.
> Parisotti: Se tu m'ami
> Schubert: Die Vögel, D691
> Liszt: O Lieb', so lang du lieben kannst, G298
> Giordani: Caro mio ben

June 26.
> Schubert: Seligkeit, D433
> Bizet: Pastorale
> Mozart: Warnung, K433

June 30. EMI Studio No. 1. Chorus and Philharmonia Orchestra conducted by Charles Mackerras.
> Trad: O come all ye faithful
>> LP: 33CX1482, ASD3798, 35530, S-36750, 100453-1. C: TC-ASD3798, EG7 63574-4, 100453-4. CD: CDM7 63574-2, CDM63574, 763574-2.
>
> Silcher (orch. Mackerras): Die Lorelei
> Gruber: Stille Nacht

July 1.
> Gruber: Stille Nacht
>> LP: 33CX1482, ASD3798, 35530, S-36750, 100453-1. C: TC-ASD3798, EG7 63574-4. 100453-4. CD: CDM7 63574-2, CDM63574, 763574-2.

July 2. Kingsway Hall. Chorus and Philharmonia Orchestra conducted by Otto
Ackermann
  Sieczynsky: Wien, du Stadt meiner Träume
    LP: 33CX1570, SAX2283, ASD2807, 35696, S-35696, SVP1180,
    SAXF158, 100478-1, 2C 053 00 478. EP: SEL1648, ESL6267. SP:
    SCD2128. C: TC-ASD2807. CD: CDC7 47284-2, CDC47284, 1C 567 747
    284-2.
  Lehár: Der Zarewitsch – Einer wird kommen
    LP: 33CX1570, SAX2283, ASD2807, 35696, S-35696, SVP1180,
    SAXF158, 100478-1, 2C 053 00 478. EP: SEL1652, ESL6260. C:
    TC-ASD2807. CD: CDC7 47284-2, CDC47284. 1C 567 747 284-2.
  Lehár: Der Graf von Luxemburg – Heut' noch werd'ich Ehefrau
    LP: 33CX1570, SAX2283, ASD2807, 35696, S-35696, Set S-3754,
    SVP1180, SAXF158, 100478-1, 2C 053 00 478. EP: SEL1652, ESL6260.
    C: TC-ASD2807. CD: CDC7 47284-2, CDC47284, 1C 567 747 284-2.
  J. Strauss II: Der Zigeunerbaron – Saffis Lied
July 3.
  Lehár: Der Graf von Luxemburg – Hoch, Evoë Angèle Didier
    LP: 33CX1570, SAX2283, ASD2807, 35696, S-35696, SVP1180,
    SAXF158, 100478-1, 2C 053 00 478. EP: SEL1652, ESL6260. C:
    TC-ASD2807. CD: CDC7 47284-2, CDC47284, 1C 567 747 284-2.
  J. Strauss II (arr. Benatzky): Casanova – The Nuns' Chorus; Laura's Song
    LP: 33CX1570, SAX2283, ASD2807, YKM5014, 35696, S-35696,
    SVP1180, SAXF158, 100478-1, 2C 053 00 478. EP: SEL1642, ESL6263.
    SP: SCD2128. C: TC-ASD2807. CD: CDC7 47284-2, CDC47284, 1C 567
    747 284-2.
  Zeller: Der Vogelhändler – Ich bin die Christel von der Post; Schenkt man
    sich Rosen in Tirol
    LP: 33CX1570, SAX2283, ASD2807, 35696, S-35696, SVP1180,
    SAXF158, 100478-1, 2C 053 00 478. EP: SEL1642, ESL6263. C:
    TC-ASD2807. CD: CDC7 47284-2, CDC47284, 1C 567 747 284-2. Ich
    bin die Christel is on LP: Set S-3754.
July 4.
  Heuberger: Der Opernball – Im chambre separée
    LP: 33CX1570, SAX2283, ASD2807, 35696, S-35696, Set S-3754,
    SVP1180, SAXF158, 100478-1, 2C 053 00 478. EP: SEL1648, ESL6267.
    C: TC-ASD2807. CD: CDC7 47284-2, CDC47284, 1C 567 747 284-2.
  Suppé: Boccaccio – Hab' ich nur deine Liebe
    LP: 33CX1570, SAX2283, ASD2807, 35696, S-35696, SVP1180,
    SAXF158, 100478-1, 2C 053 00 478. EP: SEL1652, ESL6260. C:
    TC-ASD2807. CD: CDC7 47284-2, CDC47284, 1C 567 747 284-2.
  J. Strauss II: Eine Nacht in Venedig – Seht, o seht
  Lehár: Giuditta – Meine Lippen, sie küssen so heiss
July 5.
  Lehár: Giuditta – Meine Lippen, sie küssen so heiss
    LP: 33CX1570, SAX2283, ASD2807, 35696, S-35696, SVP1180,
    SAXF158, 100478-1, 2C 053 00 478. EP: SEL1648, ESL6267. C:
    TC-ASD2807. CD: CDC7 47284-2, CDC47284, 1C 567 747 284-2.
  Zeller: Der Obersteiger – Sei nicht bös

LP: 33CX1570, SAX2283, ASD2807, CFP4277, SEOM13, 35696,
S-35696, Set S-3754, SVP1180, SAXF158, 100478-1, 2C 053 00 478. EP:
SEL1648, ESL6267. C: TC-ASD2807. CD: CDC7 47284-2, CDB7
62646-2, 1C 567 747 284-2.

Millöcker (arr. Mackchen): Die Dubarry – Was ich im Leben beginne; Ich
schenk' mein Herz
LP: 33CX1570, SAX2283, ASD2807, 35696, S-35696, SVP1180,
SAXF158, 100478-1, 2C 053 00 478, Set S-3754. C: TC-ASD2807. CD:
CDC7 47284-2, CDC47284, 1C 567 747 284-2, 1C 567 747 284-2. Was
ich im Leben is on LP: Set S-3754.

July 9-13, 15. La Scala Theatre, Milan.
Maria Callas (soprano)....................................Turandot
Giuseppe Nessi (tenor)......................................Altom
Nicola Zaccaria (bass).......................................Timur
Eugenio Fernandi (tenor).....................................Calaf
Elisabeth Schwarzkopf (soprano)...............................Liù
Mario Boriello (baritone)......................................Ping
Renato Ercolani (tenor).......................................Pang
Piero de Palma (tenor).............................Emperor/Pong
Giulio Mauri (bass).......................................Mandarin
Elisabetta Fusco (soprano)..................................Voice I
Pinuccia Perotti (soprano).................................Voice II
La Scala Orchestra and Chorus conducted by Tullio Serafin.
Puccini: Turandot
LP: 33CX1555-7, Set RLS741, Set EX291267-3, Set 3571, 33FCX766-8,
C90934-5, 33QCX10291-3, 33WCX1555-7, 1C 153 291 267-3, 2C 153 00
969-71, 2C 153 291 267-3, Set 291267-3. C: Set TC-RLS741, Set
EX291267-5. CD: Set CDS7 47971-8, Set CDCB47971, Set 747971-8,
Set 667 747 971-8, Excerpts on LP: 33CX1792, Set (E) SLS5104, Set
3814, 33FCX30148, C80578, 33WSX559, 33QCX10466, 33QCX10108,
1C 187 28 985-86M, OL3242. EP: SEBQ215, SEBQ127, SELW1533,
C50151. SP: SCBQ3028, SCB3036. C: EG7 63657-4. CD: Set CMS7
63790-2, CDM7 63657-2.

July 30. Festspielhaus, Salzburg.
Dietrich Fischer-Dieskau (baritone)..................Count Almaviva
Elisabeth Schwarzkopf (soprano)..................Countess Almaviva
Irmgard Seefried (soprano)..............................Susanna
Erich Kunz (baritone).......................................Figaro
Murray Dickie (tenor)....................................Don Basilio
Georg Stern (bass)..Bartolo
Sieglinde Wagner (mezzo-soprano).......................Marcelina
Christa Ludwig (mezzo-soprano).........................Cherubino
Alois Pernerstorfer (bass-baritone).......................Antonio
Anny Felbermayer (soprano)..............................Barbarino
Erich Majkut (tenor)......................................Don Curzio
Vienna State Opera Chorus, Vienna Philharmonic Orchestra conducted by
Karl Böhm.
Mozart: Le nozze di Figaro

LP: Melodram Set MEL709, Giuseppe di Stefano Records Set GDS31019, Gala Set GL100.601. CD: Orfeo C296923D. Excerpts on LP: Melodram Set MEL047. Excerpts on CD: Verona 27092-4, Virtuoso 269.7152.

August 10. Festspielhaus, Salzburg.
    Tito Gobbi (baritone)..Falstaff
    Rolando Panerai (baritone)......................................Ford
    Luigi Alva (tenor)...Fenton
    Tommaso Spataro (tenor)................................Dr Caius
    Renato Ercolani (tenor).................................Bardolph
    Mario Petri (bass-baritone)................................Pistol
    Elisabeth Schwarzkopf (soprano).............................Ford
    Anna Moffo (mezzo-soprano)...............................Nanette
    Anna Maria Canali (mezzo-soprano)....................Meg Page
    Giulietta Simoniato (mezzo-soprano)..............Mistress Quickly
    Vienna State Opera Chorus, Vienna Philharmonic Orchestra, conducted by
        Herbert von Karajan.
        Verdi: Falstaff
            CD: Hunt Set CDKAR226.

September 2-7, 9-11. Kingsway Hall.
    Elisabeth Schwarzkopf (soprano).........................Countess
    Eberhard Wächter (baritone)...............................Count
    Nicolai Gedda (tenor)..................................Flamand
    Dietrich Fischer-Dieskau (baritone)......................Olivier
    Hans Hotter (baritone)...............................La Roche
    Christa Ludwig (mezzo-soprano)...........................Clairon
    Rudolf Christ (tenor)......................................Taupe
    Anna Moffo (soprano).............................Italian Soprano
    Dermot Troy (tenor)...............................Italian Tenor
    Karl Schmitt-Walter (baritone).........................Majordomo
    Wolfgang Sawallisch......................................Servant
    Edgar Fleet (tenor)......................................Servant
    Dennis Wicks (bass).....................................Servant
    Ian Humphries (tenor)...................................Servant
    John Hauxvell (baritone)................................Servant
    Geoffrey Walls (bass)...................................Servant
    Lesley Fyson (tenor)....................................Servant
    Edward Darling (tenor)..................................Servant
    David Winnard (bass)....................................Servant
    Philharmonia Orchestra conducted by Wolfgang Sawallisch.
        Strauss: Capriccio
            LP: 33CX1600-02, OC230-2, Set 3580, C90997-9, 33WCX1600-02,
            OS3110-3, 1C 151 143 524-3M, 143524-3. CD: Set CDS7 49014-8, Set
            CDCB49014. Excerpts on LP: OH233. C: EG7 63657-4. CD: Set CMS7
            63790-2, CDM7 63657-2, Set 749014-8,

December 22. Concertgebouw, Amsterdam. Felix de Nobel (piano).
    Mozart: Als Luise die Briefe, K520; Un moto di gioia, K579

Schubert: An Sylvia, D891; Der Einsame, D800; Rosamunde, D797 – Der
    Vollmond strahlt; Die Vögel, D691; Gretchen am Spinnrade, D118
Strauss: Ruhe, meine Seele, Op. 27 No. 1; Schlechtes Wetter, Op. 69 No. 5;
    Hat gesagt, bleibt's nicht dabei, Op. 36 No. 3
C: Verona 427021. CD: Verona 27021.

1958

In early 1958 Schwarzkopf was in London to do more work on the song
recitals with Gerald Moore. She also took part in a Festival Hall concert
where she sang 'Voi che sapete' from *Le nozze di Figaro* in an ornamented
version arranged by the conductor Charles Mackerras. She liked the
arrangement at the time, and remembers singing it on other occasions.
She also gave a number of recitals in Basel, Düsseldorf, Hamburg, Berlin
and Frankfurt with her teacher and mentor Michael Raucheisen, marking
his farewell to the concert platform. Excerpts from one of the two Berlin
recitals have been published in various 'pirate' editions.

The round of concerts and recitals on the continent continued until the
beginning of April, when Schwarzkopf and Moore tackled Wolf's *Italien-
ishes Liederbuch* once more, this time in the Abbey Road studios. At the
end of May there were more Bach cantata recordings with Thurston Dart,
all of which remained unpublished with the exception of No. 199, *Mein
Herze schwimmt im Blut*, which only appeared 30 years later as part of the
75th birthday set. Dame Elisabeth now regards this as an outstanding
example of her singing at its best, particularly in a technical sense. Also
in May she recorded excerpts from Wagner's *Lohengrin* with Christa
Ludwig. 'Especially notable for Christa – out of this world – I'm not too bad
either.' She had sung the opera in Milan five years previously with
Karajan, so the music was familiar to her.

The sequence of concert and stage appearances continued as ever. In
May and June there were performances of *Le nozze di Figaro* under Giulini
and more *Falstaffs* with Karajan, both at the Vienna State Opera, and it
was Salzburg once more in July and August. On 27 July Schwarzkopf sang
a Wolf recital in the Mozarteum with Gerald Moore, and 35 years later this
was issued by EMI, with the singer's warm approval. Her operatic appearances at Salzburg were in *Così fan tutte* and *Le nozze di Figaro*, both
conducted by Karl Böhm.

Elisabeth then travelled to Vienna, where she took part in productions
of *Don Giovanni, Così fan tutte* and *Falstaff*, as well as in a recording of

Beethoven's *Missa solemnis* under Karajan, who was also the *Falstaff*
conductor. On one-never-to-be-forgotten day she had stage rehearsals for
the Verdi opera from 10 a.m. to 1 p.m., followed by a recording of the
'Benedictus' from the *Missa solemnis* in the afternoon. Notwithstanding
an earlier promise, and knowing full well that his soloist would be taxed
to the limit, Karajan made Schwarzkopf sing out with her full voice at the
morning rehearsal. Somehow she got through the 'Benedictus' later that
day, with 'a noose round my neck'.

January 6. Hochschule für Musik, Berlin. Michael Raucheisen (piano).
    T. Arne: The Tempest – Where the bee sucks
      LP: Melodram Set MEL082, Discoreale DR10038.
    Purcell: Music for a while
      LP: Melodram Set MEL082, Discoreale DR10038.
    Schubert: Didone abbandonata, D51 – Vedi quanto adoro; Misero
        pargoletto, D42
      LP: Melodram Set MEL082, Discoreale DR10038, Discocorp RR208,
      Discocorp RR537.
    Strauss: Hat gesagt, bleibt's nicht dabei, Op. 36 No. 3
      LP: Melodram Set MEL088.
    Strauss: Schlechtes Wetter, Op. 69 No. 5
      LP: Melodram Set MEL088.
    Trad. (arr. Quilter): Drink to me only with thine eyes
      LP: Melodram Set MEL082, Discoreale DR10038.

January 11. EMI Studio No. 1A. Gerald Moore (piano).
    Wolf: Die Spröde; Mignon 3; Blumengruss
      LP: 33CX1657, SAX2333, Set SLS5197, 35909, 1C 037 03 725,
      EAC40089, AA8292. C: 1C 237 03 725. Mignon 3 is on LP: Set 1546133.
      Die Spröde and Mignon 3 are on C: EG7 63653-4. CD: Set CMS7
      63790-2, CDM7 63653-2.
January 12.
    Rachmaninov: To the children, Op. 26 No. 7
      LP: 33CX5268, SAX5268, 36345, EAC80012, AA8070.
    Wolf: Nachtzauber
January 13.
    Trad. (arr. Weatherley): Danny Boy
      LP: 33CX5268, SAX5268, 36345, Set 1546133, EAC80012, AA8070,
      EAC70145, EAC47031-41, EAC6017. C: EG7 63654-4. CD: CDM7
      63654-2.
    Trad. (arr. Brahms): Deutsche Volkslieder – No. 42, In stiller Nacht

January 16. Royal Festival Hall, London. Goldsbrough Orchestra conducted by
    Charles Mackerras.
    Mozart: Le nozze di Figaro – Voi che sapete (ornamented version of aria)
      LP: Voce VOCE116.

April 1-3, 5-7. EMI Studio No. 1. Gerald Moore (piano).
  Wolf: Italienisches Liederbuch

April 15. Great Hall, Conservatorio, St Pietro a Maiella, Naples. Naples
  Scarlatti Orchestra conducted by Ugo Rapallo.
    Bach: Cantata No. 202, Weichet nur, betrübte Schatten – Weichet nur,
      betrübte Schatten; Cantata No. 92, Ich habe in Gottes Herz und
      Sinn – Meinem Hirten bleib' ich treu
    CD: Melodram CDM16529.
    Mozart: Nehmt meinen Dank, K 383
    CD: Melodram CDM16529.

May 24. EMI Studio No. 1. Philharmonia Orchestra conducted by Thurston Dart.
    Bach: Cantata No. 199, Mein Herze schwimmt im Blut
    Bach: Cantata No. 92, Ich habe in Gottes Herz und Sinn – Meinem Hirten
      bleib' ich treu
    Bach: Cantata No. 208, Was mir behagt, ist nur die muntre Jagd – Schafe
      können sicher weiden

May 25. EMI Studio No. 1. Christa Ludwig (mezzo-soprano), Philharmonia
  Orchestra conducted by Heinz Wallberg.
    Wagner: Lohengrin – Euch Lüften, die mein Klagen
      LP: 33CX1658, SAX2300, T520, ST520, Set SXDW3049, 35086,
      S-35806, 33FCX821, 1C 181 52 291-2. 2C 181 52 291-2, 152291-3. C:
      TC-SXDW3049. CD: CDM7 69501-2.

May 26. EMI Studio No. 1. Philharmonia Orchestra conducted by Thurston Dart.
    Bach: Cantata No. 199, Mein Herze schwimmt im Blut
      C: EG7 63655-4. CD: Set CMS7 63790-2, CDM7 63655-2.

June 25. Kurzaal, Scheveningen, Holland. Netherlands Chamber Orchestra,
  conducted by Szymon Goldberg.
    Haydn: Cantata, Berenice che fai, HobXXIVa/28
    LP: Discocorp Set RR208.
July 27. Mozarteum, Salzburg. Gerald Moore (piano).
    Wolf: Im Frühling; Auf eine Christblume 1; Lied vom Winde; Philine;
      Kennst du das Land?; Der Schäfer; Blumengruss; Frühling übers
      Jahr; Anakreons Grab; Phänomen; Ganymed; Mühvoll komm'ich
      und beladen; In dem Schatten meiner Locken; Bedeckt mich mit
      Blumen; Wer tat deinem Füsslein weh?; Wehe der, die mir
      verstrickte; Nun lass uns Frieden schliessen; Mausfallen
      Sprüchlein; Tretet ein, hoher Krieger; Singt mein Schatz wie ein
      fink; Du milchjunger Knabe; Wandl' ich in dem Morgentau; Das
      Kohlerweib ist trunken; Wie glänzt der helle Mond
    CD: CDH7 64905-2. *The last six items are on CD: Stradivarius
    STR10009.*

August 24 or 31. Residenz, Salzburg.
    Elisabeth Schwarzkopf (soprano)........................Fiordiligi
    Christa Ludwig (mezzo-soprano)........................Dorabella

Rolando Panerai (baritone). . . . . Guglielmo
Luigi Alva (baritone). . . . . Ferrando
Graziella Sciutti (soprano). . . . . .Despino
Carlo Schmidt (bass). . . . . Don Alfonso
Vienna State Opera Chorus, Vienna Philharmonic Orchestra conducted by
Karl Böhm.
> Mozart: Così fan tutte
> *Excerpts on LP: LP52.*

September 12-16. Musikvereinsal, Vienna. Christa Ludwig (mezzo-soprano),
Nicolai Gedda (tenor), Nicola Zaccaria (bass), Singverein der Gesellschaft
der Musikfreunde, Philharmonia Orchestra conducted by Herbert von
Karajan.
> Beethoven: Missa solemnis, Op. 123
> LP: 33CX1634-5, ST914-5, Set SLS5198, CFPD4420-1, Set 3595, Set
> S-3595, 33FCX828-9, SAXF177-8, 102581-3, C91019-20, STC91019-20,
> 33WCX1634-5, 33QCX10369-70, SAXQ7317-8, 820558-9, 1C 137 00
> 627-8, 2C 181 00 627-8, 2C 193 02 581-2, 2C 167 02 581-2, OS3069-70.
> T: TT914-5. C: Set TC-SLS5198, TC-CFPD4420-1.

December 29. La Scala Theatre, Milan.
Elisabeth Schwarzkopf (soprano). . . . . .Iole
Fedora Barbieri (mezzo-soprano). . . . . .Dejanira
Ettore Bastianini (baritone). . . . . .Lichas
Franco Corelli (tenor). . . . . .Hyllus
Agostino Ferrin (bass). . . . . Priest of Jupiter
Jerome Hines (bass). . . . . Hercules
Vittorio Tatozzi (bass). . . . . .First Trachinian
La Scala Chorus and Orchestra conducted by Lovro von Matačić.
> Handel: Hercules (sung in Italian)
> *LP: Giuseppe di Stefano Set GDS3001, Ed Smith Set EJS395, Set
> HOPE239.*

1959

Schwarzkopf's first recording engagement this year was in April. The
repertoire was Verdi and Puccini arias, and Walter Legge engaged Nicola
Rescigno as conductor, who had worked in Italian repertoire very successfully with Maria Callas. It was his support, no doubt, which contributed
to the fact that these sessions were highly succesful artistically (though
not all the items were published). Indeed, Dame Elisabeth regards this
particular version of Mimì's aria as containing 'some of my best and most
imaginative singing'. In May a continual round of engagements took her
to Scandinavia, and then to Vienna in June, where she sang in *Le nozze di*

Figaro and *Così fan tutte* under Böhm. In early September there was a notable occasion in Lucerne when Sir Thomas Beecham, who had conducted the Philharmonia's first concert, returned to them for only the second and in fact the last time in order to conduct a performance of Handel's *Messiah*. This was the only occasion on which Elisabeth sang under his baton as a soloist.

Then in mid-September came the recording of *Le nozze di Figaro* under Giulini, followed by a Festival Hall concert performance. *Figaro* went ahead with few problems, but almost immediately there was a scheduled recording of *Don Giovanni* under Otto Klemperer. Three days of sessions went by, and then Klemperer was taken ill. In the crisis that followed Walter Legge persuaded Giulini to undertake his second Mozart recording. He did so with great reluctance and trepidation, since it was a score which he had never conducted, and he normally needed a long period of preparation. There were also two scheduled Festival Hall performances of the work, and in order to relieve Giulini of those responsibilities Legge engaged a second conductor, the young Colin Davis. Davis's early career was undoubtedly helped by the success he made of this opportunity.

In the recording Giulini's tempi were much faster than those of Klemperer. Another conductor, Antonino Tonini, was at the keyboard for the recitatives, 'and I think we lapsed into some quite good Italian'. Schwarzkopf had to be the foil for Sutherland's 'creamy voice', and so cultivated a 'sharp, unfriendly tone'. 'That Elvira does not get any sympathy from the listener. It's well sung, but the voice is rather cutting for my taste. That was the only occasion when I had to give a different voice from my normal one with Elvira. The normal thing was rather what I did with Furtwängler' (in the 1954 live performance from Salzburg). She remembers Giulini as a very effective conductor who brought a high degree of dramatic impetus to both Mozart operas. She remembers too how self-critical he was, and how he suffered in the quest to realise his own high standards.

Almost immediately after those sessions she went back to the United States for a briefer than usual visit, singing Fiordiligi in four performances with the Chicago Lyric Opera. Three of the four were under Matačić, but the first was conducted by Krips, and she remembers this occasion as one of her happiest experiences on stage: 'He always made it so easy for the singers. I felt I was just floating through it. It was the only time when singing was a physical pleasure.' Then it was back to the Royal Opera House in London for the first time in eight years for six performances of *Rosenkavalier* conducted by Georg Solti.

April 22-23. Kingsway Hall. Philharmonia Orchestra conducted by Nicola
   Rescigno.
      Verdi: Otello – Emilia, te ne prego; Piangea cantando; Ave Maria
         (with Margreta Elkins, mezzo-soprano).
            LP: 33CX5286, SAX5286, Set SXDW3049, 36434, S-36464, Set S-3754,
            1C 181 52 291-2, 2C 181 52 291-2, 152291-3. C: Set TC-SXDW3049.
April 23-24.
      Puccini: La bohème – Donde lieta uscì
April 24.
      Puccini: Gianni Schicchi – O mio babbino caro
            LP: 33CX5286, SAX5286, Set SXDW3049, 36434, S-36464, Set S-3754,
            1C 181 52 291-2, 2C 181 52 291-2, 152291-3. C: Set TC-SXDW3049.
      Puccini: La bohème – Si, mi chiamano Mimi
            LP: 33CX5286, SAX5286, Set SXDW3049, 36434, S-36464, Set S-3754,
            1C 181 52 291-2, 2C 181 52 291-2, 152291-3. C: Set TC-SXDW3049.
April 24-25.
      Puccini: Turandot – Signore, ascolta
April 25.
      Puccini: Turandot – Tu che di gel
      Verdi: La traviata – Addio del passato

May 18. EMI Studio No. 1A. Gerald Moore (piano).
      Strauss: Ruhe, meine Seele, Op. 27 No. 1; Heimliche Aufforderung, Op. 27
         No. 3

September 16-19, 21-25, 27, November 21. Kingsway Hall.
      Eberhard Wächter (baritone)........................Count Almaviva
      Elisabeth Schwarzkopf (soprano)..................Countess Almaviva
      Fiorenza Cossotto (mezzo-soprano).......................Cherubino
      Giuseppe Taddei (baritone)................................Figaro
      Anna Moffo (soprano).....................................Susanna
      Dora Gatta (soprano)..................................Marcellina
      Ivo Vinco (bass)...Bartolo
      Renato Ercolani (tenor)..................... Don Basilio/Don Curzio
      Piero Cappuccilli (baritone)..............................Antonio
      Elisabetta Fusco (soprano)..............................Barbarina
      Gillian Spencer (soprano)...............................First Girl
      Diana Gillingham (soprano)............................Second Girl
      Philharmonia Chorus and Orchestra conducted by Carlo Maria Giulini.
         Mozart: Le nozze di Figaro
            LP: 33CX1732-5, SAX2381-4, Set SLS5152, Set 3608, Set S-3608,
            33FCX862-5, SAXF114-7, 1C 165 00 514-7, 2C 165 00 514-7, Set
            103465-3, 1C 197 03 464-6, OS3036-8, Set SMS1010. C: Set
            TC-SLS5152, Set 4X3X3608. CD: Set CMS7 63266-2, Set CDMB63266,
            Set 763266-2, Set 653 763 261-2. Excerpts on LP: 33CX1934, SAX2573,
            ALP2008, ASD558, SXLP30303, YKM5002, Set S-3754, AV34006, 1C
            061 01 392, 1C 063 00 839, 1C 147 30 636-7, 143671-1, 1C 061 100
            839-1. C: TC-SXLP30303, 4AV34006, 1C 263 00 839. CD: Set CDC7
            47950-2, 747950-2, 567 747 950-2.

October 2-4. EMI Studio No. 1.
 Eberhard Wächter (baritone)..........................Don Giovanni
 Joan Sutherland (soprano)............................Donna Anna
 Luigi Alva (tenor)................................. Don Ottavio
 Gottlob Frick (bass).............................. Commendatore
 Elisabeth Schwarzkopf (soprano)......................Donna Elvira
 Giuseppe Taddei (baritone)............................. Leporello
 Piero Cappuccilli (baritone)..............................Masetto
 Graziella Sciutti (soprano).................................. Zerlina
 Philharmonia Chorus and Orchestra conducted by Otto Klemperer.
  Mozart: Don Giovanni

October 7-15, November 23-24. EMI Studio No. 1.
 Eberhard Wächter (baritone)..........................Don Giovanni
 Joan Sutherland (soprano)............................Donna Anna
 Luigi Alva (tenor).....................................Don Ottavio
 Gottlob Frick (bass).............................. Commendatore
 Elisabeth Schwarzkopf (soprano)......................Donna Elvira
 Giuseppe Taddei (baritone)............................. Leporello
 Piero Cappuccilli (baritone)..............................Masetto
 Graziella Sciutti (soprano)................................. Zerlina
 Philharmonia Chorus and Orchestra conducted by Carlo Maria Giulini.
  Mozart: Don Giovanni
    NB: Schwarzkopf did not attend the session on
    November 24.
   LP: 33CX1717-20, SAX2369-72, Set SLS5083, Set 3605, Set S-3605,
   33FCX875-8, SAXF192-5, C91059-62, STC91059-62, 1C 137 100 504-3,
   Set 100504-3, 33WCX518-21, SAXW9503-6, 1C 165 00 504-7, 1C 181 00
   504-7, 2C 165 00 504-7, OS5331-4. C: Set TC-SLS5083, 4X3X3605. CD:
   Set CDS7 47260-8, Set CDCC47260, Set 7472608-4, Set 667 747 260-8.
   Excerpts on LP: 33CX1918, SAX2559, SXLP30300, ASD3915,
   YKM5002, S-36948, Set S-3754, STC80714, 1C 061 02 056, 1C 037 03
   069, AV34038, 1020 561. C: TC-SXLP30300, TC-ASD3915, EG7
   63078-4, 1C 237 03 069, 1C 261 763 078-4, 102056-1. CD: CDC7
   43950-2, CDM7 63078-2, CMS7 63747-2, 747950-2, 567 747 950-2,
   763078-2, 555 763 078-2.

December 19, 21, 23. EMI Studio No. 1. Gerald Moore (piano).
 Wolf: Italienisches Liederbuch
  LP: 33CX1714, SAX2366, 35883, S-35883, EAC40100, Set AA9539-42.
December 23.
 Wolf: Der Genesene an die Hoffnung

1960

Late 1959 and early 1960 was a busy period for Elisabeth Schwarzkopf, even by her own highly industrious standards. In the New Year she was in Vienna for two performances of *Rosenkavalier* and one of *Don Giovanni*, both conducted by Heinrich Hollreiser, and a single performance of *Le nozze di Figaro* under Karajan. She travelled to the United States, via a television appearance in Montreal, and remained in America until the end of March, fulfilling a demanding schedule of recital and concert engagements. This time there were no stage appearances. The Handel items with Paray are the only souvenir of that visit. 'I have some photos where we look so genuinely delighted with one another, so I think we both must have liked it very much, and so did the public, no doubt.'

From early April she was back in Europe for more concert and recital performances. In May she spent almost the whole of her time with the Vienna State Opera. There were performances of *Le nozze di Figaro* under Karajan and *Così fan tutte* under Böhm; she took the role of the Countess in Strauss's *Capriccio* on stage for the first time in a new production under Böhm and there were two more performances of *Rosenkavalier* under André Cluytens and Hollreiser.

At the end of the month there was a special occasion. In 1952 she had sung the soprano part in the last movement of Mahler's Fourth Symphony with the Concertgebouw Orchestra conducted by Bruno Walter. Walter was now poised to conduct his farewell performance in Vienna with the Vienna Philharmonic, and he asked her not only to sing in Mahler's Fourth, but also to perform three other Mahler songs in the same concert. There was a connection between the two artists in that Walter was Maria Ivogün's great mentor, and he felt that he should convey his knowledge of Mahler to an Ivogün pupil. Together Walter and Schwarzkopf went through all the Mahler songs for soprano, with Walter at the piano. Elisabeth felt that hers was not a Mahler voice, with the exception of the Fourth Symphony, which needed a lighter timbre. At the concert she was conscious that she hurried one or two bars in the Fourth Symphony, and as for the three songs, 'No, no, no, I wasn't at all happy. It wasn't the tension of the occasion, I knew it was not for my voice. I could have said no, but with Bruno Walter one doesn't say no. Besides, I didn't know it with my brains. I knew it with my instinct that it was quite beyond me, but I thought nevertheless something might come out which was of value.'

On the very next day after the Mahler concert she was back in the Musikvereinsaal for another concert. This time it was with the Philharmonia Orchestra on a Viennese visit under Giulini, and the repertoire, Strauss's *Vier leztze Lieder*, brought her back to home ground.

She sang on a number of occasions with Jacqueline Bonneau in Paris, and remembers one of the songs sung in the Strasbourg recital. 'A French accompanist for German Lieder who didn't speak German is quite some undertaking, but she did it respectably and very well. We took a very fast tempo for *Auf dem Wasser zu singen* – oh dear, oh dear, that will be full of 'h's I am sure – a very fast little brook – maybe we found that tempo right at the time. She was nice and comfortable and friendly, and we rehearsed a lot, even with Walter [Legge].'

At Salzburg this was the year when *Rosenkavalier* was filmed, and there were some disturbing behind-the-scenes machinations and disputes before Schwarzkopf's itinerary was finally settled. In the event she gave four performances of *Don Giovanni* under Karajan, four of *Così fan tutte* under Böhm, and just one of *Rosenkavalier* with Karajan, without any stage rehearsal, before the production was filmed. The soundtrack was recorded over two mornings. Dame Elisabeth remembers, somewhat wryly, that the only part of the score which Karajan repeated was the orchestral passage at the beginning of Act 3. The filming, in a series of single 'takes' lasting the length of each reel, was undertaken as a second stage in proceedings. The singers used half voices throughout and did their best to synchronise with the soundtrack.

Dame Elisabeth finds some fault with the film's visual production, since in a Hofmannsthal comedy it should be possible to see the characters reacting to one another, whereas the camera tends to concentrate on the face of whoever is singing at a given time. Nevertheless, she feels that the film provides a more mature portrayal of the Marschallin than the 1956 recording, and it created goodwill for her in many countries.

In September Schwarzkopf took part in Viennese performances of *Capriccio*, *Don Giovanni* and *Rosenkavalier*, and then spent her by now customary spell with the San Franciso Opera. She sang in *Rosenkavalier* under Silvio Varviso, in *Così fan tutte* under Kurt Herbert Adler, and in *Le nozze di Figaro* under Krips. And as usual the San Francisco productions moved on briefly to Los Angeles. With the Dallas Civic Opera she then sang two performances of Donna Elvira under Nicola Rescigno, and there were several recitals in which she was accompanied by John Wustman. As in the previous year, there is just one brief souvenir of her US visit in brief excerpts from a New York concert performance of Handel's *Hercules*. Then at the end of the year it was back to Vienna for more performances of *Rosenkavalier, Capriccio* and *Così fan tutte*.

February 18. Ford Auditorium, Detroit. Detroit Symphony Orchestra conducted by Paul Paray.
>   NB: This concert did not take place in 1962, as some
>   sources suggest.
>   Handel: Giulio Cesare – V'adoro, pupille; Hercules – My father
>   *LP: Rococo 5374.*

May 29. Musikvereinsaal, Vienna. Vienna Philharmonic Orchestra conducted by Bruno Walter.
>   Mahler: Des Knaben Wunderhorn – No. 9, Wo die schönen Trompeten
>   blasen
>   Mahler: Rückert Lieder – No. 1, Ich atmet' einen linden Duft; No. 4, Ich
>   bin der Welt abhanden gekommen
>   *LP: Bruno Walter Society Set BWS705, Discocorp RR537, Discocorp Set*
>   *RR208. CD: Discocorp Set CD705, Verona 27075, Music and Arts*
>   *5OC37-7914-5.*
>   Mahler: Symphony No. 4
>   *LP: Bruno Walter Society Set BWS705. CD: Discocorp Set CD705,*
>   *Verona 27075, Music and Arts 5OC37-7914-5, Wing Discs WCD1-2.*

June 15. Palais des Fêtes, Strasbourg. Jacqueline Bonneau (piano).
>   Schubert: *An die Musik, D547; *Auf dem Wasser zu singen, D774;
>   *Fischerweise, D881; Rosamunde, D797 – Der Vollmond strahlt;
>   *Claudine von Villa Bella, D239 – Liebe schwärmt auf allen Wegen;
>   Der Einsame, D800; Seligkeit, D433; *Du bist die Ruh', D776
>   Wolf: Herr, was trägt der Boden hier; †St Nepomuks Vorabend; †Nun lass
>   uns Frieden schliessen; In dem Schatten meiner Locken; Wiegenlied
>   im Sommer; *Geh, Geliebter, geh jetzt; †Mausfallen Sprüchlein
>   Strauss: †Freundliche Vision, Op. 48 No. 1; Ruhe, meine Seele, Op. 27 No.
>   1; Zueignung, Op. 10 No. 1; †Schlechtes Wetter, Op. 69 No. 5
>   *CD: Chant du Monde LDC278899. Items marked * are on Nota Blu*
>   *93.50911-2. Items marked † are on Nota Blu 93.50923-4.*

July 27. Landestheater, Salzburg.
>   Elisabeth Schwarzkopf (soprano)............................. Fiordiligi
>   Christa Ludwig (mezzo-soprano)............................. Dorabella
>   Graziella Sciutti (soprano)..................................Despina
>   Waldemar Kmentt (tenor)................................. Ferrando
>   Hermann Prey (baritone)................................Guglielmo
>   Karl Dönch (baritone)................................. Don Alfonso
>   Vienna State Opera Chorus and Vienna Philharmonic Orchestra conducted
>   by Karl Böhm.
>   Mozart: Così fan tutte

LP: Movimento Musica Set 03.026, Melodram Set MEL708. Excerpts on
LP: Melodram Set MEL082, Melodram Set MEL088. CD: Melodram
MEL16501, Gala GL100501.

August 3. Altes Festspielhaus, Salzburg.
Eberhard Wächter (baritone)..........................Don Giovanni
Leontyne Price (soprano)............................... Donna Anna
Elisabeth Schwarzkopf (soprano)......................Donna Elvira
Cesare Valletti (tenor)................................Don Ottavio
Walter Berry (bass).................................... Leporello
Graziella Sciutti (soprano)................................. Zerlina
Rolando Panerai (baritone)................................Masetto
Nicola Zaccaria (bass)............................... Commendatore
Vienna State Opera Chorus, Vienna Philharmonic Orchestra conducted by
Herbert von Karajan.
    Mozart: Don Giovanni
        LP: Historical Recording Enterprises Set HRE274-3, Movimento Musica
        Set 03.001, Murray Hill Set C6007, Paragon DSV52010-1. CD:
        Movimento Musica Set 013.6012, Curcio OP6.

August 6. Neues Festspielhaus, Salzburg.
Elisabeth Schwarzkopf (soprano).................Die Feldmarschallin
Otto Edelmann (bass)...................................Baron Ochs
Sena Jurinac (soprano)......................................Octavian
Alfred Poell (baritone)...................................... Faninal
Anneliese Rothenberger (soprano)............................Sophie
Judith Hellwig (soprano)...............................Leitmetzerin
Renato Ercolani (tenor)................................... Valzacchi
Hilde Rössl-Majdan (contralto)...............................Annina
Erich Majkut (tenor)...................... Marschallin's Majordomo
Siegfried Frese (tenor)........................Faninal's Majodomo
Alois Pernerstorfer (bass-baritone) ....Police Commissioner
Josef Knapp (baritone) .... Notary
Giuseppe Zampieri (tenor)...........................Italian Tenor
Fritz Sperlbauer (tenor)................................Landlord
Vienna State Opera Chorus, Vienna Philharmonic Orchestra conducted by
Herbert von Karajan
    Strauss: Der Rosenkavalier
        CD: Hunt Set KAR227.

August. Neues Festspielhaus, Salzburg.
Elisabeth Schwarzkopf (soprano).................Die Feldmarschallin
Otto Edelmann (bass)...................................Baron Ochs
Sena Jurinac (soprano)......................................Octavian
Alfred Poell (baritone)..................................... Faninal
Anneliese Rothenberger (soprano)............................Sophie
Judith Hellwig (soprano)...............................Leitmetzerin
Renato Ercolani (tenor)....................................Valzacchi
Hilde Rössl-Majdan (contralto)...............................Annina
Erich Majkut (tenor)...................... Marschallin's Majordomo

Siegfried Frese (tenor)...........................Faninal's Majodomo
Alois Pernerstorfer (bass-baritone)................Police Commissioner
Josef Knapp (baritone).....................................Notary
Giuseppe Zampieri (tenor)............................Italian Tenor
Fritz Sperlbauer (tenor)...................................Landlord
Vienna State Opera Chorus, Vienna Philharmonic Orchestra conducted by
Herbert von Karajan
    Strauss: Der Rosenkavalier
    VHS Video: Rank 7015E.

August 13. Mozarteum, Salzburg. Gerald Moore (piano).
    Schubert: Fischerweise, D881; Seraphine an ihr Klavier, D342; Das Lied
       im Grünen, D917; Seligkeit, D433.
    CD: Stradivarius STR10009.

December 2. Town Hall, New York. Chester Ludgin (baritone), Christa Ludwig
    (mezzo-soprano), Richard Verreau (bass), Walter Berry (bass), John Parella
    (bass), American Opera Society Chorus and Orchestra conducted by Nicola
    Rescigno.
    Handel: Hercules – Daughter of Gods; How blest the maid; Ah, think what
       ills
    LP: Discocorp Set RR208.

1961

In mid-January Elisabeth and Gerald Moore started on a new LP collection, entitled 'Hugo Wolf: Songs from the Romantic Poets'. The programme
as it later appeared on the published record was divided into three sections,
which comprised *Alte Weisen*, a group of six Gottfried Keller settings, six
songs for a female voice and four more Goethe Lieder. After carrying out
mainly concert engagements in France, Germany and England, including
a performance of Brahms's *Deutsches Requiem* on 3 March, Schwarzkopf
went back to the USA for a stay of just over a month. Again it was the
concert hall rather than the opera house on which her activities were
centred. She was back in London in late April for another concert with
Klemperer, which this time included Mahler's Fourth Symphony. Sessions
for the Brahms *Requiem*, Bach's *St Matthew Passion* and Mahler's Second
and Fourth Symphonies continued this year in her absence, usually
supervised by Walter Legge, although there were sessions for each work
where she was very much a participant.

There were a number of personnel problems involved in the Bach
recording, and many editing sessions. 'Walter was beside himself. Satur-

day, Sunday, every day listening to the *Matthew Passion*. I don't think he could suffer any *Matthew Passion* again in his life, after that. To get the right takes, all those sequences, and what goes where – it was gruesome.'

To be present for only part of a recording, and not to be able to experience the work as a whole, except later in an associated concert performance, was something she was able to take in her stride. 'One is a professional, and delivers as one would deliver always. Perhaps in a concert one puts in something more of a projecting quality of expression and sound – I don't mean loudness, I mean projection, which is different from loudness. In my case I was certainly different in a hall with an audience, although I did not ever cater for the audience. It was not disregard for them, but I was so aware that they would get more if I concentrated one hundred per cent on the music. No, I gave up catering for the audience quite early in my life. It may have looked as if I did it that way, because you can't sing other than to the audience, you see – you can't turn round. The conductor has the great advantage of being able to turn his back to the audience, and not having to look in their faces, which we have to do. Somebody reading newspapers in Rome; ladies in Turin waving their fans in different tempi – it is very disconcerting. Naturally in the song repertoire there are things which go directly to somebody or to some people, but you can't sing other than in the direction of the audience. Maybe they will think it was sung to them personally. It wasn't ever, no.'

During May she sang in five performances of *Rosenkavalier* under Böhm at La Scala. Part of June was spent with the Vienna State Opera, where she sang in productions of *Don Giovanni, Capriccio, Così fan tutte*, and *Rosenkavalier*. The performance of *Figaro* recorded live under Giulini was one of four given in Amsterdam, Rotterdam and The Hague. She gave eleven performances in Salzburg this year. There was a Lieder recital with Gerald Moore once more, and performances of *Rosenkavalier* and *Così fan tutte*, both under Böhm.

For some time now her operatic repertoire had been fined down to just a few roles – Donna Elvira, Fiordiligi, the Contessa in *Figaro*, the Marschallin, Countess Madeleine and Alice Ford. In September it was *Così, Rosenkavalier* and *Figaro* at the Vienna State Opera, and during a November stay in the USA there were performances of *Così* and *Don Giovanni* at the Chicago Lyric Opera. The year ended once more in Vienna, with *Così, Capriccio* and *Rosenkavalier*.

January 15. EMI Studio No. 1. Gerald Moore (piano).
> Wolf: Singt mein Schatz wie ein Fink; Du milchjunger Knabe
>> LP: 33CX1946, SAX2589, Set SLS5197, 36308, AA8078, Set AA9539-42.
> Wolf: Tretet ein, hoher Krieger

January 15-16.
    Wolf: Das Kohlerweib ist trunken
January 16.
    Wolf: Mausfallen Sprüchlein
        LP: 33CX1946, SAX2589, Set SLS5197, 36308, EAC70223, AA8078, Set
        AA930258, Set AA9539-42. C: EG7 63653-4. CD: Set CMS7 63790-2,
        CDM7 63653-2.
    Wolf: Wandl'ich in dem Morgentau
        LP: 33CX1946, SAX2589, Set SLS5197, 36308, AA8078, Set AA9539-42.
    Wolf: Morgentau
        LP: 33CX1946, SAX2589, Set SLS5197, 36308, AA8078. C: EG7
        63653-4. CD: Set CMS7 63790-2, CDM7 63653-2.
    Wolf: Wie glänzt der helle Mond
January 17.
    Wolf: Die Spinnerin; Das Vöglein
        LP: 33CX1946, SAX2589, Set SLS5197, 36308, AA8078, Set AA9539-42.
        C: EG7 63653-4. CD: Set CMS7 63790-2, CDM7 63653-2.
    Wolf: Wiegenlied im Winter
January 18.
    Wolf: Wie glänzt der helle Mond; Wiegenlied im Winter
        LP: 33CX1946, SAX2589, Set SLS5197, 36308, A8078, Set AA9539-42.
        C: EG7 63653-4. CD: Set CMS7 63790-2, CDM7 63653-2. Wie glänzt is
        on LP: Set 1546133. *Wie glänzt is on CD: Nota Blu 93.50923-4.*
    Wolf: Sonne der Schlummerlosen; Wiegenlied im Sommer
January 20.
    Wolf: Sonne der Schlummerlosen
        LP: 33CX1946, SAX2589, Set SLS5197, 36308, AA8078.
    Wolf: Nachtzauber; Die Zigeunerin
January 21.
    Wolf: Die Zigeunerin; Zur Ruh', zur Ruh'!
January 22.
    Wolf: Zur Ruh', zur Ruh'!
    Schubert: Liebe schwärmt auf allen Wegen, D239; Lachen und Weinen,
        D777; Der Jüngling an der Quelle, D300; Du bist die Ruh', D776
January 30.
    Wolf: Der Schäfer
        LP: 33CX1946, SAX2589, Set SLS5197, 36308, AA8078.
    Wolf: Als ich auf dem Euphrat schiffte
    Brahms: Von ewiger Liebe, Op. 43 No. 1
    Wagner: Wesendonk Lieder – No. 4, Schmerzen; No. 5, Träume
February 14.
    Wagner: Wesendonk Lieder – No. 4, Schmerzen
    Brahms: Von ewiger Liebe, Op. 43 No. 1

April 25. Kingsway Hall. Philharmonia Orchestra conducted by Otto Klemperer.
    Mahler: Symphony No. 4 in G – fourth movement
        LP: 33CX1793, SAX2441, ASD2799, 35829, S-35829, S-60359, Set
        S-3754, 33FCX941, SAXF259, 33QCX10473, STC91191, 1C 063 00 553,
        2C 069 00 553, 2C 165 52 219-26, EAC50035. C: EG7 69672-4,
        100553-4, 245 769 667-4. CD: CDM7 69667-2, 555 769 667-2.

April 26. Kingsway Hall. Philharmonia Orchestra conducted by Otto Klemperer.
Brahms: Ein deutsches Requiem, Op. 45
> NB: Sessions for this work involving Dietrich
> Fischer-Dieskau (baritone), and the Philharmonia
> Chorus and Orchestra also took place on January 2,
> March 21, 23 and 25.

LP: 33CX1781-2, SAX2430-1, Set SLS821, Set 3624, Set S-3624, 33FCX915-6, SAXF233-4, 33QCX10455-6, SAXQ7355-6, STC91224-5, 2C 167 01 295-6, 290279-3, 1C 161 00 545-6, 1C 153 101 295-3, OS3191-2, SCA1117-8, AA8328-9, AA9092-3. C: Set TC-SLS821, 4XS-3624, 290279-5. CD: CDC7 47238-2, CDC47238, 74238-2, 567 747 238-2. Excerpts on LP: Set S-3754.

May 4-6, 8, 10-12. Kingsway Hall. Philharmonia Orchestra conducted by Otto Klemperer.
Bach: St Matthew Passion, BWV244
> NB: Sessions for this work involving other artists
> took place on November 21, 25-26, 1960: January
> 3-4 and April 14-15, 1961. See November 28 for
> complete listing.

July 3. Amsterdam.
Elisabeth Schwarzkopf (soprano)..................Countess Almaviva
Hermann Prey (baritone)...........................Count Almaviva
Giuseppe Taddei (baritone)................................. Figaro
Graziella Sciutti (soprano)................................ Susanna
Stefania Malagu (mezzo-sop).............................Cherubino
Joseph Rouleau (bass).....................................Bartolo
Mimi Aarden (contralto)................................ Marcellina
Frans Vroons (tenor)..................................Don Basilio
Chris Taverne (tenor)................................. Don Curzio
Ge Smith (bass)..Antonio
Wilma Driessen (soprano)............................... Barbarina
Netherlands Chamber Choir, Hague Residentie Orchestra conducted by
Carlo Maria Giulini.
Mozart: Le nozze di Figaro
CD: Verona 27092-4.

October 10. RAI Studios, Naples. Naples Scarlatti Orchestra conducted by Carlo Franci.
Mozart: Ch'io mi scordi di te? ... Non temer, K505; Così fan tutte – Per
pietà, ben mio; Così fan tutte – E amore un ladroncella
CD: Melodram CDM16529.

November 28. Kingsway Hall. Christa Ludwig (mezzo-soprano), Helen Watts (contralto), Peter Pears (tenor), Wilfred Brown (tenor), Nicolai Gedda (tenor), Alfredo Kraus (tenor), Geraint Evans (baritone), Dietrich Fischer-Dieskau (baritone), John Carol Case (baritone), Walter Berry (bass), Hampstead Parish Church Choir, Philharmonia Chorus and Orchestra conducted by Otto Klemperer.

Bach: St Matthew Passion, BWV244
   LP: 33CX1799-1803, SAX2446-50, Set SLS827, Set 3599, Set S-3599,
   33FCX924-8, SAXF243-7, 33QCX10458-62, SAXQ7358-62,
   STC91200-3, 1C 153 01 312-5, 2C 165 01 312-5, OS3120-5, AA9366-9,
   EAC77245-8. C: Set TC-SLS827. CD: Set CMS7 63058-2, Set 653 763
   658-2. Excerpts on LP: 33CX1881, SAX2525, CX5253, SAX5253,
   S-36162, Set S-3754, SMC 81021, E80693-4, 1C 037 00 580. EP:
   SEL1707. C: IC 237 00 580.

1962

1962 was not a particularly prolific recording year for Elisabeth
Schwarzkopf, any more than the previous two years. She was as busy as
ever in concert and operatic appearances, however. In March she went to
the USA for just over a month. There were no stage appearances this time,
but a number of engagements with orchestra and recitals with her current
US accompanist, John Wustman. In June she sang in Vienna State Opera
performances of *Figaro*, *Così fan tutte*, *Rosenkavalier* and *Capriccio*. The
recital in Amsterdam late that month was one of several she gave with
Felix de Nobel as accompanist. 'Oh yes, he was very, very good. He was a
wonderful connoisseur of Hugo Wolf, and Walter and I were astonished to
find someone who had such knowledge.'

The recording of *Die lustige Witwe* followed in July. The Yugoslav
conductor Lovro von Matačić impressed her in operetta; in fact she puts
him in the same class as Ackermann, who had now unfortunately died. 'He
was very Austrian in his approach, insofar as he was a gentleman of
nobility and charm, at all times – a quite different charm from English
charm, it's the Viennese/Austrian charm which is quite apart from anything else, but some of the Yugoslavs had it – they belonged to the 'Alte
Kaiser Reich' of Franz Josef in their education. Walter took voices which
were not necessarily the right ones for Danilo. The first [in the 1953
recording] was Kunz, our most beloved Figaro and Leporello for many,
many years, the second was another baritone, Wächter. So they had to sing
other notes than are prescribed sometimes, but in operetta you can go
lower, if the personality warrants it. You can do it in opera only in very
few places, but in operetta you do it all the time, if there's a great
personality, with grace and wit and charm.'

Her only operatic appearances at the Salzburg Festival this year were
in *Così fan tutte*, though she gave the by now customary recital with Gerald
Moore and also sang Strauss's *Vier letzte Lieder* with the young István

Kertész conducting. Hard on the heels of Salzburg came the commercial recording of *Così*. There were cast changes, some necessitated by contractual obligations, but Christa Ludwig was fortunately able to take the part of Dorabella. 'Christa was the continuous Dorabella of all time. She did it with so many Fiordiligis in her life. She knew it all, she had this incredible talent to scale her voice down to suit a smaller voice, which mine was plainly – smaller than hers. And with whoever she sang it, she never used a big Wagnerian voice in *Così*, and it is a big achievement to be able to scale a voice down and retain all the timbre and all the sound and all the beauty of the voice.' Ludwig also enjoyed a non-artistic advantage. 'She was quite tall, so she could always wear slippers. And in a long opera like *Così* we envied her. For us it was four hours on high heels. A terrible predicament, that was.'

On the evening after the last recording session there was a Festival Hall concert performance of *Così*, and within a matter of days Schwarzkopf was on stage at San Francisco in *Rosenkavalier*, with János Ferencsik conducting, and then in *Don Giovanni* under Leopold Ludwig. There was also the usual round of recitals, and then it was back to England and to the EMI studios for more work with Gerald Moore, primarily on the Wolf recital, before a series of *Rosenkavalier* performances at the Théâtre de la Monnaie in Brussels under André Vandernoot.

March 2. Musikstudio Funkhaus, Hannover. Hermann Reutter (piano).
  Schubert: An die Musik, D547; Der Einsame, D800; Seligkeit, D433;
    Gretchen am Spinnrade, D118
  Trad. (arr. Brahms): Deutsches Volkslieder, No. 6 – Da unten im Tale;
    Liebestreu, Op. 3 No. 1; Vergebliches Ständchen, Op. 84 No. 4
  Strauss: Ruhe, meine Seele, Op. 27 No. 1; Wiegenlied, Op. 41 No. 1;
    Meinem Kinde, Op. 37 No. 3; Schlechtes Wetter, Op. 69 No. 5; Hat
    gesagt, bleibt's nicht dabei, Op. 36 No. 3; Zueignung, Op. 10 No. 1
  Wolf: Mignon 1; Mignon 2; Mignon 3; Philine; Kennst du das Land?; Herr,
    was trägt der Boden hier; Bedeckt mich mit Blumen; In dem
    Schatten meiner Locken; Wer rief dich denn?; O, wär dein Haus;
    Wiegenlied im Sommer; Die Zigeunerin; Nachtzauber
  All the above items are on LP: Movimento Musica Set 02.017. CD:
  Movimento Musica Set 051.015. The Brahms and Schubert items are on
  CD: Verona 27075.

March 8. EMI Studio No. 1. Gerald Moore (piano).
  Wolf: Nachtzauber; Der Zigeunerin
March 9.
  Wolf: Hochbeglückt in deiner Liebe; Nimmer will ich dich verlieren
    LP: 33CX1946, SAX2589, Set SLS5197, 36308, S-36308, AA8078.
  Wolf: Als ich auf dem Euphrat schiffte

Schubert: Der Jüngling an der Quelle, D300
March 12.
Schubert: An Sylvia, D891
Trad. (arr. Brahms): Volkskinderlieder – No. 4, Sandmännchen

March 15. Kingsway Hall. Hilde Rössl-Majdan (contralto), Philharmonia Chorus
and Orchestra conducted by Otto Klemperer.
Mahler: Symphony No. 2
NB: Schwarzkopf did not attend sessions for this
work which took place on November 22-24, 1961,
and March 24, 1962.
LP: 33CX1829-30, SAX2473-4, Set SLS806, Set 3634, Set S-3634,
33FCX948-9, SAXF948-9, CCA948-9, STC91268-9, 1C 163 00 570-71,
2C 165 52 519-26, 2C 181 00 570-1, Set 100570-3, AA8098-9,
AA7415-16, SCA1085-6, EAC77257-8. C: EG7 69662-4, 245 769 662-4.
CD: CDM7 69662-2, CDM69662, 555 769 662-2, 100570-2. Excerpts on
LP: Set S-3754.

April 25. Kingsway Hall. Philharmonia Orchestra conducted by Antonio Tonini.
Puccini: Turandot – Tu che di gel sei cinta; Signore ascolta
Verdi: La traviata – Addio del passato
April 27.
Puccini: La bohème – Donde lieta uscì
Rossini: Guillaume Tell – Sombre forêt (sung in Italian)

June 29. Concertgebouw, Amsterdam. Felix de Nobel, piano.
Wolf: Morgentau; Das Vöglein; Wiegenlied im Sommer; Wiegenlied im
Winter; Mausfallen Sprüchlein; Mignon 1; Mignon 2; Mignon 3;
Kennst du das Land?; Wer rief dich denn?; Nun' lass uns Frieden
schliessen; Die Zigeunerin
CD: Verona 27021. C: Verona 427021.

July 2-7, 9, 12. Kingsway Hall.
Elisabeth Schwarzkopf (soprano)......................Hanna Glawari
Eberhard Wächter (baritone)...............................Danilo
Hanny Steffek (soprano)................................. Valencienne
Josef Knapp (baritone)................................... Mirko Zeta
Nicolai Gedda (tenor)...................................... Camille
Kurt Equiluz (tenor).. Cascada
Hans Strohbauer (tenor)...................................... Raoul
Franz Boheim (baritone)..................................... Njegus
Eilidh McNab (soprano).. Dodo
Philharmonia Chorus and Orchestra conducted by Lovro von Matačić.
Lehár: Die lustige Witwe
LP: AN101-2, SAN101-2, Set SLS823, Set 3630, Set S-3630, 2C 153 00
001-2, 2C 181 00 001-2, Set 290797-3, 1C 153 00 001-2, 1C 036 03 192,
EAC47211-2. CD: Set CDS7 47178-8, Set CDCB37178, 667 747 178-8.
Excerpts on LP: ALP2252, ASD2252, SEOM 1, 36340, S-36340,
AV34044, Set S-3754, 1C 187 28 494-5, SME2224. C: 4XS-36340,
4AV34044, 1C 237 03 192. C8: 8XS-36340.

August 8. Alte Festspielhaus, Salzburg.
    Elisabeth Schwarzkopf (soprano)......................... Fiordiligi
    Christa Ludwig (mezzo-soprano)......................... Dorabella
    Hermann Prey (baritone)................................Guglielmo
    Waldemar Kmentt (tenor)............................... Ferrando
    Graziella Sciutti (soprano)...............................Despina
    Karl Dönch (baritone)................................. Don Alfonso
    Vienna State Opera Chorus, Vienna Philharmonic Orchestra conducted by
    Karl Böhm.
    Mozart: Così fan tutte
       CD: Arkadia ADD2 CDMP455, Gala GL100503.

September 10-15, 17-18. Kingsway Hall.
    Elisabeth Schwarzkopf (soprano)......................... Fiordiligi
    Christa Ludwig (mezzo-soprano)......................... Dorabella
    Hanny Steffek (soprano)................................. Despina
    Giuseppe Taddei (baritone)............................. Guglielmo
    Walter Berry (bass).................................... Don Alfonso
    Alfredo Kraus (tenor)....................................Ferrando
    Philharmonia Chorus and Orchestra conducted by Karl Böhm.
    Mozart: Così fan tutte
       LP: AN103-6, SAN103-6, Set SLS5028, Set SLS901, Set 3631, S-3631,
       1C 163 01 182-4. 2C 167 01 182-4, Set 101720-3. C: Set TC-SLS5028.
       CD: Set CMS7 69330-2, Set CDMC69330, Set 769330-2, Set 655 769
       330-2. Excerpts on LP: ALP2265, ASD2265, ASD3915, SXLP30457,
       YKM5002, EMX2099, EMX9519, EH7 63018-1, 36167, S-36167,
       S-36948, Set S-3754, 1C 063 00 838, 27004-1, AV34002. C:
       TC-SXLP30457, TC-ASD3915, 1C 263 00 838, TC2-MOM290891-9,
       TC-EMX2099, EH7 63018-4, 4AV34002. CD: CDM7 62040-2,
       CD-EMX9519, Set CMS7 69128-2, CDH7 63018-2.

December 3. EMI Studio No. 1. Gerald Moore (piano).
    Wolf: Tretet ein, hoher Krieger; Hochbeglückt in diener Liebe
       LP: 33CX1946, SAX2589, Set SLS5197, 36308, S-36308, AA8078. Tretet
       ein is in Set AA9539-42.
    Wolf: Das Köhlerweib ist trunken
December 4.
    Wolf: Als ich auf dem Euphrat schiffte; Nimmer will ich dich verlieren
       LP: 33CX1946, SAX2589, Set SLS5197, 36308, S-36308, AA8078.
    Wolf: Die Zigeunerin; Das Köhlerweib ist trunken.
December 7.
    Wolf: Das Köhlerweib ist trunken
       LP: 33CX1946, SAX2589, Set SLS5197, 36308, S-36308, AA8078, Set
       AA9539-42.
    Wolf: Wiegenlied im Sommer
       LP: 33CX1946, SAX2589, Set SLS5197, 36308, S-36308, AA8078, Set
       AA9539-42. CD: Set CMS7 63790-2, CDM7 63653-2.
    Wagner: Wesendonk Lieder – No. 5, Träume
       LP: SAN255, S-36640, 1C 065 01 861, Set 1546133. C: EG7 63653-4.
       CD: Set CMS7 63790-2, CDM7 63654-2.

Schubert: Der Jüngling an der Quelle, D300
  LP: CX5268, SAX5268, 36345, S-36345, EAC80012, EAC47149-50,
  EAC6017, AA8070. C: EG7 63656-4. CD: Set CMS7 63790-2, CDM7
  63656-2.
Trad. (arr. Brahms): Deutsche Volkslieder – No. 42, In stiller Nacht
Brahms: Wiegenlied, Op. 49 No. 4; Von ewiger Liebe, Op. 43 No. 1

1963

In 1963 Schwarzkopf made only one commercial recording, when she sang
in Giulini's performance of the Verdi *Requiem*. For her there was particular
satisfaction in singing with an admired colleague, Christa Ludwig. In the
work there is a particular need for the soprano and mezzo to match their
voices: 'Christa and I did, to an uncanny degree.' This time there was no
need for Ludwig to scale down her voice!

Once again her performing schedule was full. Highlights of her year
included a début in February at the Paris Opéra-Comique, where she sang
in *Così fan tutte* under Serge Baudo. She also sang in *Rosenkavalier* at the
Paris Opéra under Louis Fourestier. In March and April she took part in
performances of *Don Giovanni* at La Scala, under Hermann Scherchen,
and there was another début, at the Hamburg State Opera, where
Rosenkavalier and *Così fan tutte* were once again paired. In Vienna she
sang most of her specialist parts during several visits this year. There were
two American tours, in the first of which she sang for the first time at the
Hollywood Bowl. This was one of several concerts during 1963 in which
she sang operetta items with Willi Boskovsky conducting. Their first appearance together had been in a March Festival Hall concert, and conductor and
soloist soon developed 'an uncanny togetherness' in performance.

Salzburg followed a familiar pattern, with one of her *Rosenkavalier*
performances under Karajan issued on a pirate label. It was the last year
in which she appeared as a guest with the San Francisco Opera. Performances there included *Capriccio* with Georges Prêtre, whose conducting as
a Frenchman in this very German work she had first admired in Parisian
performances the previous year. The end of the year followed a familiar
pattern in the shape of appearances at the Vienna State Opera.

July 31. Neues Festspielhaus, Salzburg.
  Elisabeth Schwarzkopf (soprano). . . . . .Die Feldmarschallin
  Otto Edelmann (bass). . . . . .Baron Ochs
  Sena Jurinac (soprano). . . . . .Octavian

Karl Dönch (baritone)..Faninal
Anneliese Rothenberger (soprano)............................ Sophie
Judith Hellwig (soprano)...................................Marianne
Renato Ercolani (tenor)................................ Leitmetzerin
Hetty Plümacher (contralto)................................ Annina
Martin Hausler (bass).....................Marschallin's Majordomo
Siegfried Frese (tenor)..........................Faninal's Majordomo
Josef Knapp (baritone).......................................Notary
Regolo Romani (tenor)................................Italian Tenor
Fritz Sperlbauer (tenor)....................................Landlord
Alois Pernerstorfer (bass-baritone)............... Police Commissioner
Vienna State Opera Chorus, Vienna Philharmonic Orchestra conducted by
Herbert von Karajan.
  Strauss: Der Rosenkavalier
    LP: Movimento Musica Set 04.004. T: Discocorp Set RR659.

September 16-21, 23-24. Kingsway Hall. Christa Ludwig (mezzo-soprano),
  Nicolai Gedda (tenor), Nicolai Ghiaurov (bass-baritone), Philharmonia
  Orchestra and Chorus conducted by Carlo Maria Giulini.
  Verdi: Messa da Requiem

1964

This was the year of Walter Legge's break with the Philharmonia Orchestra and his departure from EMI. Although these events did not occur until
April, there were portents enough to make Elisabeth's artistic endeavours
in the studio a struggle even in the early part of the year. The recollections
of her participation in the Klemperer recordings of *Messiah* and *Zauberflöte* give her no pleasure. Legge had looked forward to *Zauberflöte* as his
last great EMI recording, just as the Beecham version of the same opera
had been his first, but it was not to be, and Schwarzkopf completed the
recording simply because she was under contract to do so. In April she
attempted some Lieder sessions with Gerald Moore, but they were abandoned at her request. In September she went to Paris for the recording of
Contes d'Hoffmann, but she was not satisfied with her performance. 'I
didn't care for it much, because I was not a genuine French singer. I tried,
and thought it was perhaps all right. It wasn't my piece at all, nor was the
voice sufficient for it.' This was her last operatic recording, and the only
occasion when Walter Legge did not produce one of her commercial studio
recordings, apart of course from the wartime Telefunkens.

Her pattern of live performances was a little different this year, and a
little less concentrated. In the early months she sang in *Così fan tutte* in

Barcelona, in *Rosenkavalier* in Vienna, Geneva and Marseilles, and her concert appearances included three in the Festival Hall. In May she paid a brief trip to New Zealand, and her Salzburg performances of Rosenkavalier and *Così* during August were augmented by a concert in which she sang the Strauss *Vier letzte Lieder* with the Berlin Philharmonic under Karajan, as she had on two occasions in May. The Salzburg performance was unfortunately issued on 'pirate' CD editions. 'We transposed the first song as Flagstad had done. It was the only solution at the time, but it cannot have been good. I was in very bad form.'

Her American visit this year took place between late September and mid-December. *Rosenkavalier* performances at San Francisco and Los Angeles under Leitner were followed by several performances of the same opera at the New York Met under Thomas Schippers. This is not a production she remembers with any enthusiasm, but unfortunately the last performance from it has been issued on a 'pirate' CD set. Other appearances included a Wolf recital in New York's Town Hall with Fischer-Dieskau and Moore.

February 24-25, March 12 and 14. Philharmonia Orchestra conducted by Otto
    Klemperer.
      Handel: Messiah
              NB: Sessions for this work involving Grace Hoffman
              (mezzo-soprano), Ursula Böse (contralto), Peter
              Pears (tenor), Nicolai Gedda (tenor), Jerome Hines
              (bass) and the Philharmonia Chorus and Orchestra
              took place on March 9-10, 13, 16-19, July 20-22,
              September 28-29, October 1-2, 8-9, November 2-3.
      LP: AN146-8, SAN146-8, Set RLS915, Set SLS915, Set 3657, Set
      S-3657, CAN146-8, 2C 167 00 036-9, AA9117-9, AA9326-8,
      EAC77252-4. C: Set 4XS-3657. CD: Set CMS7 63621-2. Excerpts on LP:
      ALP2288, ASD2288, 36324, S-36324, Set S-3754, AE34465, SMC80936,
      1C 063 01 430, 2C 061 01 393, 2C 01 393, 101393-1, AA8401. C:
      4XS-36324, 2C 269 01 393, C8: 8XS-36324.

March 24, 26, 31. April 1-4, 6-7. Kingsway Hall.
    Nicolai Gedda (tenor)..................................... Tamino
    Gundula Janowitz (soprano)............................. Pamina
    Walter Berry (bass)..................................... Papageno
    Ruth-Margret Pütz (soprano)............................Papagena
    Gottlob Frick (bass)....................................Sarastro
    Lucia Popp (soprano)...........................Queen of the Night
    Gerhard Unger (tenor).....................Monostatos/First Priest
    Elisabeth Schwarzkopf (soprano)....................... First Lady
    Christa Ludwig (mezzo-soprano).......................Second Lady
    Marga Höffgen (contralto)............................. Third Lady
    Agnes Giebel (soprano)................................. First Boy

Anna Reynolds (soprano). . . . . Second Boy
Josephine Veasey (mezzo-soprano). . . . . Third Boy
Franz Crass (bass). . . . . Speaker/Second Priest/Second Armed Man
Karl Liebl (tenor). . . . . First Armed Man
Philharmonia Chorus and Orchestra conducted by Otto Klemperer.
    Mozart: Die Zauberflöte

April 7. Kingsway Hall. Artists as on September 16-21, 23-24, 1963.
    Verdi: Messa da Requiem
        LP: AN133-4, SAN133-4, Set SLS909, Set 3649, Set S-3649, 1C 165 00
        629-30, 2C 167 00 029-30. C: 4X2X3649, 2C 297 00 029-30. CD: Set
        CDS7 47257-8, CDCB47257. Excerpts on LP: HQS1407, YKM5015.

April 8 and 10. Artists as on March 24 etc.
    Mozart: Die Zauberflöte
        LP: AN137-8, SAN137-9, Set RLS912, Set SLS912, Set 3651, Set
        S-3651, 1C 157 100 031-3, 2C 165 00 031-3. C: 2C 295 00 031-3. CD: Set
        CMS7 69971-2, Set 653 769 971-2. Excerpts on LP: ALP2314, ASD2314,
        ESD1003261, 143547-1, S-36315, 1C 061 100 835-1, 2C 061 100 835-1.
        C: TC-ESD1003261, EG7 69056-4, 143547-4, 4XS-36315, 1C 245 769
        056-4, 1C 261 100 835-4. CD: CDM7 69056-2, CDM7 63451-2, 555 769
        052-2.

April 11. EMI Studio No. 1. Gerald Moore (piano).
    Schubert: Seligkeit, D433; Die Forelle, D550
April 12.
    Schubert: Die Forelle, D433; Wiegenlied, D498
    Strauss: Ruhe, meine Seele, Op. 27 No. 1; Zueignung, Op. 10 No. 1

August 1. Grosses Festspielhaus, Salzburg.
    Elisabeth Schwarzkopf (soprano). . . . . .Die Feldmarschallin
    Otto Edelmann (bass). . . . . .Baron Ochs
    Sena Jurinac (soprano). . . . . .Octavian
    Willy Ferenc (baritone). . . . . .Faninal
    Anneliese Rothenberger (soprano). . . . . Sophie
    Judith Hellwig (soprano). . . . . .Marianne
    Renato Ercolani (tenor). . . . . Leitmetzerin
    Hetty Plümacher (contralto). . . . . .Annina
    Richard van Vrooman (bass). . . . . .Marschallin's Majordomo
    Siegfried Frese (tenor) . . . . .Faninal's Majordomo
    Josef Knapp (baritone). . . . . .Notary
    Ermanno Lorenzi (tenor) . . . . Italian Tenor
    Fritz Sperlbauer (tenor). . . . . .Landlord
    Alois Pernerstorfer (bass-baritone). . . . . Police Commissioner
    Vienna State Opera Chorus, Vienna Philharmonic Orchestra conducted by
    Herbert von Karajan.
    Strauss: Der Rosenkavalier
        CD: Hunt Set CDKAR227.

August 15. Grosses Festspielhaus, Salzburg. Berlin Philharmonic Orchestra
    conducted by Herbert von Karajan.
    Strauss: Vier letzte Lieder, Op. posth.
        *CD: Paragon PDC84008, Virtuoso 2697152, Verona 27075, Nuova Era
        2251-2.*

September 1-5, 9-11. Salle Wagram, Paris.
    Nicolai Gedda (tenor)................................... Hoffmann
    Gianna D'Angelo (soprano)................................Olympia
    Elisabeth Schwarzkopf (soprano)..........................Giuletta
    Victoria de los Angeles (soprano)..........................Antonia
    Christiane Gayraud (mezzo-soprano)..................Voix de la Mère
    Renée Fauré (speaker)................................Stella/Muse
    Jean-Christophe Benoit (baritone)........................Nicklause
    Nikola Guiselev (bass)...................................Lindorf
    George London (bass).........................Coppelius/Dr Miracle
    Ernest Blanc (baritone)................................Dapertutto
    Michel Sénéchal (tenor)............................... Spalanzani
    Jean-Pierre Laffage (baritone)...................... Luther/Schemil
    Robert Geay (bass)......................................Crespil
    André Mallabrera (tenor)................................Nathanaël
    Jacques Pruvost (baritone)............................... Herman
    Jacques Loreau (tenor)...........Andres/Cochenille/Frantz/Pitichinaccio
    Jeannine Collard (mezzo-soprano)........... Second Voice in Barcarolle
    René Duclos Choir, Paris Conservatoire Orchestra conducted by André
    Cluytens.
        Offenbach: Les contes d'Hoffmann
                NB: It would appear that Schwarzkopf was not
                present at sessions held for this work on September
                21-23, October 5 and 22.
        LP: AN154-6, SAN154-6, Set SLS918, Set 3667, Set S-3667,
        SMA91459-61, 1C 157 00 145-7, 1C 157 100 045-3, 100045-3, 2C 167 12
        866-8. C: Set 4X3X-3667. CD: Set CMS7 63222-2, CDMB63222, 763222,
        653 763 222-2. Excerpts on LP: ASD2330, SXLP30538, S-36413,
        AV34077, 1C 063 01 967, 290165-1, 1C 061 101 967-1. C: EG7 63448-4.
        CD: CDM7 63448-2.

December 19. Metropolitan Opera House, New York.
    Elisabeth Schwarzkopf (soprano)..................Die Feldmarschallin
    Otto Edelmann (bass)...............................Baron Ochs
    Lisa della Casa (soprano)...............................Octavian
    Karl Dönch (baritone)...................................Faninal
    Judith Raskin (soprano)..................................Sophie
    Lynn Owen (soprano)................................... Marianne
    Andrea Velis (tenor).....................................Valzacchi
    Gladys Kriese (contralto)................................ Annina
    Norman Scott (bass)..........................Commissary of Police
    Gabor Carelli (bass)................... Feldmarschallin's Major-Domo
    Arthur Graham (tenor)......................Faninal's Major-Domo
    Gerhard Pechner (baritone)...............................Attorney

Charles Anthony (tenor). . . . . .Landlord
Barry Morell (tenor). . . . . .Italian Tenor
Metropolitan Opera Chorus and Orchestra conducted by Thomas Schippers.
    Strauss: Der Rosenkavalier
        CD: Claque Set GM3010-2.

1965

By this time Elisabeth Schwarzkopf and Walter Legge had left London
and were living on the continent. Their recording activities centred on
Berlin, where they worked with a new sound engineer, Johann Matthes.
'Walter knew of Matthes, and respected his work already very highly.
Maybe he thought that another brilliant sound engineer could give new
life to what I did. The physical side of the voice was no longer respect-
able, really. We did some good things, though, but on my side it was
hazy already.'

Highlights of the early part of that year were appearances in *Capriccio*,
Rosenkavalier and *Figaro* at the Vienna State Opera. In February there
was a sequence of *Rosenkavalier* performances at Lyons, and then at the
Théâtre de la Monnaie in Brussels. In early April Schwarzkopf was in the
United States. There were no stage appearances on this visit. She paid
another visit to America in July for a series of concerts, including two in
the Hollywood Bowl with Boskovsky.

Her first recording assignment was in late August, when she embarked
on the first Songbook in partnership with Gerald Moore. With Fischer-Dieskau and Moore she also started work on the Brahms *Deutsche Volkslieder*, which were completed the following month. Also in September
came the second recording of Strauss's *Vier letzte Lieder*, with George Szell.
'Many people maintain the first one is better. It's different of course. The
voice is much younger. I don't think the first one is better, although one
hears in the second that it is a maturer sound, but then the poems are not
poems for a young creature, the poems are that of a mature person. It is
never a girlish sound, it must suggest maturity, if anything. To look back
at all seasons of life, and not be a spring-like noise. No, I'm very satisfied
with that of course, and the main thing is that George Szell was satisfied.
And to satisfy him was really something. He knew so much about singing
– he was a singer's conductor if anyone was – incredible. And of course he
could make every orchestra play as if they were his own Cleveland, or the
Philharmonia for that matter.' In fact Walter Legge had apologised to Szell

that Berlin's premier orchestra, the Philharmonic, was not available. However, as we can hear, the Radio Symphony Orchestra played with great distinction under Szell. Elisabeth ended the year in Belgium, Switzerland and France, where she sang in *Così fan tutte* in Lyon.

August 22-27. Evangelisches Gemeindhaus, Zehlendorf, Berlin. Gerald Moore (piano).

Trad. (arr. Wolf-Ferrari): Quando a letto vo' la sera; Dimmi, bellino mio, com'io ho da dare; Dio ti facesse star tanto digiuno; Vo' fa''na palazzina alla marina; Giovanottino che passi per via; Giovanetti, cantate ore che siete; Vado di notte, come fa la luna
 LP: CX5268, SAX5268, 36345, S-36345, 1C 187 01 307-8, EAC80012, EAC60167, AA8070, SME2012-3. C: EG7 63654-2. CD: Set CMS7 63790-2, CDM7 63654-2.

Trad. (arr. Wolf-Ferrari): Quando sara quel benedetto giorno
 LP: SME2012-3.

Schubert: Seligkeit, D433
 LP: CX5268, SAX5268, 36345, S-36345, 1C 187 01 307-8, EAC80012, EAC60167, AA8070, Set AA930258, EAC70223, EAC47031-41, EAC47083-4, EAC47149-50, EAA176, AA8589.

Schubert: Die Forelle, D550
 LP: CX5268, SAX5268, 36345, S-36345, 1C 187 01 307-8, Set 1546133, EAC80012, AA8070, EAC47031-41, EAC70145, EAC47031-41, EAC40034, EAC47083-4, EAC47149-50, EAC60167, Set AA930258. C: EG7 63656-4. CD: Set CMS7 63790-2, CDM7 63656-2.

Schubert: Der Einsame, D800
 LP: CX5268, SAX5268, 36345, S-36345, 1C 187 01 307-8, Set 1546133, EAC80012, AA8070, EAC47149-50, EAC60167. C: EG7 63656-4. CD: Set CMS7 63790-2, CDM7 63656-2.

Schubert: Liebe schwärmt auf allen Wegen, D239
 LP: CX5268, SAX5268, 36345, S-36345, 1C 187 01 307-8, Set 1546133, EAC80012, AA8070, EAC47149-50, EAC60167.

Schumann: Zwei venezianische Lieder – Leis' rudern hier, Op. 25 No. 17; Wenn durch die Piazzetta, Op. 25 No. 18
 LP: CX5268, SAX5268, ASD3124, 36345, S-36345, 1C 187 01 307-8, 1C 063 02 598, Set 1546133, EAC80012, AA8070, EAC60167. C: EG7 63656-4. CD: Set CMS7 63790-2, CDM7 63656-2.

Wolf: Die Zigeunerin
 LP: CX5268, SAX5268, 36345, S-36345, 1C 187 01 307-8, Set S-3754, EAC80012, AA8070, EAC70223, EAC60167, EAA176, AA8589. C: EG7 63656-4. CD: Set CMS7 63790-2, CDM7 63653-2, Set AA930258.

Wolf: Wenn du zu den Blumen gehst
 LP: CX5268, SAX5268, 36345, S-36345, 1C 187 01 307-8, EAC80012, AA8070, EAC60167. C: EG7 63656-4. CD: Set CMS7 63790-2, CDM7 63653-2.

Debussy: Mandoline
 LP: CX5268, SAX5268, 36345, S-36345, Set 1546133, EAC80012, EAC60167, AA8070. C: EG7 63656-4. CD: Set CMS7 63790-2, CDM7 63654-2.

Schumann: Widmung, Op. 25 No. 1
  LP: CX5268, SAX5268, ASD3124, 36345, S-36345, 1C 187 01 307-8, 1C
  063 02 598. EAC80012, EAC60167, AA8070, Set AA93028, EAC70145,
  EAC47031-41, EAC47083-4.
Schumann: Wie mit innigstem Behagen, Op. 25 No. 9
  LP: ASD2634, 36752, S-36752, EAC60169. C: EG7 63656-4. CD: Set
  CMS7 63790-2, CDM7 63656-2.

August 28-30. Evangelisches Gemeindhaus, Zehlendorf, Berlin. Dietrich
  Fischer-Dieskau (baritone), Gerald Moore (piano).
  Trad. (arr. Brahms): Deutsche Volkslieder, Nos. 1-42

September 1-3. Grünewald Church, Berlin. Berlin Radio Symphony Orchestra
  conducted by George Szell.
  Strauss: Vier letzte Lieder, Op. posth.
    LP: CX5258, SAX5258, ASD2888, 36347, S-36347, 1C 063 00 608, 1C
    065 100 608-1, 1C 567 747 276-2, 2C 065 00 608, 2C 069 00 608,
    100608-1, AA8058, EAC85021. C: 2C 269 00 608. CD: CDC7 47276-2,
    CDC47276, 747276-2, 567 747 276-2.
  Strauss: Zueignung, Op. 10 No. 1; Freundliche Vision, Op. 48 No. 1; Die
    heiligen drei Könige, Op. 56 No. 6; Muttertänderlei, Op. 43 No. 2;
    Waldseligkeit, Op. 49 No. 1
    LP: CX5258, SAX5258, ASD2888, 36347, S-36347, 1C 063 00 608, 1C
    065 100 608-1, 1C 567 747 276-2, 2C 065 00 608, 2C 069 00 608,
    100608-1, AA8058. C: 2C 269 00 608. CD: CDC7 47276-2, CDC47276.

September 6-11. Evangelisches Gemeindhaus, Zehlendorf, Berlin. Dietrich
  Fischer-Dieskau (baritone), Gerald Moore (piano).
  Trad. (arr. Brahms): Deutsche Volkslieder, Nos. 1-42
    LP: AN163-4, SAN163-4, Set 3675, Set S-3675, SMAC91487-8, 1C 193
    00 054-5, 1C 153 00 054-5. CD: Set CDS7 49525-2, Set 667 749 525-2.
    Excerpts on LP: Set 1546133. No. 42 on C: EG7 63654-2. CD: Set CMS7
    63790-2, CDM7 63654-2.
September 12-13.
  Wolf: Italienisches Liederbuch

1966

At the beginning of the year Schwarzkopf travelled to the USA. Her stay
was to be a long one, lasting until early April. It was during this visit that
she made her only commercial recording in America, and her only recording for CBS. Glenn Gould wanted to accompany her in a short programme
of Strauss songs. In the event there were problems, since Gould continually
improvised on Strauss's written accompaniments. 'While we [Elisabeth

and Walter Legge] were listening [to playbacks] in the recording booth he did not come in with us, and played on, with fingerless gloves and a coat on and was fantasising all the time, never hearing with us what he had done. We couldn't even discuss with him. He couldn't do it in the *Ophelia* songs, that's why we allowed them. We tried other songs, but I have not allowed them to be published, because he was playing pure fantasy with *Morgen* and what have you – he said that the printed notes were "shorthand writing" for what Strauss really meant.'

Soon after she returned from America, Schwarzkopf and Fischer-Dieskau worked together on Wolf's *Italienisches Liederbuch*. The baritone was now under contract to DG, and in return for 'loaning' him to EMI an arrangement was made for Elisabeth and Fischer-Dieskau to record the *Spanisches Liederbuch* for DG a few months later. Work also began on the second Songbook, and here the pianist was Geoffrey Parsons. Gerald Moore was about to retire and Parsons was being groomed as his successor as Schwarzkopf's accompanist on record – he had already accompanied her in a number of public recitals. 'Walter could exert all the teaching he had in mind, because Geoffrey took it all freely, and lapped it all up – and could do it technically. Some people can't because they are not in love with the piano. It was a very happy partnership.'

In May and June there were performances of *Così* at Drottningholm, and *Rosenkavalier* at the Paris Opéra. In July there was a brief trip to New York for a Carnegie Hall recital with John Wustman, and a concert in the Stravinsky Festival, where Elisabeth sang excerpts from *The Rake's Progress* and took part in a performance of the complete *Pulcinella* ballet music under Lukas Foss. In August she returned to the Kingsway Hall, where she worked with an old conductor colleague, Alceo Galliera, but with a new orchestra, the London Symphony. They recorded 'Tatiana's Letter Scene' from Tchaikovsky's *Eugene Onegin* in German. 'It's OK, I think, for a German singer. I was trying to do it at one point in Russian. Slava Richter was trying to teach me, but it was no good. I can't just do a parrot thing: I did it once in Helsinki with *Luonnotar*, but that isn't the same as Russian, and hasn't the same emotional content.'

Later that year Schwarzkopf sang in *Rosenkavalier* at the Stockholm Royal Opera, and one of the performances has been issued on a 'pirate' edition. In the context of some stagings she had to endure she remarks that 'it was a nice, normal performance, thank God, where the scenery was in unison with what was happening on the stage'. David Oistrakh and his wife were present at one of the performances. Elisabeth then sang in *Rosenkavalier* at the Gran Teatro in Barcelona, and there were also performances of *Così* at the Théâtre de la Monnaie in Brussels.

January 14. New York City. Glenn Gould (piano).
> Strauss: Lieder der Ophelia, Op. 67 Nos. 1-3
> > LP: CBS 76983, CBS Set M2X35914, Japanese CBS 46DC5304-5. CD:
> > Sony Set CD52657, Sony Set SM2K52657.
> Strauss: Heimliche Aufforderung, Op. 27 No. 3; Morgen, Op. 27 No. 4; Wer
> > lieben will, Op. 49 No. 7; Winterweihe, Op. 48 No. 4

April 10-17. Evangelisches Gemeindhaus, Zehlendorf, Berlin. Dietrich
Fischer-Dieskau (baritone), Gerald Moore (piano).
> Wolf: Italienisches Liederbuch

April 21-29. Evangelisches Gemeindhaus, Zehlendorf, Berlin. Geoffrey Parsons
(piano).
> Mahler: Rückert Lieder – No. 1, Ich atmet' einen linden Duft; Des Knaben
> > Wunderhorn – No. 6, Des Antonius von Padua Fischpredigt; No. 10,
> > Lob des hohen Verstandes
> > LP: ASD2404, S-36545, 1C 187 01 307-8, EAC60168, AA-8602,
> > EAC80013. Nos. 1 and 10 are on Set 6072, No. 6 is on Set S-3754. Nos.
> > 1 and 6 are on C: EG7 63654-4. CD: Set CMS7 63790-2, CDM7 63654-2.
> Strauss: Ach, was Kummer, Op. 49 No. 8; Wer lieben will, Op. 49 No 7;
> > Meinem Kinde, Op. 37 No. 3
> > LP: ASD2404, S-36545, 1C 187 01 307-8, EAC60168, AA-8602,
> > EAC80013. Meinem Kinde is on C: EG7 63656-4. CD: Set CMS7
> > 63790-2, CDM7 63656-2.
> Wolf: Verborgenheit; Nimmersatte Liebe; Selbstgeständnis
> > LP: ASD2404, S-36545, 1C 187 01 307-8, EAC80013, EAC60168,
> > AA-8602. Verborgenheit is on Set S-3754.
> Schubert: An mein Klavier, D342
> > LP: ASD2404, S-36545, 1C 187 01 307-8, Set 1546133, EAC60168,
> > AA-8602, EAC47149-50, EAC80013, Set AA930258. C: EG7 63656-4.
> > CD: Set CMS7 63790-2, CDM7 63656-2.
> Schubert: Erlkönig, D328
> > LP: ASD2404, S-36545, Set S-3754, 1C 187 01 307-8, Set 1546133,
> > EAC800133, AA930258, EAC60168, AA-8602, EAC47149-50. C: EG7
> > 63656-4. CD: Set CMS7 63790-2, CDM7 63656-2.
> Wolf: Das verlassene Mägdlein; Gesang Weylas
> Schubert: Geheimnis, D491; Hänflings Liebeswerbung, D552

September 16-17. London Symphony Orchestra conducted by Alceo Galliera.
> Tchaikovsky: Eugene Onegin – Tatiana's Letter Scene (sung in German)
> > LP: CX5286, SAX5286, Set SXDW3049, 36464, S-36464, AV34009, 1C
> > 181 52 291-2, 2C 181 52 291-2, 152291-3. C: Set TC-SXDW3049, EG7
> > 69501-4, 4AV34009, 245 769 501-4. CD: CDM7 69501-2, CDM69501,
> > 79501-2, 545 769 501-2.

November 5. Opera House, Stockholm.
> Elisabeth Schwarzkopf (soprano)................Die Feldmarschallin
> Arne Tyren (bass)......................................Baron Ochs
> Elisabeth Söderström (soprano)...........................Octavian
> Mattiwilda Dobbs (soprano)................................Sophie

Erik Sundquist (baritone)................................ Faninal
Ileana Peterson (soprano)............................ Leitmetzerin
Olle Sivall (tenor)...Valzacchi
Margareta Bergström (contralto)........................... Annina
Sven Erik Vikström (tenor).......................... ...... .Italian Tenor
Lars Carlsson (tenor)...................... .Marschallin's Majordomo
Gunnar Lundberg (tenor)...................... .Faninal's Majordomo
Bo Lundborg (bass)..Notary
Anders Naslund (bass)......................... Police Commissioner
Stockholm Opera Chorus and Opera Orchestra conducted by Silvio Varviso.
   Strauss: Der Rosenkavalier
    Excerpts on LP: Legendary LR168.

December 16-17, January 2-10, 1967. Berlin. Dietrich Fischer-Dieskau
   (baritone), Gerald Moore.
   Wolf: Spanisches Liederbuch
     LP: DG SLPM139329-30, DG 2726 071, DG 2707 035, DG 413
     226-1GX2. C: DG 3372 071, DG 413 226-4GX2. CD: DG 423 934-2GGA2.

1967

The early part of 1967 was taken up with the last *Spanisches Liederbuch* sessions, and then Schwarzkopf took over a recital in Zürich for an indisposed Teresa Berganza. There were also concerts in Salzburg and Rome before preparations took place for the Gerald Moore farewell concert at the Festival Hall.

The idea for this event had been conceived in Walter Legge's fertile brain, but alas he was hampered by physical infirmity, since he had suffered a heart attack three weeks before the concert was due. He sat in a Zürich hospital with 'great heaps of duets and trios', and completed preparations with a secretary sitting by. He was allowed to travel to London for the event, but only by train, since he was forbidden to fly. At rehearsals he forgot his condition and was running up and down stairs at the Hall. After the concert he suffered a second, though less severe attack in the middle of the night, and had to be rushed to hospital in London. Elisabeth's burden was compounded by the fact that she was in essence the concert's hostess, and had to accommodate the two 'guest' singers in the choice of repertoire. Nevertheless, she still felt it to be a memorable concert, and it was of course a unique gesture to honour an accompanist in this way.

Soon after the this concert Elisabeth embarked on an American tour which lasted just under a month. There were no operatic appearances, but a diverse programme of recitals, mostly accompanied by Martin Isepp, and concerts. Miami, Chicago, New Orleans and Los Angeles were among the centres visited, and there were two concert performances of Gluck's *Orfeo* under Jonel Perlea in Carnegie Hall. After a brief visit to Scandinavia Schwarzkopf stayed nearer home for her recitals, and then returned to the USA in July for two performances of *Rosenkavalier* with the Cincinatti Summer Opera. She remembers Mildred Miller as a particularly good Octavian. An extended tour of Australia and New Zealand followed, from mid-July until early September. Her accompanist in Australia was Geoffrey Parsons, who was making a return trip to his native land. After the completion of the *Italienisches Liederbuch* recording in early October Schwarzkopf gave a recital with Parsons in Ascona, which was recorded and issued on a 'pirate' edition. She does not care for the performances on this CD, which were made routine by the 'impossible acoustics', and she regrets that they have been made available. Recording sessions with Parsons in late October saw the completion of the second Songbook and the beginning of work on the third. In late November she appeared twice in *Rosenkavalier* in Lyon, and the year ended with more performances of the same work at the Théâtre de la Monnaie.

February 20. Royal Festival Hall, London, SE1. Gerald Moore (piano). Live recording from Gerald Moore's farewell recital.
> Mozart: (a) La partenza, K436; (b) Più non si trovano, K549
> > (with Victoria de los Angeles, soprano, Dietrich Fischer-Dieskau, baritone).
>
> Rossini: Les soirées musicales – (c) No. 9, La regata veneziana; (d) No. 10, La pesca; (e) Duetto buffo di due gatti
> > (with Victoria de los Angeles, soprano).
>
> Schumann: (f) Spanisches Liederspiel, Op. 74 – No. 4, In der Nacht; (g, h, i) Vier Duette, Op. 78, Nos. 1-3
> > (with Dietrich Fischer-Dieskau, baritone).
>
> Wolf: (j) Kennst du das Land?; (k) Sonne der Schlummerlosen; (l) Das verlassene Mägdlein; (m) Die Zigeunerin
>
> Haydn: (n) An den Vetter; (o) Daphnens einziger Fehler
> > (with Victoria de los Angeles, soprano, Dietrich Fischer-Dieskau, baritone).
>
> LP: AN182-3, SAN182-3, Set SLS926, 1C 165 100 068-3. Items (b), (c), (d), (e), (g), (h), (k), (l), (m), (n) and (o) are on LP: ASD143594-1, C: TC-ASD143594-4. Items (a), (b), (c), (d), (e), (f), (g), (h), (i), (n), (o) are on LP: 2C 069 01 678. Items (b), (c), (d), (e), (g), (h), (j), (k), (l), (m), (n) and (o) are on CD: CDC7 49238-2, CD-EMX2233, 567 749 238-2.

September 27 – October 3. Evangelisches Gemeindhaus, Zehlendorf, Berlin.
  Dietrich Fischer-Dieskau (baritone), Gerald Moore (piano).
    Wolf: Italienisches Liederbuch
      LP: SAN210-1, Set SLS937, Set S-3703, 1C 165 01 871-2. C: EG7
      63732-4. CD: CDM7 63732-2.

October 10. Saal der Gemeindschule, Ascona, Switzerland. Geoffrey Parsons
  (piano).
    Mozart: Abendempfindung, K523; Das Veilchen, K476; Warnung, K433;
      Ich möchte wohl der Kaiser sein, K539
    Schubert: Der Einsame, D800; An Sylvia, D891; Rosamunde, D797 – Der
      Vollmond strahlt; Seligkeit, D433
    Schumann: Wie mit innigstem Behagen, Op. 25 No. 9; Venezianische
      Lieder – Leis' rudern hier, Op. 25 No. 17, Wenn durch die Piazzetta,
      Op. 25 No. 18; Der Nussbaum, Op. 25 No. 3; Die Kartenlegerin, Op.
      31 No. 2
    Wolf: Kennst du das Land?; Das verlassene Mägdlein; In dem Schatten
      meiner Locken; Trau nicht der Liebe; Wie lange schon war immer;
      Die Zigeunerin
    Wolf-Ferrari: Il canzoniere, Op. 17 – Preghiera
      CD: Ermitage ERM109.

October 24-28. Evangelisches Gemeindhaus, Zehlendorf, Berlin. Geoffrey
  Parsons (piano).
    Mozart: (a) Das Veilchen, K476; (b) Mein Wunsch, K539
    Wolf: (c) Lebewohl
    Schumann: (d) Die Kartenlegerin, Op. 31 No. 2
    Stravinsky: (e) Pastorale
    Mussorgsky: (f) In dem Pilzen
    Tchaikovsky: (g) Pimpinella, Op. 38 No. 6
      All the above items were issued on LP: ASD2404, S-36545, 1C 187 01
      307-8, EAC60168, AA-6802, EAC80013. Items (a) and (b) are on LP: Set
      6072. Item (d) is on LP: Set 1546133. Item (a) is on LP: EAC40034,
      EAC47083-4, EAC47031-41. Item (d) is on C: EG7 63656-4. CD: Set
      CMS7 63790-2, CDM7 63656-2. Item (g) is on C: EG7 63654-4. CD: Set
      CMS7 63790-2, CDM7 63654-2.
October 28.
    Strauss: Lieder der Ophelia, Op. 67 Nos. 1-3
      LP: ASD2634, S-36752, EAC60169, EAC80014, AA-8807. C: EG7
      63656-4. CD: Set CMS7 63790-2, CDM7 63656-2.

1968

The first two months of this year found Schwarzkopf in North America. There were recitals with Geoffrey Parsons in New York's Carnegie Hall and Lincoln Center, as well as elsewhere. Her performances included Mahler's Fourth Symphony with William Steinberg and the Pittsburgh Symphony Orchestra, and two concerts with the Detroit Symphony Orchestra under Sixten Ehrling.

Then it was back to London for the Mahler and Mozart recording sessions with George Szell. Szell found the LSO in a less than perfect state and gave the orchestra a difficult time. On one occasion in the Mahler songs he felt that the harp was out of tune, and despite the player's denial dismissed him instantly. Dame Elisabeth has mixed feelings about the Mozart items: 'You can hear that it is too late, if you have a discerning ear, but it is musically good, fine, but it is not the young voice any more, and for Mozart that is not so good – it should be the voice in fuller bloom.'

In April Schwarzkopf and Parsons undertook their first tour of Japan, lasting just under a month. There were performances in America during July, including items from the Blossom Music Center later issued on 'pirate' labels, and then in August Schwarzkopf and Parsons gave five performances in Buenos Aires (where they experienced 'the best acoustics in the world' in the Colon Theatre) and Rio de Janeiro. The next set of Berlin recording sessions saw the completion of the third Songbook. Performances in Paris, Rome and London completed another busy year. One of the London performances, now issued on a 'pirate' CD, took the form of a centenary tribute to the eminent critic Ernest Newman, who had been Walter Legge's mentor in the 1930s and later a close friend.

March 8-9, 11-12. Kingsway Hall. Dietrich Fischer-Dieskau (baritone), London Symphony Orchestra conducted by George Szell.
  Mahler: Des Knaben Wunderhorn, Nos. 1-10, 13, 14
    LP: SAN218, ASD100098-1, S-36547, 1C 065 00 098, 2C 069 00 098, EAC70200, EAC-163, AA9258-31. C: TCC-ASD100098-4, 2C 269 00 098. CD: CDC7 47277-2, CDC47277, 74277-2, 567 747 277-2. Excerpt on LP: Set S-3754.

March 10-14, 18. Kingsway Hall. London Symphony Orchestra conducted by George Szell.

Mozart: Alma grande e nobil core, K578; Vado ma dove? ... O Dei, K583;
Ch'io mi scordi di te? ... Non temer, K505
(with Alfred Brendel, piano); Nehmt meinem Dank, K383
LP: ASD2493, S-36643, 1C 063 01 959, 2C 069 01 959. C: 2C 269 01
959. CD: CDC7 47950-2, CDH7 63702-2, 747950-2, 567 747 950-2.
Strauss: Meinem Kinde, Op. 37 No. 3; Ruhe, meine Seele, Op. 27 No. 1;
Wiegenlied, Op. 41 No. 1; Morgen, Op. 27 No. 4
(with Edith Peinemann, violin); Das Rosenband, Op. 36 No.1; Das
Bächlein, Op. 88 No. 1; Winterweihe, Op. 48 No. 4
LP: ASD2493, S-36643, 1C 063 01 959, 2C 069 01 959, EAC85021. C:
2C 269 01 959. CD: CDC7 47276-2, CDC47276, 567 747 276-2. Meinem
Kinde is on LP: Set S-3754. C: EG7 63656-4. CD: Set CMS7 63790-2,
CDM7 63656-2. Wiegenlied is on LP: EAC70145.

July 26 or 28. Music Center, Blossom, USA. Cleveland Orchestra conducted by
George Szell.
Mozart: Le nozze di Figaro – Giunse alfin; Don Giovanni – In quali eccessi
... Mi tradi; Così fan tutte – Amor e un androncello
LP: Rococo 5374. CD: Arkadia CDGI745.

October 20-27. Evangelisches Gemeindhaus, Zehlendorf, Berlin. Geoffrey
Parsons (piano).
Liszt: (a) Die drei Zigeuner, G320
Mahler: Lieder und Gesänge aus der Jugendzeit – (b) No. 6, Um schlimme
Kinder artig zu machen
Grieg: (c) Ich liebe dich, Op. 5 No. 3; (d) Mit einer Wasserlilie, Op. 25 No.
4; (e) Letzter Frühling, Op. 33 No. 2
Schubert: (f) Hänflings Liebeswerbung, D552; (g) Ach, um deine feuchten
Schwingen, D717; (h) Was bedeutet die Bewegung? D720
Chopin: 17 Polish Songs, Op. 74 – (i) No. 1, Mädchens Wunsch; (j) No. 16,
Litauisches Lied
Loewe: (k) Kleiner Haushalt, Op. 71
All the above items were issued on LP: ASD2634, S-36752, EAC80014,
EAC60169, AA8807. (f), (g), (h) are on LP: EAC47149-50. (c) is on LP:
EAC40034, EAC70145, EAC47031-41, EAC47083-4. (a), (c), (e), (i) are
in Set AA930258. (b) is on C: EG7 63654-4. CD: Set CMS7 63790-2,
CDM7 63654-2. (f), (g), (h) are on C: EG7 63656-4. CD: Set CMS7
63790-2, CDM7 63656-2. (k) is on C: EG7 63654-4. CD: Set CMS7
63790-2, CDM7 63654-2.
Strauss: Die Nacht, Op. 10 No. 3; All'mein Gedanken, Op. 21 No. 1;
Wiegenliedchen, Op. 49 No. 3
Wolf: Storchenbotschaft; Nun' lass uns Frieden schliessen

December 2. Royal Festival Hall, London SE1. Geoffrey Parsons (piano).
Wolf: Was für ein Lied soll dir gesungen werden; Im Frühling; Phänomen;
Wandl' ich in dem Morgentau; Kennst du das Land?; Wiegenlied im
Sommer; Anakreons Grab; Die Zigeunerin; Sagt, seid Ihres, feiner
Herr; In dem Schatten meiner Locken; Ach, im Maien; O wär dein
Haus; Nein, junger Herr; Wir haben beide lange Zeit

Schubert: Was bedeutet die Bewegung?, D720; Ach, um deine feuchten
  Schwingen, D717; Gretchen am Spinnrade, D118
Strauss: Ophelia Lieder, Op. 67; Meinem Kinde, Op. 37 No. 3; Das
  Rosenband, Op. 36 No. 1; Ach, was Kummer, Op. 49 No. 8
CD: Eklipse AKTRP4.

1969

Schwarzkopf toured the USA during February and March. From April to
June her activities were concentrated in Europe, including a recital at
Nohant, south-west of Paris, which has been issued on a 'pirate' CD. Here
she had a new partner, the pianist Aldo Ciccolini. 'I enjoyed working with
him very much. He had different ideas which I followed gladly. He was a
specialist in fairly modern French music, but he played Schumann won-
derfully well, and for the *Nussbaum* we took gladly, freely, this tempo
which he started. We were startled when he started playing, since it was
ever so much slower than everybody had done it before including me, but
I think it was genuinely right. That tempo which he took really by instinct
or knowledge ... and ours, just by habit, had become faster and faster, and
was a virtuoso piece instead of a Schumann *Albumblatt.*' At Nohant there
were acoustic problems once more, and Dame Elisabeth does not care for
the performances overall.

In July she returned to the USA for a month, and her concerts included
two featuring arias from operettas – one in the Hollywood Bowl under
Anton Paulik, the other at the Ravinia Festival under Franz Allers. In
September she gave two Festival Hall performances of Strauss's *Vier letzte
Lieder* with the LSO under Barbirolli. There was also a Lieder recital with
Parsons in the Festival Hall before a brief return visit to the USA, where
she appeared at Lincoln Center, New York.

June 29. Nohant, France. Aldo Ciccolini (piano).
  Schubert: Der Einsame, D800; Rosamunde, D797 – Der Vollmond strahlt;
    An Sylvia, D891; Seligkeit, D433
  Schumann: Wie mit innigstem Behagen, Op. 25 No. 9; Der Nussbaum, Op.
    25 No. 2
  Liszt: Die drei Zigeuner, G320; Es muss ein Wunderbares sein, G314
  Chopin: 17 Polish Songs, Op. 74 – (i) No. 1, Mädchens Wunsch; (j) No. 16,
    Litauisches Lied
  Wolf: Kennst du das Land?; Wenn du zu den Blumen gehst; In dem
    Schatten meiner Locken; Die Zigeunerin

Strauss: Ruhe, meine Seele, Op. 27 No. 1; Meinem Kinde, Op. 37 No. 3;
    Morgen, Op. 27 No. 4; Hat gesagt, bleibt's nicht dabei, Op. 36 No. 3:
    Ach, was Kummer, Op. 49 No. 8
Mozart: Ich möchte wohl der Kaiser sein, K539
    CD: Arkadia CDGI802.1.

1970-1979

In January 1970 Elisabeth Schwarzkopf and Geoffrey Parsons were back
in Japan for a month-long recital tour. Schwarzkopf made a few appearances in America before returning to Europe and to some April recording
sessions in Berlin, which have not yielded any published material. There
were recitals in Paris and Lyon, and a Mozart concert in Strasbourg. In
the recording sessions which began at the end of August Schwarzkopf and
Parsons worked on the fourth Songbook, and commenced a collection which
would be entitled 'Songs I Love'. In November she made her first tour of
South Africa for many years.

In January 1971 she was in the USA and Canada once more, and as
always there were new centres to visit as well as the more familiar
performing venues. A deferred visit to Australia with Geoffrey Parsons
took place in May, and in the latter part of the year performances were
confined to Britain and the near continent. She had not given any stage
performances for a few years, but she now appeared in a farewell series of
six *Rosenkavalier* performances in the Théâtre de la Monnaie under
Georges Sebastien. The production even had a special title, 'Adieu à la
Scène', of which she was quite unaware before her arrival in Brussels.

January 1972 saw her and Parsons back in Japan for another visit. A
series of American performances followed, and then after some more local
appearances it was back to America in November and December. Not only
had Schwarzkopf made her last stage appearance, but there were to be no
more performances with orchestra – except for a special performance of
the single Wolf song *Kennst du das Land* at a Covent Garden gala evening,
'Fanfare for Europe', in January 1973. On this occasion a fellow participant
was Sir Laurence Olivier, who lamented the fact that he had to project
his voice into the auditorium through the less penetrative medium of
speech.

There may have been fewer engagements in 1973, but there were still
new places to visit – Prague, Bucarest and even Korea. In the March
recording sessions Schwarzkopf at last completed the collection 'Songs I

Love'. Her 1974 recording sessions involving the two Schumann song cycles gave her less satisfaction, particularly *Frauenliebe und Leben*. 'It wasn't for me, and besides it needs a mezzo-ish voice, not with the mezzo sound all the time, but with the resilience, and the reserve of power in the mezzo range, which I never had. I made up by darkening the colour and all sorts of things.' There were more visits to America and Japan during the year, and a first visit to Istanbul. 1975 included a long American visit, her last as a singer, but fewer engagements in general.

Schwarzkopf was well aware, at this stage in her career, that she had to change her vocal technique in order to cope with the passing of the years. 'My voice was on the waning side, and all kinds of muscular powers had gone, and the breathing had gone. You can hear that the voice was getting old, surely. And one doesn't like that and one tries to make do with all kinds of funny vowels, and oh dear it is really an awful thing. Everybody has different difficulties, certainly, so the problems will be different for every singer. Anyway, mine was mainly intonation, I think, and breathing power, not the timbre so much as the intonation which I tried to make do with all kinds of colouring of vowels, and so on, which no non-singer can ever understand – why one does it. They wouldn't, it's no good explaining to anyone who is not a singer.'

A pattern of quite widely spaced engagements was now the norm, and there were just two more recording sessions in 1977 and 1979. The Decca company very much wanted to have one of her records in its catalogue, and persuaded her to put together a last recital. It was called, simply, 'To my Friends'. 'In that there is already the excuse that it's only for you who like me. Others may find great fault in it and rightly so, but maybe you like me enough to have it.' The record was completed in January 1979.

On 19 March Schwarzkopf and Geoffrey Parsons gave a recital in the Zürich Opera House. Three days later Walter Legge died, and there would be no more performances from his wife. Legge had encouraged her to go on. ' "You can do it, meine Schatz, you can do it, you sing that – you'll do it better." He was wrong there, I wouldn't have been better than people in full bloom of the voice. He thought there would be some moments which would be more memorable. But if you don't have the voice you cannot put over what you would like to – you make ways round it technically, and by that time it has already vanished.'

1970

February 15. CBC Studios, Toronto. John Newmark (piano).
   Schubert: An die Musik, D547; Die Forelle, D550; Seligkeit, D433
   Schumann: Der Nussbaum, Op. 25 No. 3
       LP: Rococo 5388.
Same televised concert as above. Orchestra conducted by Martin Rich.
   Mozart: Warnung, K433
       LP: Rococo 5388.

April 6-16. Evangelisches Gemeindhaus, Zehlendorf, Berlin. Geoffrey Parsons
   (piano).
       Schubert: Was bedeutet die Bewegung? D270; Ach, um deine feuchten
           Schwingen, D717; Hänflings Liebeswerbung, D552
       Grieg: Ich liebe dich, Op. 5 No. 3; Mit einer Wasserlilie, Op. 25 No. 4;
           Letzter Frühling, Op. 33 No. 2
       Chopin: 17 Polish Songs, Op. 74 – No. 1, Mädchens Wunsch; No. 16,
           Litauisches Lied
       Loewe: Kleiner Haushalt, Op. 71
                   NB: These were re-recordings of items recorded in
                   October 1968, but it would seem that the earlier
                   versions were published. Other unpublished items
                   may also have been recorded at these sessions.

August 27-31, September 1-8.
       Mozart: Der Zauberer, K472; Abendempfindung, K523
       Brahms: Wie Melodien zieht es mir, Op. 105 No. 1; Immer leiser wird mein
           Schlummer, Op. 105 No. 2; Der Jäger, Op. 95 No. 4; Liebestreu, Op. 3
           No. 1; Ständchen, Op. 106 No. 1; Vergebliches Ständchen, Op. 84 No. 4
       Trad. (arr. Brahms): Volkskinderlieder – No. 4, Sandmännchen
       Wolf: Im Frühling; Auf eine Christblume
       Grieg: Erstes Begegnen, Op. 21 No. 1; Zur Rosenzeit, Op. 48 No. 5; Mit
           einer Primula veris, Op. 26 No. 4; Lauf der Welt, Op. 48 No. 3
       Strauss: Die Nacht, Op. 10 No. 3; Wiegenliedchen, Op. 49 No. 3
       All the above items were issued on LP: ASD2844, 1C 063 02 331, 1C
       065 102 331-1, EAC80015, EAC60170. Die Nacht and Im Frühling are
       on LP: Set 1546133. Abendempfindung is on LP: EAC47031-41.
       Sandmännchen is on LP: EAC47031-41. Vergebliches Ständchen is on
       LP: EAC47031-41, EAC47083-4. Ständchen is on C: EG7 63654-4. CD:
       Set CMS7 63790-2, CDM7 63654-2. Im Frühling is on C: EG7 63653-4.
       CD: Set CMS7 63790-2, CDM7 63653-2. Die Nacht and Wiegenliedchen
       are on C: EG7 63656-4. CD: Set CMS7 63790-2, CDM7 63656-2.
September 1-8.
       Wolf: Denk' es, o Seele; An eine Aeolsharfe
       LP: ASD3124, 1C 063 02 598, Set 1546133, EAC80177, EAC60172. C:
       EG7 63653-4. CD: Set CMS7 63790-2, CDM7 63653-2.

1973

March 1-10.
  Wolf: Keine gleicht von allen Schönen; Der Gärtner; An der Schlaf; Auf
    einer Wanderung; Begegnung; Sonne der Schlummerlosen; Auftrag
  Schubert: Gretchen am Spinnrade, D118; Wehmut, D772; Meeres Stille,
    D216; An Sylvia, D891; Erntelied, D434
  Schumann: Der Nussbaum, Op. 25 No. 3
    All the above items were issued on LP: ASD3124, 1C 063 02 598,
    EAC80177, EAC60172. All four Schubert items are on LP:
    EAC47149-50. Meeres Stille, Gretchen am Spinnrade and Sonne der
    Schlummerlosen are on LP: Set 1546133. Gretchen am Spinnrade is on
    LP: EAC47031-41, EAC40034, EAC47083-4. Der Nussbaum is on LP:
    EAC47031-41, EAC47083-4. Sonne der Schlummerlosen, Auf einer
    Wanderung and Begegnung are on C: EG7 63653-4. CD: Set CMS7
    63790-2, CDM7 63653-2. Meeres Stille, Gretchen am Spinnrade and
    Der Nussbaum are on C: EG7 63656-4. CD: Set CMS7 63790-2, CDM7
    63656-2.

1974

January.
  Schumann: Frauenliebe und Leben, Op. 42
    LP: ASD3037, S-37043, RL32010, 1C 063 02 547, 2C 069 02 547,
    EAC80035.
April.
  Schumann: Liederkreis, Op. 39
    LP: ASD3037, S-37043, RL32010, 1C 063 02 547, 2C 069 02 547,
    EAC80035. Note: Four unspecified songs by Schubert, and one Wolf
    song were also recorded at these sessions. These were test recordings
    using the then new Neumann Dummy Head.

1975

December 12-22.
  Brahms: Am jüngsten Tag, Op. 95 No. 6; Ach und Du, Op. 85 No. 3; Auf die
    Nacht in dem Spinnstub'n, Op. 107 No. 5; Schwalbe, sag mir an, Op.
    107 No. 3; Ruft die Mutter, Op. 69 No. 9; O wüsst ich doch den Weg
    zurück, Op. 63 No. 8; Therese, Op. 86 No. 1; Dunkel, wie dunkel, Op.
    43 No. 1; Blinde Kuh, Op. 58 No. 1; Feinsliebchen trau du Nicht, Op.

105 No. 3; Guten Abend, gute Nacht, Op. 49 No. 4; Geuss nicht so laut, Op. 46 No. 4; Meine Liebe ist grün, Op. 63 No. 5; O Frühlingsabend-Dämmerung, Op. 71 No. 3; Der Schmied, Op. 19 No. 4; Ei schmollte mein Vater, Op. 69 No. 4; Der Tod, das ist die kühle Nacht, Op. 96 No. 1; Wehe, so willst Du mich wieder, Op. 32 No. 5; O kühler Wald, Op. 72 No. 3; Volkslied, O brich nicht Steg, Op. 7 No. 6

1977

January 5. Rosslyn Hill Chapel, Hampstead, London NW3. Geoffrey Parsons (piano).
> Wolf: Lebewohl; Das verlassene Mägdlein
>> LP: Decca SXL6943, US London OS26592, Teldec 6.42576AW. C: Decca KSXC6943. CD: Decca 430 000-2DM.

January 6.
> Wolf: Fussreise; Auf ein altes Bild
>> LP: Decca SXL6943, US London OS26592, Teldec 6.42576AW. C: Decca KSXC6943. CD: Decca 430 000-2DM.

January 7.
> Wolf: Jägerlied
>> LP: Decca SXL6943, US London OS26592, Teldec 6.42576AW. C: Decca KSXC6943. CD: Decca 430 000-2DM.
> Wolf: Gebet

January 13.
> Wolf: Heimweh

January 14.
> Wolf: Bei einer Trauung
>> LP: Decca SXL6943, US London OS26592, Teldec 6.42576AW. C: Decca KSXC6943. CD: Decca 430 000-2DM.

January 15.
> Wolf: Selbstgeständnis; Storchenbotschaft
>> LP: Decca SXL6943, US London OS26592, Teldec 6.42576AW. C: Decca KSXC6943. CD: Decca 430 000-2DM.
> Wolf: Ein Stündlein wohl vor Tag

January 16.
> Wolf: Nimmersatte Liebe
>> LP: Decca SXL6943, US London OS26592, Teldec 6.42576AW. C: Decca KSXC6943. CD: Decca 430 000-2DM.
> Wolf: Schlafendes Jesuskind; Mausfallen Sprüchlein

January 17.
> Wolf: Elfenlied
>> LP: Decca SXL6943, US London OS26592, Teldec 6.42576AW. C: Decca KSXC6943. CD: Decca 430 000-2DM.
> Wolf: Nixe Binsefuss

1979

January 2. Sofiensaal, Vienna. Geoffrey Parsons (piano).
> Wolf: Mausfallen Sprüchlein
>> LP: Decca SXL6943, US London OS26592, Teldec 6.42576AW. C: Decca
>> KSXC6943. CD: Decca 430 000-2DM.
> Wolf: Storchenbotschaft; Jägerlied

January 3.
> Loewe: Die wandelnde Glocke, Op. 20 No. 3
>> LP: Decca SXL6943, US London OS26592, Teldec 6.42576AW. C: Decca
>> KSXC6943. CD: Decca 430 000-2DM.
> Kilpinen: Kleines Lied

January 4.
> Loewe: Tom der Reimer, Op. 133

January 6.
> Brahms: Mädchenlied, Op. 107 No. 3
>> LP: Decca SXL6943, US London OS26592, Teldec 6.42576AW. C: Decca
>> KSXC6943. CD: Decca 430 000-2DM.
> Brahms: Am jüngsten Tag, Op. 95 No. 6
> Wolf: Der Genesene an die Hoffnung

January 7.
> Wolf: Herr, was trägt der Boden hier

January 8.
> Wolf: Heimweh; Nixe Binsefuss
>> LP: Decca SXL6943, US London OS26592, Teldec 6.42576AW. C: Decca
>> KSXC6943. CD: Decca 430 000-2DM.

January 9.
> Grieg: Ein Schwann, Op. 25 No. 2
>> LP: Decca SXL6943, US London OS26592, Teldec 6.42576AW. C: Decca
>> KSXC6943. CD: Decca 430 000-2DM.
> Wolf: Bedeckt mich mit Blumen
> Marx: Venetianisches Wiegenlied

January 10.
> Brahms: Blinde Kuh, Op. 58 No. 1; Therese, Op. 86 No. 1
>> LP: Decca SXL6943, US London OS26592, Teldec 6.42576AW. C: Decca
>> KSXC6943. CD: Decca 430 000-2DM.
> Strauss: Heimkehr, Op. 15 No. 5
> Marx: Venetianisches Wiegenlied

Index of Works

References to the pages of this book appear in **bold** type.

Index of Artists